"Chock full of illustrative examples and suggestions backed by solid research, this book fills a yawning gap in the literature of understanding what goes into success in long-term relationships for individuals with Asperger Syndrome. Even more so with the second edition, this important resource is a must read for anyone involved with or supporting a person on the autism spectrum to achieve a deep, meaningful, and loving relationship."

—*Stephen M. Shore, EdD, internationally-known educator, author, consultant, and presenter on issues related to the autism spectrum*

"I read Ms. Stanford's book some years ago as a graduate student training to be a Couples' Counselor. Now updated, she has created an insightful guide on the broad range of the Autism Spectrum as described in DSM-5. Based on numerous stories about Asperger's and long-term relationships, this book continues to serve as a valuable resource for clinicians, adults with AS and their partners alike."

—*Eva Mendes, Couples' Counselor and Asperger / Autism Specialist*

T0385260

Asperger Syndrome
(Autism Spectrum Disorder)
and Long-Term Relationships

2ND EDITION

Ashley Stanford
Foreword by Liane Holliday Willey

Jessica Kingsley *Publishers*
London and Philadelphia

This edition published in 2015
by Jessica Kingsley Publishers
73 Collier Street
London N1 9BE, UK
and
400 Market Street, Suite 400
Philadelphia, PA 19106, USA

www.jkp.com

First edition published in 2003
by Jessica Kingsley Publishers

Library of Congress Cataloging in Publication Data
A CIP catalog record for this book is available from the Library of Congress

British Library Cataloguing in Publication Data
A CIP catalogue record for this book is available from the British Library

ISBN 978 1 84905 773 8
eISBN 978 1 78450 036 8

Printed and bound by CPI Group (UK) Ltd, Croydon, CR0 4YY

MIX
Paper from responsible sources
FSC® C013604

To my family

You are my breath of fresh air
When life becomes stale.
You are the twinkle in my eye
When I smile.
You are my straight path
When my world stretches out in all directions.
You are my past, my present, and my eternity.
I relish every day with you.

I write of him
who fights
and vanquishes his sins,
who struggles on
through weary years
against himself…
and wins.

Caroline Bigelow LeRow,
Pieces for Every Occasion

Contents

Foreword

I am the only child of a neurotypical (NT) woman and a man who had Asperger Syndrome (AS). As a child, I found that life with a mismatched set of parents could be quite challenging. My mother craved a social life and my father craved thinking in silence. For 40 years my mother was convinced my father was intentionally setting up communication barriers and bad-mannered responses to her family and friends as part of a passive aggressive scheme to express his sour feelings toward their marriage. After I was diagnosed in 1998, my mother very slowly began to believe my father was never her antagonist out of ill will. Rather, she came to realize he was a man who saw and reacted to the world in ways an NT is not innately able to understand. This was an awakening that settled my mother's resentment and (as my father would put it) her disapproval of his ways. By the time my father passed away, my folks were no longer adversaries. They were faithful friends who had finally learned to accept one another, even when they were unable to gauge life in the same way.

I'm glad my parents were able to find a mutual friendship, but I'm sad they were never able to see one another for who they really were. If only my mother had had Ashley's book when she was a young married woman. I can only imagine how much happier and content she would have been. I can only wonder how life might have been for my dad who, despite his best efforts to be a kind and fair man (he often succeeded), was never quite able to understand how he confounded his wife so deeply.

Many things can divide a relationship between an NT and a person with AS. Among some of the challenges are distinct differences in the two individual's personal space and intimacy needs (or lack thereof), social awareness and social desire, empathy margins, commitment to a favored interest, sensory information tolerance or needs, and real confusion over nonverbal communication. My parents, like my husband and I, suffered setbacks in each of these areas.

I'm known as a very straightforward and verbal Aspie. In fact, there was a time when I thought about dissecting my relationship's ups and downs. But the undertaking soon proved to be too tricky and baffling for me. I could articulate how I felt about the relationship, but I couldn't begin to guess how my husband felt. I knew my needs, but couldn't predict his. Thankfully, Ashley Stanford rose to the task and wrote a book that will undoubtedly save and protect NT/AS relationships. Ashley is more than prepared to answer logically, empathetically, and whole-heartedly not only all the questions I thought I had on the subject, but even far more than I had ever imagined were possible.

When Ashley asked me to provide the foreword for her first edition of *Asperger Syndrome (Autism Spectrum Disorder) and Long-Term Relationships*, I was a bit nervous. I was very worried Ashley might have written things that would upset me. As my father with Asperger Syndrome (Autism Spectrum Disorder) is wont to say, neurotypicals have a better press agent than people with Asperger Syndrome (Autism Spectrum Disorder). In other words, I worried I might read a dozen or a hundred things that would upset my heart. I hear, far too often, far too many complaints about a partner with Asperger Syndrome (Autism Spectrum Disorder).

Ashley's book quickly settled any qualms I may have had. While I methodically made my way through her book, I kept comparing myself to a child happily digging through a big community sand box that held trinket after trinket of lovelies. With every turn of the page, Ashley's book just kept pouring out the trinkets. More and more and more goodies just kept surfacing. And believe you me, my 30 years of marriage tied to raising three kids has needed every trinket Ashley provides!

I cannot possibly make a list of all the things Ashley's book covers. There are too many! Good idea, after well-researched concept, followed by illustrative example and elaborated suggestions—these all pile one on top of the other until a tower strong and solid enough to withstand all sorts of interpersonal uproar stands smack bang in front of the reader.

This book is a keeper. A must-have. It is the very book I would hand any adult involved in a relationship affected by Asperger Syndrome (Autism Spectrum Disorder). It really is that good. And I do not say that lightly. As proof of my belief in this book, I will close by saying the following: people often ask my husband how he manages to remain married to me, his wife with Asperger Syndrome (Autism Spectrum Disorder). Next time they do, I am going to suggest he refers them to Ashley's book.

Liane Holliday Willey, author of *Pretending to be Normal: Living with Asperger's Syndrome (Autism Spectrum Disorder)*, *Safety Skills for Asperger Women*, and *Asperger Syndrome in the Family*, and editor of *Asperger Syndrome in Adolescence*

Acknowledgments

As I am a private person, I will probably never meet the people to whom I am most indebted—the researchers and writers who worked hard to define and quantify the condition we have been referring to as Asperger Syndrome but that now fits under the umbrella term of Autism Spectrum Disorder (ASD): Tony Attwood, Simon Baron-Cohen, Uta Frith, Lorna Wing, Ami Klin, and so many others. They have been my source of inspiration when unfamiliar terms and conflicting information became confusing. To transform this book from a manuscript into a publishable book, I turned to the professionals at Jessica Kingsley Publishers. They are heroes in the field of Autism Spectrum Disorder as they build a continuous flow of current information and support for us all. Finally, I acknowledge the kind words of encouragement from my family and friends. They never gave up on me.

Note The author of this work has chosen to use a pen name to guard the privacy of her family. While some readers may grasp for a stronger author voice, those who truly understand the intricacies of Asperger Syndrome (Autism Spectrum Disorder) and the social difficulties it entails will recognize and respect the need for privacy.

Preface

My background is in technical communication and curriculum development. I thrive when I am solving problems, both technical and educational. When I discovered my husband had Asperger Syndrome, now re-diagnosed as Autism Spectrum Disorder, I attacked the "problem" as natural-born researchers often do: I looked online, in bookstores, asked around the community nearby, muddled my way through research reports, and searched the world at large for helpful information. I found plenty of strategies that sounded helpful, but proved disastrous at home.

As many of us do, I lost hope quickly. I found discouragement at every turn: "People with Asperger Syndrome shouldn't marry," and, "Most ASD marriages end in divorce." I was looking for answers, not opposition. In my research I noticed that there are constant breakthroughs and improvements in what is available to children with ASD and their parents, but I found precious little in the way of marital help. I began digging for what worked and suffering through what did not work.

Back in my early married days, a good friend of mine, an airline stewardess, advised me with a common metaphor: "Put on your own air mask first, sweetie." I have adopted this as a mantra for how I approach my ASD-linked marriage. By putting on my own air mask first, I make myself a stronger person who is then capable of helping others around me. I am of no use to anyone otherwise. This book is my air mask—a conglomeration of most of the understandings and solutions that have helped me build a healthier, happier marriage.

This book does not have answers for everyone. No one does. All I can offer is an open-minded and positive view of the many options for how to make ASD-linked adult relationships work. I believe that the most reliable solutions come from wrapping our minds around the full extent of the diagnosis, then brainstorming for solutions within that framework that will work for us personally. My goal as a writer was to organize insights and potential solutions into one easy format. You never know when one chance thought or story will give you the breath of fresh air you need.

Be forewarned: this book has no answers for how a person with ASD can be "cured" or "recover." This book is not going to enlighten your partner with ASD to his "errant ways" and it definitely is not going to change his or her behavior. It is going to change *your understanding* and, in turn, both you and your partner will benefit. We cannot improve our partners directly; we can only improve ourselves.

I am writing mainly to the partners of those with ASD. It does not matter if you are male or female, although I mainly use "him" since the statistics for the diagnostic rate currently dictate that males are more commonly diagnosed with ASD. I also make little differentiation between a marriage and a long-term relationship. From what I have seen, the dynamics are about the same. I hope that as you read you will be able to see beyond the titles of "him" and "her," "marriage" and "relationship."

Choosing appropriate terminology for labeling people is the most annoying problem when writing. No matter what terminology I choose, I will offend someone. Are we NTs (neurotypicals)? Not quite. Few readers will be neurologically typical. Are we the partner without ASD? Not really. I don't define myself through my husband's diagnosis. What are we then? For simplicity I have chosen to use NT (usually) to refer to any person or partner who is not diagnosed or diagnosable as having ASD. It is woefully inadequate, but it is a compromise for the sake of simplicity and readability.

It is equally awkward to label people with Asperger Syndrome or Autism Spectrum Disorder. Previously, before the DSM-5 (the manual used to diagnose conditions) revised how they classify people with this set of traits, we had the option of referring to people with Asperger Syndrome as Aspies, a pleasant, fun term similar to "genius," "artist," or "intellectual." Those easier days are past and now we refer to the more correct term: a person with Autism Spectrum Disorder, shortened to ASD for simplicity. It is awkward but in our daily lives we handle things far more difficult than awkward terminology.

The information in this book is useful for both ASD/NT couples and ASD/ASD couples due to the fact that there is significant carry-over between the two. Even if you started out as an ASD/NT relationship, you may end up functioning like an ASD/ASD couple at times. People who marry those with ASD begin to take on certain traits as time ticks by, becoming "Aspergated" (a term from the pre-DSM-5 days) as they live with their partner with ASD day after day, year after year. No matter what combination of traits you combine within your relationship, insights can be gained by familiarizing yourselves with the intricacies of the diagnostic criteria and pondering the implications for long-term relationships.

Since this book is based on the very personal experiences of people who are often in painful situations, all names and descriptive details have been omitted. I have chosen to indicate only "a man" or "a woman." All we need is the essence of the experience—what has worked for them. Some stories are specific examples from a few select couples that I know personally, many are personal experiences of my husband and me, and some are based on experiences that are so common that you will probably think I am writing about you.

Disclaimer Please note that the common examples come from widely published information pertaining to Asperger Syndrome (Autism Spectrum Disorder). They are noted by "For example..." These examples are fictitious and are based on information that is classified as common knowledge. These can be verified easily by reading about ASD (see the final chapter of this book). With the less interesting facts, uncommon details are added to help bring life to the examples. The examples cited as "One woman said...", or otherwise identified as belonging to a particular individual, come from personal friends of the author or from the author's personal experience. No real quotes or example quotes were taken from any other source. The Internet was not used as a source for quotes as there is no way to verify the validity behind these sources.

1

One Day I Woke Up

One day I woke up to find that the man sleeping beside me was still a stranger. I knew the rote information about his past—when he was born, where he went to school, his favorite color—but I did not know him. I did not know his hopes for the future, his regrets, his aspirations, nothing personal.

He knew next to nothing about me. He had never asked. He only knew what I offered. We had been married eight years.

This bothered me. I did not have any preconceived notions of wedded bliss, but this seemed odd. We spent more hours together than most couples. We communicated. Ask either of us any type of rote information about the other and we would pass the test with flying colors. "What is her blood type? Social security number? Driver's license number? What were his grades in college? What courses did he take?" We knew every technical detail about each other but we knew nothing deeply personal. I had never heard him say, "I feel…" or "I wish…" I had been patiently awaiting a deeper level of bonding but it still had not happened. Something was missing. I suspected it had something to do with spirituality or repressed emotional problems in one or both of us, but I was at a loss for answers.

I spent the next three years examining his childhood. Was it something his mother did? Did he learn to repress everything? It seemed that his heart was under some sort of elusive shield that I could not lift. The more I searched for answers, the more frustrated I became. His mother was a saint. His father was supportive and a superb role model. They were good parents and helped their son develop into a strong man. There had not been any trauma in his childhood that would have caused the anomalies that I was seeing in him and in our relationship.

I spent the next two years frustrated. I read nearly every marriage therapy book I could get my hands on, all of them proving a disappointment. I went into therapy only to walk away with a sense that both my husband and I were in a territory unfamiliar to the therapists. Everywhere I turned, the answer was the same: "This is odd."

During this time my husband's sister discovered that her son had Autism. With a diagnosis of High-Functioning Autism and Hyperlexia, she dove deep into the Autism community and found the resources she needed to help her child function and even thrive. After several years, she mentioned Asperger Syndrome. Did her brother—my husband— have it?

I surfed the web for information on Asperger Syndrome. The diagnostic criteria were shockingly familiar—my mind whispered, "This is him." Everything made sense. Everything fell into place. I felt deep pangs of regret for all the times I misspoke, for all the times I underestimated and overestimated him. He was trying his best to be the husband I wanted and needed but there were certain things about the way his brain works that made life extremely difficult for both of us. I never understood why we could not just take off and spend the day in the city. Or go on a hike. Or have a small change in plans. Why was everything so difficult? Now I was flooded with all the reasons.

As many people do who have just discovered that one of them has Autism Spectrum Disorder, my husband and I followed the predictable path. I did full-time research about ASD while my husband continued with his life, interested, but not interested enough to do anything about it. I read books by Tony Attwood, Liane Holliday Willey, Uta Frith, Simon Baron-Cohen, Ami Klin, Lorna Wing, Temple Grandin, and many others. I read into the wee hours of the night while he snoozed beside me. As I read, I understood why he did not seem to care. He already knew all this information. He was who he was and he was at peace with it. I was the one banging my head against the wall in frustration over my lack of understanding. He could not share this information with me because he could not verbalize it. He only understood ASD as "the" way of being. He did not have anything else to compare it to because he literally could not see other people's way of seeing.

As I learned about ASD, I kept extensive journals, notes, and documentation. I learned that there is a booming population of individuals with ASD who are frustrated by a lack of understanding on an adult level. I decided to put my technical writing career on hold to pull together a book that may possibly help others like me who are searching for understanding. People with ASD and their partners had formed a community identity—the main aspect of their identity is that they (myself included) are desperate to find answers before they lose their significant other to the cold misunderstandings that shut out the best of us.

Finding answers has been exhausting but the benefits have been a thousand-fold. In the process, we have found that our children also exhibit various shades of ASD and we have been able to restructure several parts of our lives, accessing the support of professionals, to better help them grow into their potential. As others in my situation have also discovered, the journey is grueling but well worth the effort. This journey has forced me to open my eyes.

I believe that someday we will wake up as a civilization and realize that the diagnosis for Autism Spectrum Disorder contains traits and skills that now confuse us, but are at the core of human progress. Geniuses throughout history who have been identified previously as highly eccentric are now being recognized as having had ASD and are being authoritatively diagnosed postmortem. I believe that as we become more sophisticated in our perceptions, we will realize some of the brilliance behind the particular neural wiring of the ASD brain. When I first met my husband, I sensed in him an intense ability to think differently. If I learn even a little about his brilliance, then I will have gained a rare and precious insight, an expansion of view into what it means to be human.

2

||||||||||||||||||||||||||||||||||||||||||||||||||||||||||||||||||||||||||||||||||||||||||||||||||||||||||

What does Asperger Syndrome (Autism Spectrum Disorder) Look Like in an Adult?

Asperger Syndrome (Autism Spectrum Disorder) in an adult may be harder to detect than it is in a child because an adult has had decades to consciously restructure behaviors, hiding the more obvious symptoms. As you look at the diagnostic criteria, be aware that you often need to look underneath the adult layers of self-preservation strategies and avoidance tactics. If at all possible, get accurate information about the person's childhood. Information about childhood is crucial because it shows whether or not the apparent ASD traits are consistent or if the apparent indicators are just a life phase.

WHAT IS ASPERGER SYNDROME (AUTISM SPECTRUM DISORDER)?

In the most general terms, Asperger Syndrome affects a person's ability to make and maintain relationships. In 1944 a man named Hans Asperger, a Viennese pediatrician, defined this particular neurological condition. It was not until 50 years later, in 1994, that the American Psychiatric Association recognized this syndrome as legitimate and included it in their diagnostic manual. In 2013 the diagnosis shifted from Asperger Syndrome to Autism Spectrum Disorder, placing AS under the ASD umbrella, effectively removing the term Asperger Syndrome from future use.

Previously, Asperger Syndrome was said to be on the Autism Spectrum; i.e. there are several types of Autism, and Asperger Syndrome happened to be one of them. People with Asperger Syndrome self-identified as "Aspies," which was a term of endearment for many. Originally, people with Asperger Syndrome were said to have "a dash of Autism" (Asperger 1979, p.49). When this book was first published, the most common opinion at the time of writing was that Asperger Syndrome and High-Functioning Autism (HFA) were so similar that they could be used synonymously for most purposes (Attwood 1998, p.150). In this book's second edition much has changed. The updates to the diagnostic criteria are explained in detail later in this book.

ASD may be difficult to identify in higher-functioning individuals because of the subtle nature of the symptoms. There are no physical signs of the disorder: no wheelchair, no glasses, no crutch. It takes a well-trained eye to see the lack of gestures, poor eye contact, odd communication style, and other indicators that trigger recognition of the condition. The lack of obvious outward signs can either be considered a blessing or a curse. On the one hand it allows the person with ASD to hide the condition, sneaking through the normalcy detectors that exist in the world, while on the other hand a lack of recognition that the person with ASD has a differently wired brain can lead to incorrect assumptions and misunderstandings. One minute your partner appears as normal as can be, and the next minute he appears rude and callous, oblivious to the accepted rules of social behavior. Because a person with ASD can achieve apparent normalcy, it can be hard to explain to friends and family that the odd behavior is not deliberate.

The following list may trigger recognition of some outward manifestations of the condition. Keep in mind that not all symptoms apply to all people with ASD—and individuals present each symptom in varying ways. People with ASD can be as different as any of us can, but they do share certain specific traits due to the diagnostic criteria. It is unlikely that all of the following apply. It is a list of the observable conditions that one may see in someone with ASD.

- Socially awkward—may not make or keep friends.

- Preoccupation with a particular subject.

- Difficulty reading social cues, facial expressions, or body language.

- Unable to fluently take turns when conversing with others.

- Finds emotions confusing, uninteresting, or nerve-wracking.
- Misreads allowable body space between people.
- Naïve/gullible.
- Often unaware of others' feelings.
- Easily upset by changes in routines and transitions.
- May prefer to stay home.
- Imaginary play does not come naturally—may not enjoy playing with children at any age.
- Possibly prefers technical reading, science fiction or other genres over best-selling fiction.
- May not make social connections with others.
- May not make emotional connections with partner and children.
- Literal in speech and understanding.
- Stilted, formal manner of speaking.
- May have difficulties with grammar, spelling, pragmatics, semantics, etc.
- Obsessive, repetitive routines.
- Tendency to rock, fidget, or pace.
- A lack of hand gestures when speaking.
- Overly sensitive to certain sensations—sounds, lights, smells, colors, etc.
- May not enjoy holding hands.
- May be finicky about the softness of clothing or the taste of foods.
- Physically awkward/clumsy.
- Unusually accurate memory for certain details.

When looking at this list, you probably found that many of the people you know fit the traits in some fashion or another. Be careful—many symptoms can be caused by environmental factors or may be a simple life phase. ASD is based in a person's neurology, how the brain is wired, and is generally consistent from childhood through adulthood. One of the most accurate ways to know if someone has ASD is to use the official diagnostic criteria, included in this book for your convenience.

Since you picked up this book, it is likely that this list sparked some, "So *that's* what it is," recognition for you. Now, let's get on to the core of Autism Spectrum Disorder—the diagnostic criteria.

DIAGNOSTIC CRITERIA

One morning I ate my breakfast while reading articles on Autism in *The New York Times*, on the BBC, and several other valuable news sources. There were several articles written in the last few years about young adults dating and finding love, establishing relationships that they hoped would be long term. As I read about couple after couple, I realized that some of the partners who considered themselves as having Asperger Syndrome may receive the Autism Spectrum Disorder diagnosis or may not. It would depend on the diagnostician, the way the person presented their symptoms on the day(s) of the evaluation, and many other factors.

No matter what a diagnostician said, these couples experienced issues related to emotional reciprocity, problematic communication, and perhaps most relevant for intimate relationships, sensory issues. None of the young adults in the news articles were receiving services related to their diagnosis, at least none were mentioned, and the vital undercurrent of the articles was that the diagnosis served one main purpose—to help people with ASD understand themselves and to help others to understand the purpose behind ASD-driven behavior.

My guess is that it is confusing and difficult to not know for sure if you have ASD. If one's diagnosis is questionable, it might lead one to feel unsure and unsettled. I am actually grateful that my husband's diagnosis is unquestionable. There is no doubt that he fits all criteria. The only item to debate is the level of current severity.

In 2013, the criteria used most often to diagnose ASD became stricter, making higher-functioning people with Autism less likely to receive a diagnosis of ASD. For those people who received a diagnosis of Asperger Syndrome or High-Functioning Autism in previous years but who are no longer sure of their ASD diagnosis, I invite and encourage you to continue reading this book. Those with conditions similar to ASD and those who exhibit only some of the ASD criteria can still gain insights from this book.

The most widely used diagnostic criteria are found in the DSM-5 (American Psychiatric Association 2013), but there are many sets of diagnostic criteria. Everyone chooses the set of diagnostic criteria and rating scale that they prefer. I have chosen to build this book on the diagnostic criteria published by the American Psychiatric Association because they are the most widely used by clinicians.

Following are the diagnostic criteria for Autism Spectrum Disorder, diagnostic code 299.00 as listed in the *Diagnostic and Statistical Manual of Mental Disorders*, 5th edition (DSM-5).

DIAGNOSTIC CRITERIA FOR 299.00 AUTISM SPECTRUM DISORDER

A   Persistent deficits in social communication and social interaction across multiple contexts, as manifested by the following, currently or by history (examples are illustrative, not exhaustive; see text):

1. Deficits in social-emotional reciprocity, ranging, for example, from abnormal social approach and failure of normal back-and-forth conversation; to reduced sharing of interests, emotions, or affect; to failure to initiate or respond to social interactions.

2. Deficits in nonverbal communicative behaviors used for social interaction, ranging, for example, from poorly integrated verbal and nonverbal communication; to abnormalities in eye contact and body language or deficits in understanding and use of gestures; to a total lack of facial expressions and nonverbal communication.

3. Deficits in developing, maintaining, and understanding relationships, ranging, for example, from difficulties adjusting behavior to suit various social contexts; to

difficulties in sharing imaginative play or in making friends; to absence of interest in peers.

Specify current severity:
Severity is based on social communication impairments and restricted, repetitive patterns of behavior.

B   Restricted, repetitive patterns of behavior, interests, or activities, as manifested by at least two of the following, currently or by history (examples are illustrative, not exhaustive; see text):

1.   Stereotyped or repetitive motor movements, use of objects, or speech (e.g., simple motor stereotypies, lining up toys or flipping objects, echolalia, idiosyncratic phrases).

2.   Insistence on sameness, inflexible adherence to routines, or ritualized patterns of verbal or nonverbal behavior (e.g., extreme distress at small changes, difficulties with transitions, rigid thinking patterns, greeting rituals, need to take same route or eat same food every day).

3.   Highly restricted, fixated interests that are abnormal in intensity or focus (e.g., strong attachment to or preoccupation with unusual objects, excessively circumscribed or perseverative interests).

4.   Hyper- or hyporeactivity to sensory input or unusual interest in sensory aspects of the environment (e.g., apparent indifference to pain/temperature, adverse response to specific sounds or textures, excessive smelling or touching of objects, visual fascination with lights or movement).

Specify current severity:
Severity is based on social communication impairments and restricted, repetitive patterns of behavior.

C   Symptoms must be present in the early developmental period (but may not become fully manifest until social demands exceed limited capacities, or may be masked by learned strategies in later life).

D   Symptoms cause clinically significant impairment in social, occupational, or other important areas of current functioning.

E   These disturbances are not better explained by intellectual disability (intellectual developmental disorder) or global developmental delay. Intellectual disability and autism spectrum disorder frequently co-occur; to make comorbid diagnoses of autism spectrum disorder and intellectual disability, social communication should be below that expected for general developmental level.

Note   Individuals with a well-established DSM-IV diagnosis of autistic disorder, Asperger's disorder, or pervasive developmental disorder not otherwise specified should be given the diagnosis of autism spectrum disorder. Individuals who have marked deficits in social communication, but whose symptoms do not otherwise meet criteria for autism spectrum disorder, should be evaluated for social (pragmatic) communication disorder.

Specify if:

With or without accompanying intellectual impairment.

With or without accompanying language impairment.

Associated with a known medical or genetic condition or environmental factor.

Associated with another neurodevelopmental, mental, or behavioral disorder.

Reprinted with permission from the Diagnostic and Statistical Manual of Mental Disorders, Fifth Edition (Copyright © 2013). American Psychiatric Association. All Rights Reserved.

Please note that the chapters in this book are based directly on the official DSM-5 diagnostic criteria. It is surprisingly easy to get lost in tangents and areas of marriage and family life that are not directly related to the diagnosis criteria. This book uses the diagnostic criteria as the spine for this book's content. Each diagnostic criterion is discussed in detail.

There is a good chance that if you are new to ASD, you will have a hard time understanding the intricacies of the diagnostic criteria. To help us all, Simon Baron-Cohen made a simplified list of the key features of Asperger Syndrome. This list is extremely helpful in that it condenses and clarifies so many of the diagnostic issues into one easy format. For a person to be considered as potentially having ASD, all ten descriptions must apply and the difficulties must be significantly interfering with daily life.

1. I find social situations confusing.

2. I find it hard to make small talk.

3. I did not enjoy imaginative story-writing at school.

4. I am good at picking up details and facts.

5. I find it hard to work out what other people are thinking and feeling.

6. I can focus on certain things for very long periods.

7. People often say I was rude even when this was not intended.

8. I have unusually strong, narrow interests.

9. I do certain things in an inflexible, repetitive way.

10. I have always had difficulty making friends.

You may want to hand this list to your partner or you may want to ask him verbally if he recognizes these traits in himself. If you have a good relationship, and it happens to be a good day, both of you may gain life-changing insights. There is also the possibility that your partner, despite his best intentions, may feel the need to lie, hide, or obfuscate the truth if he feels his partner's judgments are looming. If your partner feels that you will use this information against him later, he is likely to duck and dodge, maybe even start a fight to get you to drop it. If you think your partner will be defensive and therefore not give you honest answers, it may be quicker and easier to do an initial analysis through a therapist or counselor. As you will see in later chapters, defensiveness is natural, and is a common self-protection measure regardless of the diagnosis.

There is another pitfall that can occur with any diagnostic scale or list of key questions. The partner with ASD may interpret the questions so literally that it skews the meaning. For example:

> The Simon Baron-Cohen test was so much easier for us to understand! I read the list to my husband and he bellowed a resounding, "Yes," or, "Of course!" to every single one except the one that says: "People often say I was rude..." He said, "No," but I pointed out that currently there is no one to say he was rude. His colleagues understand him, and the children and I have learned that saying, "You're rude," does not do a bit of good, so no one points it out anymore. For us to determine if this feature fits my husband, we looked in his past, back when he used to have to interact with others who did not understand him as well. Sure enough, we often heard the comment: "You're rude." He's still just as rude as he always was; he just does not hear about it anymore.

Simon Baron-Cohen's list of key features appears simple, but it is carefully worded—take time to answer honestly yes or no to the specific criteria. Misinterpreting the diagnostic criteria on any scale is a common hazard because the person with ASD may interpret the information too literally or otherwise misread it. Here are other examples:

> My husband [ASD] answered that "No," he does not find social situations confusing. I think he misunderstood. He doesn't find social situations confusing because he rarely tries to understand them anymore. He has learned to ignore the horrible confusion he feels in social situations—he shuts down. Whenever I have seen him think about a particular social situation, he appears to be in a confused fog.

Or:

> She [ASD] answered that she "likes social chitchat," but her definition may not be the world's definition. She doesn't mind being near it, but only if it is at a certain volume level, if it is about certain topics, and if she is the only one speaking. She doesn't engage the listener in the conversation.

Or:

> On the statement about friends…she [ASD] considers everyone she ever met a friend.

Simon Baron-Cohen and others are doing phenomenal research trying to leap over the hurdles of helping both the general populace *and* the ASD community understand the diagnosis. It is not easy to write criteria that will be interpreted accurately by those with ASD and those without. For this reason, a third opinion, that of a professional, is highly valuable in making sure that the diagnostic criteria are correctly understood.

It would be infinitely easier if there was a blood test, brain scan, or other procedure that could detect ASD, but there is not. The diagnosis is based on the diagnostician's observation of a person's communication skills, behavior, and development since childhood (Tantam 1991, p.148). Even the most qualified, well-versed diagnostician may be baffled by your partner's combination of traits.

It is possible that a person has several disorders, not just ASD. A person can have ASD in combination with Attention Deficit Disorder (ADD), Generalized Anxiety Disorder (GAD), or any number of combinations of diagnoses. Distinguishing ASD traits from the traits found in other diagnoses resembles detective work.

Part of the confusion lies in the fact that some diagnosticians have a more liberal interpretation of the diagnosis and cast a wider net, while other diagnosticians follow the strictest standards for diagnosis. Also, there are plenty of professionals who have not fully acquainted themselves with the diagnostic criteria. Unfortunately, the following are common examples of misidentifying ASD in an adult:

> He can't have ASD. He can converse with us just fine.

Or:

> She can't have ASD. She writes well and can maintain eye contact.

Or:

> Since he has never been referred for medical help for this condition before now, he can't have ASD.

As we will see later on, eye contact can be faked, writing quality is not indicative of ASD, and the ability to converse can be chalked up to the learned skill of parroting back socially acceptable, memorized lines. These intelligent souls can evade a diagnosis for years, even a lifetime.

It is vital to find a diagnostician who is familiar with identifying ASD in adults. I found out the hard way that a quick, "Have you worked with Asperger Syndrome or Autism Spectrum Disorder?" is not sufficient. I learned to ask: "How many adult patients with Asperger Syndrome or Autism Spectrum Disorder have you treated?"; "What year did you treat your first patient with Asperger Syndrome or Autism Spectrum Disorder?"; "How many of these adults that you treated are now functioning effectively in society?"; "How would you define Asperger Syndrome or Autism Spectrum Disorder in a short sentence or two?" (to identify if your views are compatible). Think about what you want to get out of the diagnosis (marital counseling, validation, etc.) then ask as many pointed, specific questions as you would ask of a surgeon who is preparing to operate on you.

My preferred question was, "In your opinion, how many adults with Asperger Syndrome or Autism Spectrum Disorder are currently functioning well in society?" This question revealed the optimism or pessimism of the clinician. I wanted to work with someone who was able to identify the disability but also be able to see that adults with ASD can function happily throughout adulthood.

As you read this book, some traits will jump off the pages at you and some will sound foreign. Please read, or at least skim, all the traits, since you may or may not recognize the traits until reading others' personal experiences with them. I found that I dismissed many traits that my husband exhibited—I was not able to see them until I learned more about them. As you read, remember that all people with ASD are different in their presentation of traits.

Since there is such a wide variety in individuals, it is impossible and inappropriate to offer generic advice designed to fit all ASD-linked couples. If, while reading this book, you see a bit of information that seems off-base for your situation, skip it and move on to the next section. There are hundreds of potential answers and ideas in this book. Even if only one idea helps, it may be the solution that allows you to see clearly long enough to fix and heal your relationship.

Understanding the updated DSM-5

In 2013 the American Psychiatric Association published the fifth edition of their guidelines used for diagnosis, the DSM-5. There are other diagnostic criteria one can use, but the DSM-5 is the most widely used by clinicians.

The DSM-5 made significant and controversial changes to how Autism is diagnosed. The American Psychiatric Association took the disorders that were considered "on the spectrum" and put them all under the same umbrella. Now the term Autism Spectrum Disorder refers to Asperger Syndrome, Autistic Disorder, and Pervasive Development Disorder Not Otherwise Specified (PDD-NOS). This eliminated the points of differentiation that used to classify people with one diagnosis or another.

This means that people previously diagnosed with Asperger Syndrome may receive either a diagnosis of Autism Spectrum Disorder (most likely) or a different diagnosis such as Social (Pragmatic) Communication Disorder or other diagnosis. It also means that the higher-functioning people who were previously diagnosed with AS, HFA, or PDD-NOS may no longer fit any diagnosis.

The diagnostic criteria were changed in the hope that the new criteria would be a more accurate and reliable tool for diagnosis. The new diagnostic criteria are more rigid, requiring the person to have more symptoms. This updated edition of this book has been rearranged to mirror the new criteria and accurately represent the ramifications experienced by someone in an ASD-linked couple.

Many people in the Asperger Syndrome community were concerned about this change, and rightfully so since the change caused people to lose services and/or go through another evaluation, a highly unpleasant experience for many. On a deeply personal level, the change can cause a sort of identity crisis. People with Asperger Syndrome commonly refer to themselves and each other with the endearing term, Aspie. This term will probably remain active for a generation or two, then slowly fade out as no new children are diagnosed as having Asperger Syndrome.

Personally, the change did not affect us, not at all. My husband had his diagnosis confirmed and was done with it. There was no question in anyone's mind, but perhaps that is because he fits every criteria and they impact him daily. Beyond that, he has never sought community identity so the term Aspie is only a word for him. For me, I felt deep sympathy for the families who went through hardship as the diagnosis update caused difficulties in attaining needed support.

In any case, a change such as this is bound to be difficult in a community where inflexibility and a strong distaste for change is part of everyday life.

Is Asperger Syndrome (Autism Spectrum Disorder) prevalent?

Many years ago, in 2001, Patricia Romanowski Bashe and Barbara L. Kirby in *The OASIS Guide to Asperger Syndrome* stated, "Most authorities place the incidence of AS somewhere around 1 in 250 to 1 in 500 persons. However, because AS is still an underdiagnosed condition, it may be more prevalent" (p.12). More recently, the Centers for Disease Control and Prevention (CDC 2014) stated that 1 out of 68 children have ASD.

ASD appears to be more prevalent in men than women. Originally Hans Asperger believed that the condition he was observing occurred only in males but he later changed that opinion. By the mid-1980s, it was noted that for every ten males diagnosed with AS, a single female is diagnosed AS, thus a 10:1 male to female ratio (Wing 1981). By 2014 the CDC showed that males were five times more likely to have ASD than females, thus a 5:1 male to female ratio (CDC Press Release, March 27, 2014).

The adult population

The bulk of the research being conducted is for children only. A common complaint:

> How are we adults with ASD supposed to raise our children with ASD when we can't even function ourselves? Where's the help for us? Do they think we just outgrow it? I don't think so!

Even the top researchers in the field are aware that "a great deal of the literature on autism and related conditions spoke of children, almost as if children with autism did not grow up to become adults" (Klin, Volkmar and Sparrow 2000, p.18).

One of the reasons why the focus is on children is because of dedicated parents working hard to build support systems for their children as quickly as possible, while the children still have the cognitive pliability to be receptive to intervention methods. One of the secondary reasons is that there is public funding for children in the public school system in the USA and many other nations. Unless severely disabled, adults do not have state and federal dollars accessible to them for services for non-debilitating disabilities. Even the cost of the diagnosis may be prohibitive, let alone treatment, especially for adults who may lack health care due to lack of employment or underemployment. Unfortunately, funding is often at the nerve center of our ability to correctly identify our human condition.

Besides lack of funding and a lesser desire to focus on adults, there are many other factors contributing to underdiagnosis of our adult population. For example:

I don't need a diagnosis. What good would it do me?

Or:

I've looked everywhere and there doesn't appear to be a single qualified ASD diagnostician in my state.

Or:

My insurance says, "It doesn't do any good to diagnose an adult."

There is also a possibility that the adult with ASD is not supported by those around him when it comes to seeking a diagnosis. As one woman explains:

My mother-in-law is a nice lady, but she refuses to see Asperger Syndrome in her son. She keeps saying things like, "I know you have this great new idea for what may be bothering him, but trust me, sweetie, he's a normal man." She'll cite how he learned to talk early and how he was so analytical, even as a baby. She'll brag about how he played on his own all day long. She'll say that he was "so focused on his studies that he never even took time to date— now that's dedication!" She never found out how scared, confused, and miserable he was. She brushed off his depression and suicide attempts as "normal teenage behavior." From her vantage point, he was normal. Even though he has discovered his Asperger Syndrome, she refuses to consider the fact that there's more to my husband than his practiced surface exterior.

Some researchers say that our adult population with ASD is underdiagnosed (Bashe and Kirby 2001, p.12; Bauer 1996). Adults who suspect ASD in themselves or their partner, and are ready to seek a diagnosis, need qualified professionals who can give an accurate diagnosis along with suggestions for therapies, treatments, or improvements.

We also need a better general awareness of the condition and how it presents in other life stages besides childhood. Hans Asperger (1944) explained:

> Naturally, intelligence and personality develop and, in the course of development, certain features predominate or recede, so that the problems presented change considerably. Nevertheless, the essential aspects of the problem remain unchanged. In early childhood there are the difficulties in learning simple practical skills and in social adaptation. These difficulties arise out of the same disturbance which at school age cause learning and conduct problems, in adolescence job and performance problems, and in adulthood social and marital conflicts. (Trans. Frith 1991, pp.67–68)

Ironically, even the highest functioning person with ASD will still need significant support as an adult. Even though he may learn his way past the more obvious traits, he may need increased support in order to attain a level of balance and happiness in a demanding adult NT world. As Digby Tantam, renowned ASD researcher, explains:

> Asperger Syndrome is a developmental disorder with its origins in infancy, but it may cause the greatest disablement in adolescence and young adulthood, when successful social relationships are the key to almost every achievement. Abnormalities that are mild enough to be disregarded in childhood may become much more conspicuous in adolescence. (Tantam 1991, p.148)

Over the last decade much more support has been built to help adults with ASD in long-term relationships. I have learned to be selective in where I turn for answers. I used to browse the bookstores, looking under the topics of divorce, codependency, depression, and anger management (offshoots of what often happens in an ASD-linked marriage when the

ASD is not considered as part of the equation). At one point I counted nearly a hundred such books in my personal library. Unfortunately, these books do not and cannot address the intricacies of ASD. Using the common literature for marriages and relationships makes you look whiny and needy on the one hand while putting down the partner with ASD as uncaring and uncommitted. Looking at your partner with ASD through an NT lens makes both of you highly unattractive.

Misdiagnosis

There are many different syndromes and disorders that can be mistaken for ASD because they are so similar; these are called differential diagnoses. Without an official analysis you may think that your partner is narcissistic, schizophrenic, has ADD (attention deficit disorder) and all its cousins, NLD (nonverbal learning disorder), avoidant personality disorder, OCD (obsessive compulsive disorder), ODD (oppositional defiance disorder), and many others. With all the confusion, many couples end up with a diagnosis of DRC (don't really care). They throw up their hands in despair and separate or divorce.

There are many conditions that can imitate ASD. You may even have "acquired ASD" or "environmental ASD" (be careful, I don't think those are official terms yet). One woman explains her environmental ASD as follows:

> Although I do not have the neurological condition of Asperger Syndrome, there are diagnosticians who would easily diagnose me with Asperger Syndrome. I'm socially awkward. I have one obsessive interest. I lack friends. I often sound pedantic. Looking back, it's revealed that I don't give eye contact because I was trained not to: both father and mother were too busy to ever look at me. I followed the rules and did not speak unless spoken to. Yet, I believe that I have the "cognitive flexibility" of which the researchers speak.

As with any newly recognized condition there will be misdiagnoses, overdiagnoses, and underdiagnoses. A diagnosis can be a matter of opinion, making it tricky to quantify what is ASD and what shades into normalcy. Let's look at what we can exclude.

- ASD symptoms may vary from day to day but they are consistent over time. They are not part of a bad day or a phase.

- The person with ASD typically does not want to be different; the actions that appear to be ASD driven are not intentional.

- ASD is more than eccentricity or unconventional behavior.

- ASD is not a character flaw. It is a neurobiological condition.

- Everybody has little activities they do (routines) to calm themselves down and deal with stress. The difference is that a person with ASD has an exceptionally difficult time stopping these behaviors when he wants to or needs to.

- ASD is not a cold or the flu—it does not go away. Coping behaviors can be learned, but you do not outgrow ASD naturally. There are many methods to train someone out of the more obvious ASD traits with the hope of rewiring their brain to be more like an NT brain (called "recovery"), but this is a huge area of debate.

It is essential to stick to the basic diagnostic criteria and avoid the confusing mishmash of assumptions that occur when we assume that all people with ASD are alike. Some of the following contrasts help us see the variety:

My partner [ASD] is an absolute clean freak. He can't stand a mess in the house. It drives him batty. My friend calls him a "neatnik."

But a person with ASD can also appear as follows:

She [ASD] is so phenomenally messy. She has piles upon piles of stuff throughout the house. She's a pack rat and she has saved everything that has come across her path for the last two decades. She knows where stuff is, but nobody else does.

Another example of variation not related to the diagnosis:

She [ASD] is an excellent writer. She may have problems in social situations, but put her in front of a keyboard and she is quite eloquent.

But a person with ASD can also exhibit a lack of writing abilities:

> I doubt he [ASD] could write a coherent paragraph if his life depended on it. He can't seem to string the words together.

Variation may also occur in speech:

> He [ASD] is nearly silent. I have to prod him to get anything more than a yes or no answer [hypoverbal].

In contrast to:

> I wish my partner [ASD] wasn't so talkative! She talks non-stop. She talks during movies, she talks during church services, and she even needs to talk herself to sleep [hyperverbal].

Another issue that is not part of the diagnosis is the issue of anger. For example:

> He [ASD] is violently explosive…he is also abusive.

But compare this to another male who also has ASD:

> I don't think I've ever seen him [ASD] angry, let alone violent. Sure, he has been peeved or annoyed, but not actually angry.

There are many secondary traits, i.e. traits that occur because of ASD, but are not part of the ASD diagnosis. It is vital to focus on the diagnostic criteria and not get too entangled in tangents. Why is this so important? Focusing on the core of the diagnosis allows us to accurately identify what our partners with ASD can change and what they cannot change. It gives us a realistic framework within which we can build our relationships.

What causes Asperger Syndrome (Autism Spectrum Disorder)?

Asperger Syndrome (Autism Spectrum Disorder) is a neurobiological condition that appears to be partly hereditary. If one of the parents has ASD, it is possible that one or more of the children and/or grandchildren will show ASD traits. It is apparently related to how the brain develops. ASD is often recognizable in early childhood—right at the point at which the child is supposed to emerge into the social world but does not.

The central issue in ASD is social impairment. There have been hordes of studies discussing how the amygdala (part of the human brain) plays a role (Klin *et al.* 2000). Apparently, in a person with ASD, the wiring in the frontal and temporal lobes of the brain are a bit out of the ordinary (Attwood 1998, p.143). There are many potential medical reasons that may explain why people with ASD are the way they are, and more medical explanations will be presented as research into the condition continues.

What causes ASD? There is a flurry of allegations as to what causes ASD—everything from vaccines to certain environmental poisons. Hereditary links appear to be strong (Asperger 1944; Folstein and Santangelo 2000, pp.159–169). No one knows for sure. Researchers will keep working to discover what causes ASD and some day we will have a better understanding of its cause.

Is there a cure?

Hans Asperger (1944, p.67) noted that "a crucial point which makes clear that the autistic personality type is a natural entity is its persistence over time." In other words, the fact that ASD does not go away is one of the signs of ASD. It is not a passing phase. It is not a temporary condition. Studies following the revival of Hans Asperger's writing proved that traits were indeed stable over time (Tantam 1991, pp.164–165). If Asperger Syndrome (as originally defined) is based in an individual's basic personality, it will not go away with time and it should be respected, not eliminated. But how do we rest comfortably on this fact when ASD is classified as a disability due to the way it wreaks havoc on the life of the socially afflicted? People with ASD can end up in homes for the disabled. They can experience clinical depression because of their social difficulties (Tantam 1991, p.172).

Although we may wish for a cure, the consensus is that no, there is none. There are pharmaceutical medications that can treat the side effects of the syndrome (anxiety, depression, etc.), and there are all sorts of solutions that may lead to living a life that could be considered recovered or otherwise healthy. The aspiration of this book, and many other books and articles that have been written in recent years, is to show potential solutions, work-arounds, and "limping methodologies" for an incurable condition that is hurting adults all over the world, and when social situations become too confusing, making them wish they could curl into the fetal position and make the rest of humanity go away!

The only cure that we are currently aware of is: *support people can help the person with ASD to survive and even thrive.* Liane Holliday Willey has given many of us insight and hope in her books. She shows how she developed into a state of residual ASD with the help of supportive family and friends. The OASIS @ MAAP website also has some insight into dealing with this incurable condition:

> Many of the weaknesses can be remediated with specific types of therapy aimed at teaching social and pragmatic skills. Anxiety leading to significant rigidity can be also treated medically. Although it is harder, adults with Asperger's can have relationships, families, and happy and productive lives.

Actions and behaviors that come naturally to NTs need to be taught through direct and specific instruction to those with ASD. For example, some people with ASD do not give eye contact naturally. They need to be taught how to give eye contact, when to give eye contact, why we give eye contact, etc. The specific behaviors can be taught, resulting in a person who is capable of functioning nicely in society, and even better in a long-term relationship.

The adult ASD-linked long-term relationship

Researchers used to think that people with ASD either could not or did not marry due to their social difficulties. Now we know better. We know that cells (large groups) of people with ASD reside in locations such as Silicon Valley in California, the Silicon Forest in Washington state, the Silicon Hills in Austin, Texas, nearly every university campus around the globe, any area with a high density of techies, scientists, engineers, mathematicians, physicists—nearly all sectors of technical advancement pull in people who tend to have ASD traits (Baron-Cohen 2001). Plenty of people with ASD are married, even happily married.

Originally, research into families impacted by ASD showed that there was a tremendously high divorce rate, with 80 percent of couples divorcing. The statistic was focused on parents of children with ASD, but it spread to cover any family impacted by ASD. The statistic was widely believed for many years, in large part due to the fact that ASD is a social communication disorder and marriage is a social contract requiring high levels of skill communicating.

Fortunately, the statistic has been proven inaccurate, removing the aura of doom from ASD-linked relationships. When I first read articles disproving the 80 percent statistics I was relieved. It made no sense to me that couples with ASD would be more likely to divorce. In fact, I saw that at least in my own situation I was more likely to remain married to my husband because of his ASD-driven loyalty. I saw similar dynamics in other couples where one partner had ASD.

WHAT IT LOOKS LIKE—WRITTEN BY AN NT PARTNER

Let's look at marriage from an insider's view, the NT viewpoint. Here is a glimpse into the life of an NT woman whose husband has ASD:

> When we go out in public, he needs me to be near him or he gets sad, distracted, and even depressed. He needs to have me walk a certain way, with our feet in step with each other. If the cadence is off, it bugs him. We need to hold hands whenever it's at all possible. Our hands have to interlock in a particular way or, well, I don't know what will happen. Something awful. Anything unexpected, loud, or confusing makes him shut down.
>
> When we're at home, we are kicked back and relaxed: pajamas at noon, relaxing on the couch, on the floor, in the computer chair. My husband is a homebody. He knows it's safe here. Even though we've had the opportunities for travel—fantastic, far away, free travel—he'd rather stay home. I travel by myself or with our children. When we are at home together it is usually peaceful and calm, with us surrounded only by the things we love. There is no tolerance for anything or anyone invading our private space and time.
>
> I've worked exceptionally hard to build a satisfying life around me. I know there are many things he can't provide so I find fulfillment in my work, my friends, my children, and my hobbies. I've learned to be more self-sufficient than most.
>
> At first glance we look like a typical American couple living the American dream, raising our children, working at jobs we love, and swimming at the neighborhood pool. But the minute you hear us talk or get even a few steps into our lives, you realize that our relationship is different, very different. You'll hear him say, "What's

your face saying?" or you'll hear me say, "Please stand three inches closer to me." I consider our marriage a successful one but it's recognizably different from the norm.

WHAT IT FEELS LIKE—WRITTEN BY A PARTNER WITH ASD

This section was supposed to be eloquently written by a spouse with ASD. Although many people with ASD have phenomenal writing talent, the people I asked said various forms of, "What do you mean—'feels like…'?" So, I asked my most reliable resource, my husband, to give me a glimpse into how a person with ASD views marriage. Since writing is painful for him, I casually turned to him as he sat at his computer and asked, "How does it feel to be married?"

He responded with, "You're crazy," without turning from the glow of his monitor. OK, wrong approach.

After several moments of silence I asked, "So, I need to fill out this section for my book. I need to know how a person with ASD views marriage. What does it feel like to be married?"

My husband sincerely wants to "be there" for me, so he leaned back in his black leather chair, folded his arms, closed his eyes, and after a moment said, "Like two pieces of a puzzle that fit together." Back to his keyboard. Silence. Familiar silence.

I have learned that my husband is perfectly content leaving a conversation unfinished or otherwise hanging so I prodded with another question, this time more specific. "What do you expect out of this marriage?"

"Nothing."

Actually, I know for a fact that he expects nothing from me. He is thrilled just being by my side. As long as I am in the marriage, he is content. Having such low expectations, actually non-existent expectations, can be freeing, but we will talk about that more in a later chapter.

I needed more information. "So what do you anticipate in our future?"

"Nothing."

"You mean you don't see any future for us?" I immediately went on red alert with that high-pitched tone of voice that he does not seem to hear. He always uses this type of terse, condensed speech, but his answer alarmed me.

He responded, "Of course we'll be together forever, but I don't expect anything in particular." Because of my persistently quizzical look (and because I was not going away) he responded with, "Things will continually improve. Our fights will dwindle and our love will grow as we learn to live with each other. Our marriage is sacred and I'm still thrilled to have you by my side." To the passerby, it might sound like he had a vision of marriage, but I could tell from his phrasing that he was repeating words he had heard in the past.

Silence. I did not know whether to call his bluff on parroting words he had learned elsewhere or just accept it. This is a common dilemma for me. I do not want to squelch his attempts at communicating, but I also do not want to accept others' words as his own. Again, he saw that I was not going away and he turned towards me. Direct eye contact—painful for him, but a generous gesture toward me. He clarified with something I know was uniquely his idea, an honest insight into his views. He said, "You've become a part of me," and the conversation was over.

So that is one ASD-influenced view of marriage. He could not write it down. It was difficult for him to even think about it. It took several pointed questions to extract even those few details from him. His response showed that he is confident in his marital future, is content with "nothing," and as long as I support and respect him, I can be part of his life. He has definitely become a treasured part of mine.

3

The Full Realization

Are ASD-linked relationships more difficult than NT relationships? Perhaps. One fact we know for sure is that Asperger Syndrome (Autism Spectrum Disorder) changes the rules of the game. One husband stated:

> You've heard of Extreme Sports? Well, I have an Extreme Marriage. My partner has Asperger Syndrome and none of the "rules of the game" apply. It is an extreme experience, pushing both of us to our physical, emotional, and spiritual limits.

Yes, it is difficult for both partners. Here is a common reaction:

> Some days I want to throw the divorce papers in his face. It shouldn't have to be this hard. Every little change in plans is an "issue."

In order to play this particular extreme sport, you either need to know the rules or be frustrated by the penalties you receive daily—the ones that make you crave divorce proceedings, as awful as they may be. Without a full realization of the intricacies of ASD you may be tempted to skip over steps (I sure did) or dismiss the problems as being less severe than they truly are (again, I am guilty). A full realization comes only when you study ASD enough to realize where your starting point is. One woman explains her full realization experience:

> I did not realize how serious this was until I read several books on childhood development. I was skimming a few books, reading how young children interact, and I realized that my husband was not doing some of the things that young children do. I backtracked in one of the books until I found where he was on their developmental scales. I went over the book with my husband and we both agreed

that he was stuck somewhere between 12 months and 18 months of age in his emotional and social development.

Although it may be an unpleasant realization, knowing where to begin may be the most crucial step of all:

> Without starting at the beginning and mastering the fundamental elements of Experience Sharing, children with Autism are unable to jump in at mid-level and grasp the intrinsic payoff of interaction. Despite their perceived high-functioning abilities in other areas of their life, not a single stage can be skipped without the entire process turning into a house of cards. (Gutstein 2000, p.53)

Depression is often mentioned in the literature regarding ASD (Tantam 1991, p.172). It seems to me that the depression stems from two sources: first, not realizing the full extent of the condition; and second, getting so caught up in the full extent of the diagnosis that you see only the negatives—the things you cannot have and never will have in your relationship.

The diagnostic criteria, by their very nature, are negative. They only point out the "Deficits in…" and the "Impairment of…" The diagnostic criteria do not point out the potential benefits of a differently wired brain. Perhaps the optimal balance is to realize the full extent of what you are dealing with and temper that realization with a hearty dose of optimism.

Optimism will not only give you the strength to see the benefits within the weighty diagnostic criteria but it will also make you a healthier person. Optimism leads to better health, a more positive outlook on the future, and a clearer ability to successfully problem-solve in difficult situations—required skills for survival in our ASD-linked relationships.

True optimism is based in reality. The reality comes from the diagnosis and how your partner presents the different ASD traits. Optimism comes from looking at the gaping chasm between the two of you, recognizing it for what it is, and beginning to build a bridge.

THE INITIAL DIAGNOSIS

There are so many issues when it comes to diagnosis. Where do we go for a diagnosis? Who is qualified to give a diagnosis? What do we do with a diagnosis? If getting a diagnosis would be difficult or painful, do we really need a diagnosis?

One of the best ways to find an up-to-date list of professionals currently practicing is to check websites that are consistently updated:

- NAS (The National Autistic Society) at *www.autism.org.uk*

- ASA (Autism Society) at *www.autism-society.org*

- OASIS (Online Asperger Syndrome Information and Support) @ MAAP at *www.aspergersyndrome.org*

- Autism Speaks at *www.autismspeaks.org*

- FAAAS (Families of Adults Affected with Asperger's Syndrome) at *www.faaas.org*

Next—who is qualified to give a diagnosis? Preferably a diagnostician who has had significant experience identifying ASD. If you have difficulty finding a qualified diagnostician, know that it is because they are rare. It may prove difficult to find a qualified diagnostician in your part of the world.

Not only do you need a diagnostician who is familiar with ASD, you need one who has seen the Autism Spectrum in its entirety. Diagnosing is an art, not a science—the ability to accurately identify one diagnosis over another takes significant experience and focused expertise. It has been said that one person can go to five different diagnosticians and get five different diagnoses. This is especially true for someone with ASD who has learned to survive in an NT world, building different personas which emerge in different situations. It takes a skilled expert to see past the practiced exterior.

As a matter of fairness to diagnosticians, arriving at a correct diagnosis can be extremely difficult. As Liane Holliday Willey states in her book *Asperger Syndrome in the Family*:

> Others of us are not so different, at least on our surfaces… We can find meaningful work, work at meaningful relationships, and play hide and go seek with society. These are the folks who really confuse the "experts." These are the ones who end up with frighteningly erroneous diagnoses that run the chronic mental illness gamut and can result, very unfortunately, in horribly inappropriate therapies.

Given our many colors, is it any wonder… (Holliday Willey 2001, p.142)

Since a correct diagnosis can be so elusive, seeing someone who is less than qualified decreases your odds of receiving an accurate diagnosis and increases your odds of an increased level of frustration. Before you dismiss the importance of seeing someone qualified, please read Chapter 10, "Help! Where to Look."

What do you do with a diagnosis? There are no medical benefits that I know of for adults with ASD other than identifying medications that can deal with the side effects of ASD (anxiety, depression, etc.). There is no financial benefit, since you probably will not find any public services available to adults with non-debilitating ASD. Perhaps the most significant benefit is your own awareness and validation. A correct diagnosis may set you on the path to marital recovery. It may help you focus your efforts, see things more clearly, and may give you access to the few counselors, therapists, and doctors who could be of help to you and your partner, especially if medication is desired or is necessary for anxiety, depression, or other common ailments that often occur when dealing with ASD.

Before you begin the potentially arduous task of finding a qualified diagnostician, ask your partner with Asperger Syndrome (Autism Spectrum Disorder) what he thinks about it. You may find:

I don't need a diagnosis at this point in my life. I have a good job. I'm fine. I don't see how having it in writing would change anything.

Do we need a diagnosis? This has been the quandary of many people who suspect they have ASD. What good does a diagnosis do anyway, other than confirm your fears? Of course, I recommend that you get a diagnosis, then push for treatment…in an ideal world. I do not want readers walking away from this book thinking that all their problems can be solved by diagnosis and treatment. Wham, bam, it is fixed. The diagnosis is only the first rung on an incredibly tall ladder. Admittedly, it may be the most important step, since an incorrect self-diagnosis could lead you in the wrong direction.

Reaction to the diagnosis

If and when you get a diagnosis, be aware that you may feel anger that you did not discover it earlier, heartache that it is too late and too far gone to patch up your marriage, or the sweet relief that many couples feel when they finally find a reason for their problems. For example:

> We had suspected something was wrong for quite a while. When the doctor said, "Asperger Syndrome," we both were so relieved. Our problems had a name.

Or you may see it as a distinct turning point:

> I feel like the first ten years of our marriage were one big unnecessary fight. Near our ten-year anniversary we found out about Asperger Syndrome. I was getting ready to leave the marriage and we found out about AS with a counselor who was helping us with the "stay together or separate" issue. Now that we know about AS we finally feel like we're making progress, finally finding answers. Getting clued into my husband's diagnosis is helping open doors for us that had been slammed shut. We're finally making visible progress.

Or it could have a negative effect:

> I wasn't surprised by the diagnosis but it did have a nasty side effect. My husband [ASD] now uses it as an excuse for poor behavior, saying, "It's the ASD. I can't help it." It's no use trying to convince him that he can't blame everything on ASD.

Or it could be devastating:

> The ASD diagnosis felt like a life sentence. The doctor might as well have said, "You are hereby sentenced to the next 40 years in emotional isolation with no possibility of parole."

Personally, my husband and I felt relief. Immense relief. My husband's bizarre traits had a name. I finally understood that he wore striped shorts, t-shirts, shin-high black socks and sandals for a reason: they were all soft and did not assault his senses. I was able to see that he was not dressing to offend me (it really was visually offensive). Instead, he was trying to self-comfort so he could be a better husband. We purchased soft clothing in muted colors, mostly black, and the problem, along with all its related difficulties, was solved. We would still be fighting about his striped shorts to this day if it weren't for the diagnosis. What a relief! Literally hundreds of small, annoying issues were cleared up and wiped away with the revelation of my husband's condition. I felt relief that I had found the reasons and he felt relief that someone (a book, a website, etc.) was able to explain these reasons for him.

Everyone responds to the ASD diagnosis differently. Some are relieved; some are distressed. Some rarely think about it; some are consumed by it. No response is right; no response is wrong. It is all part of the journey.

Denial

Some may reject a diagnosis even though their behaviors are screaming, "I have ASD." Some may choose to cover themselves in a thick blanket of denial. Why?

One reason may be related to the nature of the condition and how it is presented. They may only hear the words "lifelong," "disability," and "dysfunction." In the newly diagnosed person's mind this may be a huge insult, a condemnation, or an ugly label that is trying to stick to them. Denial may be their only option to protect themselves against something they perceive as a death sentence to their former way of being.

Another possibility is that your partner with ASD may have difficulties opening up to new possibilities. It may be an issue of inflexibility. Your partner may have struggled hard to achieve the current state of being and may be scared by someone rocking his view of self and future.

Another potential reason for denial may be in how they found out about the condition. If they were confronted by it, blindsided with it, or otherwise told about ASD without preparation for the information, then the denial may be a knee-jerk reaction that never wears off. The newly diagnosed person's first impression of new information is extremely important since they tend to stick with their first belief (Attwood 1998, pp.117–118). People with ASD may lack the cognitive flexibility to change the initial impression.

So, how do we present the ASD diagnosis for a positive first impression? Mentioning it verbally might not be a good idea since verbal communication tends to be the weakest modality for people with ASD. Mentioning a "syndrome" or "disorder" might be a bad idea also.

Perhaps you could use an article such as "The Discovery of 'Aspie' Criteria" (Attwood and Gray 1999). This delightful article explores the benefits of ASD rather than listing the negative effects of the syndrome. The article contains "discovery criteria": the positive counterpart of diagnostic criteria. I accessed this helpful article at www.tonyattwood. com.au, printed it, and set it on the kitchen counter where I knew my husband would see it. I turned it to the page where the discovery criteria were listed because he will ignore a block of text, but he will skim a list. Sure enough, when my husband read over the discovery criteria, his face lit up and he muttered, "Now, *that's* more like it."

The reason that the discovery criteria may be a better introduction to ASD is that the initial recognition is so vital. As Dr Attwood and Dr Gray explain in the article, "Knowing that others recognize and acknowledge personal strengths, could provide needed confidence to build and explore personal talents and tackle challenges."

The hidden condition

Asperger Syndrome (Autism Spectrum Disorder) is often called the hidden condition because many people with ASD, especially adults, have learned to hide the tell-tale traits from the scrutiny of others. For example:

> To the casual observer I am intelligent, kind and clever, but inside I'm dying. The pressure to perform in public is so powerful that it crushes my spirit. I feel like I'm using every ounce of strength just to have a four-minute conversation with someone.

Most of the ASD traits occur internally, inside one's head. For example, "lack of eye contact" is not an obvious behavioral issue—it is often due to the person with ASD not expecting to see any information in another person's eyes. It is a cognitive condition of not being able to interpret the nonverbal language of eye contact. Somewhere along the line, the person with ASD learns, Pavlovian style, that if he looks people "in the iris" for the right amount of time they will respond to him better. He still does not understand why we need eye contact; he just knows that it works. He does not get the emotional payoff from the eye contact that most people do. For example, when I look into a friend's eyes, I get a sense of warmth, caring, and some elusive emotional fulfillment that I cannot define. When my husband looks into someone's eyes, he is giving automated eye contact so he does not have to deal with the repercussions of being perceived as rude. He has learned NT ways, but it resounds as a hollow victory, reminding him that, no matter how hard he tries, he will never "get it."

ASD may be a hidden condition, but when you marry someone, all cards are laid out on the table, even the ASD cards. You cannot hide it in a marriage—the spouse and children are bound to find out the depth and magnitude of the condition. Once revealed, family members may assist by helping hide those issues in embarrassing situations:

> One of the reasons he can blend into the background is because the kids and I watch out for him, telling him, "Zip your pants," or, "Don't say that."

People with ASD learn the art of hiding out of sheer necessity. It is a given that they have to survive in a world that is not designed for their senses and abilities. It is a given that they have to stretch, often far beyond their liking, just to get a job or hold a conversation. As one person with ASD puts it:

> We not only bend over backwards—we do full body contortions just to perform the act…we feel intense internal pain when we are on stage. I can do it for only a short amount of time before a meltdown begins or depression sinks in.

It makes sense that in order for a person with ASD to lead a happy life, he must have a soft place to fall, a home, a refuge, and a comfort zone where his ASD-ness is respected. How do we create that? How do we manage to balance our needs with our partner's needs? How do we build a home environment that is so comforting that even the most distressed person with ASD can detox, unwind, and rejuvenate inside the walls of the home? First, we need to realize the full scale of what we are up against.

IS IT A DISABILITY?

All of us face this question at some point. We can decide to see ASD as a disability or as an unusual ability. Maybe we see it as both. This question is one of those personal, introspective issues that you will need to answer for yourself. Without analyzing your own view, you could easily give your partner conflicting messages. For example:

> My husband has ASD and we're always talking about how great it is that he can set himself apart from the crowd. Even though we talk about it as an ability, I have found that I truly see it as a "*dis*ability." My comments such as, "You can't do this?" or "What's wrong?" indicate that on a deeper level, I believe that he's "faulty" and "needs to be fixed." He picks up on my critical comments and is starting to internalize the fact that it's a "disability." He's starting to get depressed.

How you view ASD may turn out to be a deciding factor in your relationship and in your partner's view of himself. For example:

> If there's one thing I've learned about my husband [ASD] it's that he takes his cues from me. He watches what I do in public and he follows suit. He has also picked up my attitude that his ASD is an advantage to both of us. I tell him how great it is that he can be so genuinely himself and not care what other people think. He knows I enjoy the qualities that he brings to the marriage.

My personal view is this: a pessimist can see anyone as disabled. An optimist can see everyone as somehow abled. Each of us has been given gifts, traits, and challenges. There is no such thing as perfect normalcy for anyone, but there are guiding principles. My guiding principle that keeps me going during the tough times is this: I can learn from him and he can learn from me. Together, we will make each other better, stronger, and more skilled people.

PEOPLE'S JUDGMENTS

> Never explain—your friends do not need it and your enemies will not believe you anyway.
>
> Elbert Hubbard, *The Note Book of Elbert Hubbard*

All too often, people will judge your partner with ASD as "rude," "inconsiderate," "clueless," "pig-headed," you name it—the insults will come. A healthy attitude of "I don't care what they think" goes a long way to protect both you and your partner.

My most recent experience with people's judgments occurred at a social event where our little family put on a skit. Although my husband knew what he was supposed to do during the skit, he was overloaded by the lights, noise, and attention of 40 people staring at him. During a part of the three-minute skit, we were supposed to stand together as a family. Instead, he remained off to the side, staring into space, on complete overload. It was obvious that he was not participating. For a moment I paused and saw the stares of others who did not know my husband. At that moment I had the choice to side with the crowd and acknowledge his "rudeness," or I could be compassionate and inconspicuously direct the attention from him.

People judge other people. Our judgments may be completely off-base, but we still do it. Learning how to deal effectively and kindly with the judgment of others is a crucial skill to your own well-being. One woman explains:

> We've moved five times in the last two years. Every time I get to know my neighbors, within a few months they get to the comfort zone of friendship and they start saying things like, "Does he always do that?" or "Have you ever told him how rude he is?" It infuriates me to no end and we start considering another move. Now that we have children, we're going to have to stop running away from this problem. It wouldn't be good for the kids to keep moving like this.

Your partner with ASD is probably very familiar with people judging him. He has probably felt more rejection, more confusion, and more social problems than anyone else you know. Your partner may also be very good at avoiding the full impact of hurt and disappointment. For example:

> My husband [ASD] never talks about his past. Even when I ask, he quickly changes the subject. When something comes up, he'll say that he's forgotten about it or "doesn't remember." At first, I thought he had a bad memory. Then for a while I thought he was lying to me. Now I've realized that he's buried all the horrible memories of confusion from his childhood and most of his memories of adult life are gone too.

As you continue to read this book, you may be impressed with how much pain is involved when a person with ASD is thrown into the NT social blender. Most likely, the pain will not be on the surface—your partner has probably learned to be not so raw. The pain is probably buried under many layers, coming out as anger, hypercritical comments, hypersensitivity, or an inclination to keep people at a distance. For example:

> Every time we visit our therapist with a new problem, she points out that my wife's [ASD] problems are related to a misunderstanding. My wife doesn't think the way most people do and the misunderstandings lead to hurt feelings, avoidance, and deep anger. Every time we walk out of the therapist's office, the conclusion is the same: it's a buried misunderstanding of the world's social rules.

There is a possibility that people nearest and dearest to the person with ASD have judged him as being "mischievous," "disobedient," or "willfully argumentative." The strongest and most damaging judgments may have come from the parents. As one woman whose husband has ASD describes:

> [He was] raised in an overachieving family and he had serious self-esteem problems (being told he was "lazy," he "just needs to apply himself more," and so on). His parents never dreamed there could be something "wrong" with him. He "just needed to work harder," like his brothers.

The judgments from parents can be particularly damaging because these begin when the child is small, before he has had a chance to develop the critical thinking skills necessary to refute damaging feedback from others. Without the natural ability to make and keep friends, a person with ASD may be left without means of forming other positive relationships to counteract the damage that has been done by parents who are unaware or unaccepting of the ASD condition.

At some point in life, your partner with ASD may come to the painful realization that social skills are at the foundation of most human interactions. Without these social skills, he has no foundation. At best, it is a weak foundation based on guesses and rote learning. When this realization sinks in, the person with ASD may begin to feel utterly "worthless" and sink into depression. The suicide rate for people with ASD is not known for sure, but researchers agree that it is high (Attwood 1998). We need to be vigilant and seek professional help for our partners if depression sets in. People's judgments, especially the judgment of significant members of a person's family, may be the final judgment.

THE ULTIMATE TOOL

Children with ASD respond best to positive reinforcement (Attwood 1998). Honest positive reinforcement is based in the recognition of real progress. Comments such as, "Good job," mean nothing to a person with ASD. Comments such as, "That's the roundest 'O' I've seen you write so far," are most meaningful. Tracking progress for children is as easy as saving their daily worksheets. How do we track progress in an adult relationship?

I believe one of the most effective tools for improvement is something that:

- allows you to lay out your situation clearly

- shows progress

- allows you to compare and contrast past and present.

Another book I wrote, *Troubleshooting Relationships on the Autism Spectrum: A User's Guide to Solving Relationship Problems* (2013), includes an extensive section on celebrating achievements as a couple. But for the purpose of this book, I propose that an effective tool for solving marital woes is a relationship journal. Who has time to write in a journal? You may want to think of it as your own research study, grad school assignment, personal progress documentation, or documentation for tracking the progress of a two-company merger, whatever metaphor works for you. I called mine a marriage journal.

Personally, I did not have any extra chunks of time in the day, so I had to trade one activity for the journal writing time. I worked on my journal instead of arguing with my husband. When I sensed a useless argument starting, I excused myself and went to another room to write. I figured that our arguing was rarely productive and could be sacrificed for something that might prove more effective in the long run. Other people have used similar solutions.

We had been married almost a decade at the time that I started the journal. At that point in our marriage I could accurately predict how long certain arguments would take: an argument about housework—ten minutes; an argument about finances—20 minutes; an argument about something emotion-based—45 minutes or longer. If a conversation turned into an argument I would say, "Sorry, I don't have time to discuss this right now," and I would spend the time writing in my journal instead. It was time well spent.

The underlying concept of the relationship journal is as follows:

- I need to improve myself in order to manage this relationship.

- I need to improve myself in order to give my partner the rock-solid support he needs.

- I need to improve myself for the sake of improving myself.

So, the journal was focused on me: my faults, my problems, and my most urgent dilemmas. In the first few days, I filled nearly half the journal. I had more things to fix about myself than I had imagined. I had been neglected for so long that focusing on myself was actually fun.

Here is a potential structure for a relationship journal.

First page: State the purpose of your writing in a single sentence. Refer to this often to ensure that the focus of the journal does not alter.

Throughout the journal there are various types of pages: research pages, issue pages, etc. Go with the flow of how your relationship is progressing naturally. If you just read a good book, write a research page; if you just had a nasty fight with your partner, write an issue page, etc.

Research pages: As you read and research, make a note of information you want to remember—for example, Aston, *The Other Half*, "... home is a safer place to express themselves than anywhere else, and so [they] save up a whole day's worth of anxiety and let it out in a fit of anger when they get home" (2014, p.66). Record information that you want to mull over. You can reread research pages later to see how your understanding has shifted and deepened.

Issue pages: Deal with one issue at a time. The focus is on how *you* deal with the issue, not a laundry list of what your partner is doing wrong. Even if your partner is 99 percent of the problem, focus on the 1 percent over which you have control, for example, "Issue: Finances—I am out of touch with the family finances..."

Brainstorm pages: Scribble down all the ideas you can think of to solve an issue, work through a problem, or identify areas that need immediate attention. Do not edit yourself as you write. Remember your sense of humor when dealing with these heavy issues and include the silly, off-the-wall ideas. Dealing with ASD issues is outside the realm of normal experience—the most unusual ideas may prove to be the most effective solutions in the long run. For example: "I don't like to tell him the same things over and over again. Maybe I could get a parrot that could repeat it for me... His home computer can give him regular reminders for the routine tasks so I don't have to be my partner's personal assistant."

Update pages: As you stay together as a couple, there will be progress in one direction or another. Keep track of the state of your relationship on the update pages. This should motivate both you and your partner as you see your improvement. A relationship journal entry one year may state, "We had a 15-minute conversation tonight about who does the laundry and I think he actually heard me." As you look back at it a year later, you may realize that you have solved the laundry issue. You may also realize that you are now conversing for longer periods of time about more meaningful and complex issues—you may be able to accurately pinpoint real progress. Without noting progress, we tend to either exaggerate the negatives or delude ourselves into thinking that it is not so bad. Neither option is healthy. Real progress is based in reality and it takes effort to focus on the reality of the situation. By showing in a concrete, visual way that we have made progress, we can make the hurt not quite so deep and the doubt not quite so dark.

I used my marriage journal to help me see straight when anger overtook my ability to think clearly. For example, one of my frequent issue pages dealt with my husband working late. He is lucky to have attained employment in a field that is directly related to his intense interest and, as with other people with ASD, he dives so deeply into his intense interest that he loses track of the world around him.

By tracking this issue in my marriage journal I found a distinct pattern. When dinner was cold on the table and he still was not home, I started simmering. When the children went to bed without a kiss from their father, the anger would well up in my stomach. When I went to bed alone, the anger became fury. I am embarrassed to admit that at first these pages were titled, "[Obscenity] Husband Working Late Again," but as the pages repeated themselves, I was able to clarify the issue as "Anger Management," which was something I had control over.

The marriage journal helped me identify the pattern and identify what I needed—I needed to find a way to stop my reaction from escalating to such an intense level. Once I could see the pattern and identify the escalation process, I was able to brainstorm for solutions.

On a brainstorm page I wrote:

- Read a good fiction book to distract myself.

- Look at how much work I still need to do.

- Pick a fun task and become immersed in it.

- Go out to a movie with a friend and leave the kids with a babysitter.

- Be grateful that I have peace and quiet for a night.

- Pretend I am at a four-star hotel and draw a bubble bath, candles, etc.

The list grew until I had nearly a hundred delicious alternatives that could reroute the reaction. The escalations stopped, the nagging stopped, and the evenings became much more peaceful. It was not until after this issue had been solved that my husband was able to verbalize that he did not know how to deal with the anger so he deliberately worked late. Once the anger issue was cleared up, he felt free to come home whenever he wished, which was sometimes early enough to play with the children.

I usually worked on several concepts at a time. As I improved myself, my husband improved in lockstep. He responded directly to having a stronger wife. He grew stronger as I grew stronger. In hindsight, I realized that we had both been weak and fearful. Improving myself was the best thing I ever did for my husband.

Admittedly, it was extremely difficult to keep the focus on me throughout the writing process. My pen seemed to have a mind of its own as it began to drift to thoughts of how my husband's behaviors were hurting me. It took strenuous self-control to focus on healing myself. As I focused on clarifying the problems as I saw them, then worked towards meeting my own needs, I found I had little energy left to consider my partner's imperfections. I still studied ASD, but my approach was different.

I knew that my efforts had been vastly successful when one day my husband said, "You keep leaving Asperger articles around the house. Tell me about them." This was the first time he had *requested* information. I did not mind discussing what I had learned because I knew that I was his only resource—an information buffer between the hard, cold facts and his nervous soul opening just a teeny crack. Through my self-improvement efforts with the marriage journal, he saw strength in me and knew that I was secure enough to resist lashing out with "Finally!" or "Duh!" or "Figure it out yourself," all things I might have said pre-journal. We were able to talk about ASD casually and took another baby step on the road to marital recovery.

KICKING THE NORMALCY HABIT

The human brain is typically wired to interpret social interactions a certain way. This is what gives the human race continuity and cohesion. As a species we have made a huge list of rules regarding social behavior. This generally accepted list of rules gives us the parameters of normalcy. If you are going to live with someone who has ASD, you may have to pencil in some new rules and erase some incompatible rules. The brilliance of the ASD brain lies in its ability to disregard these rules. Einstein, diagnosed with ASD postmortem, was brilliant because he was able to look beyond the conventional views of physics.

In order to fully accept the ASD diagnosis, you will need to give up many of your preconceived notions of normal behavior. You will need to kick the normalcy habit. This is easier said than done. Once you do, you will be able to see beyond the behavior to the intent and motivation. One woman stated:

I believe that one of the most important skills in learning about ASD is to let go of all of our preconceived notions of…well, of everything. When I first began learning about ASD, it hit me hard that I would have to give up many of my fundamental beliefs about "normal" human behavior. It was on the level of a spiritual conversion where you sacrifice everything in order to open up to the truths. You just can't hold on to your social belief system and empathize with an Aspie at the same time. At least, I can't do it.

Some may argue that it is impossible for us to give up our ingrained notions of rational human behavior. One woman shares her experience:

I know he [ASD] can't help most of the things he does, but I still find myself getting angry. For example, I know he doesn't recognize that I need help when my arms are overflowing with groceries and I have a toddler tugging on my leg and he just walks past. I know he can't recognize it and I can even identify it as "lack of emotional reciprocity," but I still have a natural surge of anger when this happens.

Some neurologists claim that humans are hard-wired to interpret certain actions a certain way, and we cannot change our natural reactions. I believe our minds are more powerful than that. We can learn to identify our physical and psychological reaction to a situation and, in that precious split second between realization and reaction, we can change our behavior to produce a desired outcome. For example, using the previous instance of the lady whose husband with ASD walks past her without offering help:

Once I recognize the anger building up, I visualize it as acid in my stomach (probably what it really is medically) and then I'm motivated to stop it. Erupting in anger (which is what I really *want* to do) will only make the acid in my stomach hurt worse. Instead, I look for healthy options, such as saying, "Honey, please take these groceries inside for me," or I drop everything, pick up my toddler, and walk away for a few minutes until the acid is gone. There are healthy solutions—I just need to consciously choose one.

The strong man is one who is able to intercept at will the communication between the senses and the mind.

Napoleon Bonaparte, *Napoleon in His Own Words*

The flip side of the coin

Hans Asperger recognized that the individuals he was observing had certain disabilities that were counterbalanced by certain skills:

> A good professional attitude involves single-mindedness as well as the decision to give up a large number of other interests. Many people find this a very unpleasant decision. Quite a number of young people choose the wrong job because, being equally talented in different areas, they cannot muster the dedication necessary to focus on a single career. With the autistic individual, on the other hand, the matter is entirely different. With collected energy and obvious confidence and, yes, with a blinkered attitude towards life's rich rewards, they go their own way, the way to which their talents have directed them from childhood. Thus, the truth of the old adage is proved again: good and bad in every character are just two sides of the same coin. It is simply not possible to separate them, to opt for the positive and get rid of the negative. (Asperger 1944, p.89 in Frith 1991)

The coin analogy may prove to be a highly useful tool as you consider the implications of your partner's ASD. Much of the research is focused on the negative aspects of ASD. It may take a keen eye and a hearty dose of optimism to identify the flip side of the coin. For example:

> It feels like I've been through years of emotional neglect. My husband [ASD] doesn't pay attention to me. He doesn't even see me.

In this particular situation, the negative side of the coin is labeled "emotional neglect." Perhaps the positive side of the coin could be labeled "freedom." She never had to ask him if something was "OK," and she rarely had to coordinate with him. He was happy just to have her by his side.

Another example:

> I went into this marriage thinking that it was all about compromise. Wrong. I learned quickly that it was always her [ASD] way or no way. I thought we could talk about these things rationally, but no, she is as stubborn as cement.

If one side of the coin is labeled "stubborn," what is on the other side?

> Like I said, my wife is stubborn about everything, including our marriage vows. At one particularly low point in our marriage (I had lost my job, money was tight, and there were health problems) she was the strong one for us. I wanted a divorce. Looking back, I can see that I just wanted out of the situation; I didn't want out of my marriage. I'm grateful that she held it together. I know that she'll always be loyal, protective, and devoted to me and our kids.

When faced with a particularly distasteful side of a coin, it may take willpower to flip it over and look at the other side, but you may be delighted at what you find.

A paradigm shift

> Feed your faith and your doubts will starve to death.
>
> Anon

The currently acceptable view of adult relationships is that two people meet each other halfway; they share and they compromise. One woman explained how her view of marriage changed when she learned of her husband's ASD diagnosis. She discovered that her personal view of their relationship was not only inaccurate, but it was destroying any loving feelings she had for her partner.

I used to see marriage like this:

The husband and wife walk side-by-side and in the same direction, in sync with each other. I visualize the people growing taller as they achieve more in their lives. But in my mind I was growing to be a big, successful person since I was doing so well socially and career-wise. If I continued my growth without him achieving at the same rate, then I'd end up being this monstrously large tower, and he'd be a little "peon" down below. I don't want to be married to a "peon." But here is the tricky part: I want to be married to him more than I want to aggressively develop my skills, so I stayed put as a little-timer, not really accomplishing much. My view of marriage was based on the assumption that I was married to my equal. One day, while I was in the car commuting to work, it hit me—he is not my equal and never will be. We are very, very different people.

On my daily commute, I kept pondering this topic: how do my husband and I interrelate? Are we bookends as Liane Holliday Willey suggests in her book, *Pretending to be Normal* (2014)? Are we two pieces of a two-piece puzzle as my parents said? Are we a cypress and an oak tree as writer Kahlil Gibran suggests? How do we relate as a married couple?

Here is what I came up with as a way I could view "us" without seeing my husband as "lesser" than me. I know that sounds awful, but the world bases its views of personal worth on social success. It is hard not to fall into the trap of seeing people as better because they are good at making friends, schmoozing, or networking. My husband has had very few social successes; in fact people have commented before that he's "almost invisible." I don't want to be married to a "nearly invisible peon."

So here is my new visual image of us. This is the only way I can visualize us that removes the competitive part of our relationship. I got the idea for this simple visual image from the sign on a restroom door. It looked like this:

When I sat down to eat lunch that day, I recreated the image on a scrap of paper, then I scribbled words inside each of the outlines. Inside mine I wrote: ambitious, kind, friendly, loving, eager, happy, bubbly, and many other words that describe me. On my husband's I wrote: reserved, wise, good heart, literate, loves his computer, tender, and other words that describe him. Although I was sorely tempted to write all the nasty words, such as: "mean," "cruel," and "heartless," I resisted the temptation and recorded only our positive qualities. Within a few minutes of brainstorming, my figure was filled with words; his was half-full. I took this as a sign that I just did not know him well enough to fill in all of his "being."

I taped this paper to the dashboard of my car and stared at it for weeks. At stoplights, I gazed at that image while thinking of all sorts of words that could still fit inside both my husband and me. During these weeks, I came up with several other words that fit my husband well and scribbled them in. I visualized us as vessels that each contained all sorts of talents, skills, and hidden potential. I visualized what both of us "contained" rather than what height we'd climbed on the social ladder of success.

It took a few months and I noticed a shift in how I treated my husband. I started to respect him. I have to confess that I had not shown him much respect since the day we married. Literally on the second day of our marriage, I had noticed his ASD-related traits and had begun the awful habit of "looking down on him." By using the world's yardstick whereby social success equals worth, I had nearly emasculated him. I am so glad I consciously realized what I was doing before I did too much damage, not only to our relationship, but also to him personally.

Now I view my husband as the rugged, respectable man that he is. He's a strong man and has so much inside him. I am so glad that I took the time to analyze my views.

Before we dive into the specifics of the ASD diagnosis, take a minute to close your eyes and find your own visual of your relationship—free up your mind to visualize you and your partner. Is one of you bigger? Are you smiling or scowling? Does one of you have fangs? Is one of you bleeding? Are you skipping through a field of daisies? If you have difficulty visualizing you and your partner, it could possibly mean that either you are not a visual thinker or that you haven't thought about your relationship in depth. Those are just possibilities and it is only a simple visualization exercise. It could mean a thousand different things, but it may be revealing enough to give you helpful insights.

Of course, you may want to follow this up under the care of an experienced counselor or therapist. Check out the final chapter of this book: "Help! Where to Look."

4

Diagnostic Criteria A

PERSISTENT DEFICITS IN SOCIAL COMMUNICATION AND INTERACTION

A   Persistent deficits in social communication and social interaction across multiple contexts, as manifested by the following, currently or by history (examples are illustrative, not exhaustive; see text):

1.   Deficits in social-emotional reciprocity, ranging, for example, from abnormal social approach and failure of normal back-and-forth conversation; to reduced sharing of interests, emotions, or affect; to failure to initiate or respond to social interactions.

2.   Deficits in nonverbal communicative behaviors used for social interaction, ranging, for example, from poorly integrated verbal and nonverbal communication; to abnormalities in eye contact and body language or deficits in understanding and use of gestures; to a total lack of facial expressions and nonverbal communication.

3.   Deficits in developing, maintaining, and understanding relationships, ranging, for example, from difficulties adjusting behavior to suit various social contexts; to difficulties in sharing imaginative play or in making friends; to absence of interest in peers.

The first set of criteria in the diagnosis deal with social-emotional reciprocity, being able to communicate with a natural back-and-forth

71

flow, knowing what to share and what not to share, and a failure to initiate or respond to others. Here is one example of this trait in action:

> My husband is well known in his field as one of the "Gods of High Tech." He has companies calling him at least once a week to see if he'll work for them. They even call me at home and ask me, "What can we do to entice him to work for us?" I have always considered him to be a successful man in his chosen profession.
>
> Once, he had to go out to a dinner with his boss and a few colleagues (an extremely rare occurrence). Partners were invited so I gladly jumped at the chance to mingle with my husband's colleagues. I was shocked to see how bizarrely he acted. He was rude, did not answer them when they spoke to him, and he misunderstood several portions of the conversation. It is such a contradiction that someone who is so highly marketable in this field can be so inept at a simple dinner meeting.

As you look at how your partner acts in social settings, take a step back, a big step back, and analyze what is happening. Can he act politely in a social setting? How does he communicate with others? Is it different from how he communicates with you? Once you objectively analyze the situation, you will be able to focus your social endeavors better with or without your partner. The analysis may show that traits you previously saw as "negative" are actually beneficial. One woman explains:

> My husband [ASD] is extremely shy. He never speaks unless spoken to and, even then, it's often one- to two-word answers. At family reunions, if he says something, everybody will burst out with, "He spoke!" teasing him for his shy tendencies. I used to think that his quiet nature was a negative trait until I started reading about all the social gaffes that people can make when they have ASD. Now I'm thankful that my husband is so shy. It saves us a lot of embarrassment.

This woman was able to recognize that her partner had developed a unique and mutually beneficial strategy to deal with his ASD-related communication difficulties. He had learned to keep quiet. With knowledge of the ASD condition, she learned how to appreciate his coping strategy as the lifesaver it truly was.

The second set of criteria in the diagnosis deal with the most obvious outward ASD traits: eye contact, body posture, gestures, not sharing or reciprocating—all the casual components of social interaction that come naturally to most people. In this section we will explore the implications of these nonverbal signals and look for ways to work around the difficulties that can occur when nonverbal language is not natural.

Your partner with ASD may be aware of his inability to catch the nonverbal signals that you are sending his way:

> I [ASD] know that I'm missing out on all the signals she's sending my way, but I can't figure it out. All I have is an awful blank awareness that I'm missing something.

If a person is hard-wired to miss nonverbal cues, then of course they will miss the nonverbal cues of romance: a certain look with the eyes, an arm around your waist, a nudge and a wink. Nonverbal cues are a key element of romantic gestures. There are many possible examples. Here is one:

> My wife [ASD] and I are great in the romance department, but it's unusual. She doesn't seem to notice any of my advances and only takes notice of me sexually when I'm very forward and ask directly.

You may have already read the various studies that state that roughly anywhere from 75 percent to 93 percent of human communication is nonverbal. While it is a shocking fact, it often loses its meaning because it is cited so often. If we are truly going to understand ASD, we need to wrap our minds around this statistic once and for all.

Here is the mental exercise I used to help me appreciate the amount of communication my husband was missing. I refer to it as "Cell Static." Imagine you are talking with your partner on a cell phone, but the phones have a bad connection, lots of static, and you can only hear seven to 25 percent of the words. Would you understand each other? "…gr… bl…au…" Would you repeat yourself? Would it do any good to repeat yourself? The odds are the same for a person with ASD trying to hear someone else's communication. It is a bad cell phone connection.

What's the solution? Get off the cell phone.

Find ways to communicate that are out of the ordinary, not in your typical realm of communication methods. Anything but the cell phone. Find ways to compensate for the massive 75 to 93 percent that your partner is missing. Stop underestimating the power of nonverbal communication: the look in your eyes, the tilt of your head, the position of your eyebrows, the sighs, the pauses, and all the other nuances that make up the majority of your messages. As you read this book, you will explore the different parts of nonverbal communication that your partner with ASD is not hearing, seeing, or feeling. In each chapter there are explanations and suggestions for specific, outside-the-box communication ideas that may work for you both. The bottom line is that we must find a way to get off that cell phone and make a clear connection.

Finally, let's look at the third section in this part of the diagnostic criteria: what does it look like when a partner does not reach out to develop and maintain a relationship? This is an expansive part of the diagnosis because it covers so many areas: how the partner with ASD does not make friends, does not share things with others, and does not even respond to contact you have initiated. For example:

> Every weekend I reach out to my boyfriend. I try to make conversation with him and try to get him interested in something. I try to do something fun and new with him but it does not always work. He does not like to try new things and I swear he'd rather that I left him alone even though he says he likes being near me. I think he likes being near me, but not doing things with me.

In order to qualify for this section of the diagnostic criteria, the person must have actual impairment in social interactions. I asked one woman what she had observed about her partner's social abilities. Here is her response to: "How can you tell that your husband is socially impaired as the diagnosis says?"

> Want to know about "social impairment"? I'm still steaming about the other night... We went to a party for my work. All of my colleagues were there. He talked too loudly. He'd only talk to people about the new handheld device he's working on, then he walked away when people tried to talk back to him. He complained about the catered food, saying it was "gross!" He complained loudly about the temperature of the room. He stood so closely to people that one woman thought he was making an advance on her and, the worst, he passed gas loudly while talking to my boss. Now *that's* social impairment.

The above scenario contains many examples of the less attractive traits in full force: sensory issues regarding food and temperature, voice modulation difficulties, poor gauging of personal space, lack of recognition over publicly appropriate actions, and others.

Surprising? Not really. The key lies in understanding the *what* and the *why* behind the diagnostic criteria. The official diagnosis breaks it down nicely. Let's explore the first section: "Deficits in social-emotional reciprocity…"

WHAT IT MAY LOOK LIKE: SOCIAL RECIPROCITY

> *"Deficits in social…reciprocity…"*

There are so many social rules that it makes my head spin to think about them consciously. Here is a sampling:

- If someone gives you a gift, you should reciprocate in kind with a gift of a similar value and similar level of thoughtfulness.

- If someone smiles at you politely in passing, you should politely smile back.

- If someone shares an appropriate secret with you, you should share a similar secret.

- If someone is generous with you, you should be generous back in an equivalent but not identical fashion.

Determining what is appropriate in each situation is a matter of highly sophisticated judgment. Let's use the last example to illustrate how intricate social reciprocity can be. "If someone is generous with you, you should be generous back in an equivalent but not identical fashion." How? Why? Let's imagine that you were generous with your partner, making him an extra-special dinner on your anniversary night. You may, in the back of your mind, wish that he would perform a similarly generous act sometime in the next month or so. You may be surprised when your generosity is appreciated but not reciprocated.

Implications and solutions: Social reciprocity

> "Deficits in social...reciprocity..."

While there may be concrete, logical reasons why your partner does not reciprocate, it still may cause resentment in you. You may stop reciprocating entirely, which may lead to the death of the relationship. Or you may continue the one-way giving and entrench yourself in a martyr complex. Or, as many others have done, you may leave.

There have to be solutions to this dilemma. The one most frequently mentioned in the ASD literature is to tell your partner exactly what you want. Instead of wishing he would bring you roses for your birthday, tell him to bring you roses for your birthday. If your relationship is still solid, he will probably appreciate the suggestion. Take the guesswork out of difficult social situations. By telling your partner what you need, you are teaching him what is appropriate. Maybe on your next birthday, he will automatically bring you roses. Of course, they may be the exact same type of roses for the next 25 years, but at least you will get what you originally wanted, even if in excess.

Also realize that appropriate reciprocity is a common problem for all couples, ASD or not. We all tend to take each other for granted and not pitch in as we should. Common problems can range from, "I do all the housework," to, "He never compliments me." Here is one situation where comparing your ASD-linked relationship to an NT relationship may be a good idea. In an NT relationship, partners may actually be uncaring and insensitive, but at least your partner with ASD has a real excuse!

LEARNING UNIMPAIRED SOCIAL INTERACTION

Children with ASD often can be taught appropriate social interaction. One of the most popular and successful methods currently being used to teach appropriate social interaction is called "social stories" as developed by Carol Gray. The technique helps children read social situations and behave appropriately. The child learns to identify four aspects of a given scenario: descriptive (what people do), directive (desired response), perspective (others' perceptions of the story), and control (how to follow through on the desired response). For young children with ASD, the process of interpreting social situations does not come naturally as it does in most children, but it can be taught through this direct, enjoyable approach.

Can we use social stories with our partners? Probably not. Adults are typically set in their ways and do not take kindly to being treated as schoolchildren. Yet, the truth is that the social stories still need to be taught. How can we possibly help our partners understand social situations without destroying the relationship? Personally, I have found that explaining the consequences in a logical single sentence usually helps my husband with ASD survive a situation. For example, if we are at a party and my husband is standing on the periphery, I will whisper to him: "If you want to be polite, you should walk over to Joan, thank her for inviting us, and compliment her on the decorations." Of course, he makes his own decisions whether or not to put on an act or be his ASD self and ignore the social niceties.

Over the next decade or two, more methods will be developed that will help adults with ASD to navigate social situations. For now, we are left to develop our own methods based on our own best understanding.

One piece of information helped me narrow down the scope of the problem. I was looking at social interactions as one big, unpleasant whole. It was so large that it overwhelmed me. When I read Steven Gutstein's (2000, pp.34–35) definition of static versus fluid systems, it cut our perceived load in half. In a nutshell:

- *Static systems:* predictable social situations where the dialogue is pre-scripted and people are expected to perform a certain way, e.g. in line at the post office, at the checkout stand at the grocery store, or picking up the children from school.

- *Fluid systems:* unpredictable social situations where the participants determine the outcome of the interaction, e.g. a social chat between friends, an emotional encounter with your partner, playing with your child, or an impromptu meeting with the boss.

I realized that my partner with ASD did exceptionally well in static systems—he rarely made a social mistake. But fluid systems caused him to float out of control. We only needed to focus on managing and repairing the fluid interactions, which occurred much less frequently.

Despite our die-hard optimism, the weight of the difficulties found within fluid systems was often crushing because "…people with Autism perceive normal Fluid Systems not as potential sources of joy and excitement, but as overwhelming foreign environments" (Gutstein 2000, p.35). So an NT might see a holiday get-together (a fluid situation) as an enjoyable, rewarding treat, a time to relax, laugh, and enjoy the company of friends. In contrast, a person with ASD would see a get-together as a confusing, uncomfortable ordeal.

Because the fluid situations are unpleasant, the person with ASD may try to turn a fluid situation into a static situation. He may grasp for parts of the situation that he can control. For example, he may dominate the conversation in an effort to keep it static—scripted. He may try to achieve predictability in an unpredictable situation. This comes across as controlling. One couple explains:

> He [ASD] has been trying to control our home life, telling us what we can and cannot do even though it's not his business.

We were not the only ones struggling; other couples in our situation were under the same burden, looking for ways to manage the difficulties that occur when a person with ASD flounders in a fluid interaction.

WHAT IT MAY LOOK LIKE: EMOTIONAL RECIPROCITY

> "Deficits in…emotional reciprocity…"

Emotional reciprocity is the give and take, the yin and yang, the love and be loved. Without emotional reciprocity, you feel like you are married to a stranger, or even worse, a picky roommate.

Maxine Aston, a Relate counselor specializing in adult ASD relationships, explains emotional reciprocity:

> Reciprocity means to feel or give in return for the same. Most relationships depend on reciprocity to make them work—there has to be give and take. Some men and women I have come into contact with felt that they gave and their partners took.
>
>   However, no amount of nagging, bribing, emotional blackmail or ultimatums will make any difference. These will just put your

partner [with ASD] under tremendous pressure because they do not know how to show or express this thing you call empathy in the way you would wish it.

For the relationship to continue less stressfully, maintain a realistic view of the situation and do not strive for the impossible. Your partner cannot give you something they do not have, but they can protect you, care, show concern and give comfort if they are made aware that this is what is required of them. (Aston 2014, pp.115–116)

Emotional reciprocity describes the common assumption that if Partner A gives something, then Partner B will give something in return of equal value. Although NTs function successfully on this assumption every day, it may come as a bit of a surprise to your partner with ASD. Even when the partner with ASD is aware that there should be some level of give and take, he may not agree with the assumption, or know how to reciprocate. There are all sorts of hidden obstacles for the partner with ASD in this regard.

We often hear, "The key to a happy marriage is meeting each other halfway." Have you tried it in your ASD-linked relationship? Doesn't work, does it? In an ASD-linked relationship, there is no halfway, there is not even a "way." It is a completely new experience and we must forge our own paths. Some of us can simply say, "Please help me with __" and some of us have a defensive barrier in front of us.

Implications and solutions: Emotional reciprocity

> "Deficits in…emotional reciprocity…"

With a diagnosis and solid awareness, you will be able to recognize that your partner is reciprocating far more than he appears to be. For example:

NT: Eye contact is personally rewarding.

ASD: Eye contact requires conscious effort with little or no payback.

NT: Sharing information is easy and fun.

ASD: Sharing takes effort—it is a strenuous task.

NT: Uses creative speech (metaphors, sarcasm, gentle teasing) to add interest to the conversation.

ASD: Performs mental detective work to figure out what is real and what is NT-speak.

Perhaps our partners with ASD are making a much larger effort than we recognize, performing mental loopy-loops in an effort to figure out our emotional NT ways. Perhaps they work harder and more diligently than we ever realized just to meet with us on a basic emotional level. Perhaps emotional reciprocity will look different in our ASD-linked relationships than it does in the other relationships we see around us.

It may be depressing to realize that our partners may never meet us on an NT emotional playing field. As Gisela Slater-Walker (2002, p.94), an NT female married to Chris, a male with ASD, points out in *An Asperger Marriage*, "I am never going to have those 'romantic' moments where he is reading my mind." Throughout the book, Gisela points out the many things she will not experience in her marriage to a partner with ASD. Her awareness is insightful. Both Chris and Gisela explain the difficulties in the relationship and how they still have not been able to find effective counseling services that might improve their situation— Chris says, "There seems to be little prospect of this situation changing in the foreseeable future" (Slater-Walker 202, p.41).

The finality and consistent nature of ASD is counterbalanced by the realization that it is a developmental disorder. Developmental disorders are those that improve over time, as the person learns and grows. A person with ASD will learn the nuances of reciprocity as he grows, perhaps at a much slower rate than his peers, but it will occur (Attwood 1998, pp.176 and 184). Sooner or later, your partner with ASD may learn and eventually feel the sweet joys of emotional reciprocity. One woman explains her perception of this life experience:

I find it thrilling to see my husband [ASD] explore issues that others find intuitive. It is like watching someone discover the taste of chocolate—he may hate it, he may love it, but I get to be there for the first taste… Some people would be frustrated and angry that, "He's finally learning to act like an adult!" But I relish those sweet little pleasures in life and I don't have many set notions of what is appropriate for him—he is who he is.

GIVE AND TAKE

As a person with ASD progresses through school and develops into an adult, he will pick up a basic notion of social interaction, enough to get by and enough to become linked with you. Yet, there is still a large void of misunderstanding that comes when he does not understand the intricate give-and-take nature of emotion and action in an adult long-term relationship. Here are a few examples along with how they might be derailed by ASD. Note that the Take is something that your partner does for you: a gift or action you may receive if the Complication does not interfere.

Give: You make the meal.

Take: Your partner does the dishes.

Complication: Your partner may not be able to handle the complexity of the many steps in the dishwashing process: where to put the dishes, how to scrub a rarely used pan, determining the exact level of cleanliness required for an old pot, etc.

Give: You take care of the garden.

Take: Your partner mows the lawn.

Complication: Sensory issues may make mowing the lawn impossible.

Give: You express your love.

Take: Your partner expresses love in a similar fashion.

Complication: Your partner may not know the language for how to respond in a unique way but with a matching level of affection.

Give: You cry, expressing emotion you would like your partner to be aware of.

Take: Your partner puts his arm around you to console you.

Complication: Your crying is extremely disturbing to his senses (auditory sensory dysfunction).

Once you see the different types of effort that you both put into the simple daily situations in life, you can better appreciate your partner's efforts. For you, buying groceries may be simple, but for your partner with

ASD, it may be a nightmare. Here are a few examples of reciprocity by a person with ASD that may go unnoticed due to the fact that they are typically classified as relatively easy tasks in the NT realm:

Example: She [ASD] took the kids to soccer.

Level of effort: She endured a noisy car and aggravating traffic, and withstood the pressures of an inevitable meltdown for several hours, all for the sake of acting like a normal mom driving the soccer carpool.

Example: She [ASD] went with me to my yearly employee Christmas party. She talked with my colleagues and introduced herself to my boss.

Level of effort: She spent days silently agonizing over the event and weeks recovering from it. She was bombarded with sensory offenses, she endured mind-numbing voices and she held off the impending meltdown with every ounce of effort she could muster.

I have seen how both partners in a happy relationship, ASD or not, make extreme efforts to make their partner comfortable. Listen in on one woman's experience:

We went out shopping the other day, just one stop, but it was so overwhelming that when I told him we needed to go to another store next, he literally crumbled. "It's killing me!" Certain tasks are so phenomenally difficult for him, and from what I can see, he can be crushed under a load that I don't even recognize as a load.

The heavy burden of give and take can be partly lifted by an awareness of how the ASD traits raise the difficulty level of daily activities. In order to see if a particular activity is difficult for my husband, we use a rating scale of 1 to 10. If an activity is easy and enjoyable, it is a 1; an activity that takes significant effort but will not do permanent damage is a 5; an activity that is worse than walking on razor blades is a 10. For example, when I ask, "Who goes to the store for groceries?" he might say, "2," I might say "4," and he is off to the store for groceries. The rating indicates how much we will have to stretch in order to accommodate a certain task that needs to be done. A few times, we have both been in the 9s or 10s and we have decided to skip the task. The rating scale helps us communicate our emotional, mental, and physical state in a highly efficient manner.

Also, the heavy burden of give and take may be lifted, if only slightly, by encouraging your partner with ASD to imitate the actions that you need to see in order to realize a preliminary emotional satisfaction in the relationship. One woman explains:

> My husband [ASD] and I enjoy watching movies together. The whole concept of good acting is an ever-present issue for us. We poke fun at the level of acting required to look like a normal couple. Our solution is for me to script for him as if I was a movie scriptwriter creating our relationship on the spot. I say things like: "This is the part where you put your arm around me," or, "This is the part where you profess your undying love for me." It's a casual, fun way to script for him and it adds an element of lightheartedness to the otherwise depressing reality—that he needs a script to get by.

FORGIVE AND FORGET

> To forgive is to set the prisoner free, and then discover the prisoner was you.
>
> Anon

It is highly likely that you are holding on to anger, regret, grudges, frustrations, and hurt. It is heavy, isn't it? I carried around buckets full of anger for the first decade of our marriage, but then it got too heavy. It broke my back. I could not carry it all. I finally found a mental trick that helps me let go of the anger.

When my husband does something offensive, I think: "I'm going to forgive him sooner or later, so why not do it now?" I have never been able to think of a valid reason to hold out and continue the fight. The cost of continuing the fight is always far heavier than the benefit of forgiving immediately. In our topsy-turvy ASD-linked marriage, I flipped the scales once again so that I was no longer on the receiving end of his apparent crassness. I looked at forgiveness as a selfish act. I was forgiving immediately in order to save my strength for better things. Holding a grudge takes too much time and depletes my emotional reserves.

A solid understanding of ASD helped me see that in nearly all contexts it is most appropriate to forgive immediately. He will not see my grudge so it holds no value to him. What does a grudge look like in an NT relationship? One person is offended and gives the cold shoulder (body posture turned away, lack of eye contact, change in the tone of voice, lack of sharing) and the other person sees the cues and either apologizes, reacts in kind, or brings the situation out into the open—a reaction occurs in some form. Would a person with ASD see a grudge? Of course not. The nonverbal cues are missed and the NT partner gets even more frustrated, first because of the grudge, and second because the grudge is not creating the intended (NT) reaction. The grudge hurts me doubly. In order to save myself from becoming a bitter old woman, I have to find a way to let go of the grudge as if it were a chunk of dry ice simultaneously burning and freezing my hands.

Grudges are natural human reactions and, in the NT world, they serve a purpose. With most people, it is best not to forgive immediately without talking about the consequences and repercussions—doing so indicates you are a pushover, a wimp, a doormat. Humans typically learn and improve their behaviors when they see the reactions from others but people with ASD may not learn from their behaviors (Attwood 1998, pp. 117–118). Due to my husband's inability to generalize, he can make the exact same mistake repeatedly and not see the pattern. Someday he may pick up this information, but my immediate concern is to make sure that this pattern does not hurt me or make me bitter.

Of course there are behaviors that are unforgivable. For example, if he ever cheated on me, it would immediately disintegrate our union. I have made him aware of the few rules of the relationship and their specific consequences just as he has made me aware of his. For the everyday matters that are of little consequence, that are merely rude, uncomfortable, or seemingly hurtful, I have had to develop a working strategy.

Because my husband is not neurotypical our interactions are not typical. I have to look beyond normal human response and realize that it does not work with him. It goes against my natural thought processes to think in one quick, instantaneous thought, "That hurt! But I'll forget it." I have to let go of my natural, rational response to display anger and give in to the reality that normal interactions do not work for us.

"I'm going to forgive him sooner or later, so why not do it now?" Soon this became a habit. I would go through the steps without having consciously to choose the better reaction. I noticed the anger slipping away. I finally dropped that heavy load. What a relief.

THE IRONY OF CODEPENDENCY

Look at an adult ASD relationship and you may see the worrisome signs of codependency: telling each other what to say, relying on each other for basic needs, etc. Why is it that some ASD-linked codependent relationships are the happiest?

This puzzle first struck me when I surfed across Liane Holliday Willey's website, www.aspie.com. She is obviously a healthy, well-adjusted female with Asperger Syndrome, happily married with children, yet one line caught my attention. On a previous version of the site, the "About Liane" section stated, "Fifteen years and three wild and wondrous children later, I am part of a codependent family seemingly joined at the hip!" The word "codependent" jumped out as vividly as a swear word. I had learned that codependency was the evil destroyer of dreams, a crusher of souls. As I continued my research into ASD and met other couples, I saw signs of codependency in their relationships and in my own. What was it about these ASD relationships that made apparent codependency acceptable and even beneficial?

Let's break it down into some of the most easily observable behaviors. What might a codependent couple look like? Here is one example of a couple at a social gathering:

> *NT wife:* Look, there's Bob and Sally across the room standing by the big plant. Let's go over and say hi. You say hello, you're glad to see them, pause, and then ask them if their dog is doing better after surgery. Then don't say anything else unless someone asks you a question.

> *ASD husband:* OK.

To most people, this sounds absolutely ridiculous. Who does she think she is, telling her partner exactly what to say, how to say it, and when to say it? This particular scenario demonstrates an extreme situation for a person with ASD—social chitchat in a public place with people he rarely sees. With an awareness of ASD and a solid understanding that they are both in the relationship to help each other, the wife takes a preemptive strike against the problems that usually occur in a social situation— she scripts for her husband. By scripting, she gives her husband some guidance, support, and direction in a situation that makes him cringe on the inside and possibly on the outside too.

Without knowledge of ASD and the way that scripting helps a person with ASD through difficult situations, the scenario appears as a classic codependent conversation. Through an NT lens, the wife has aggressively taken over control of social situations and her husband has become the complacent puppet. Through an ASD lens, the scripting has nothing to do with control or complacency—it is a matter of survival.

ASD researcher Digby Tantam explains how scripting is appropriate in helping an adult with ASD through difficult situations:

> Words may provide people with AS with social understanding that they do not have intuitively. Clear, nonmetaphorical descriptions of why people react as they do, or how to behave in particular situations, can be useful guides for a person with AS who is at a loss and may help to prevent emotional upset or social breakdown. (Tantam 2000, p.379)

Here is another example of a couple who appear codependent but are acting based on their best knowledge of ASD:

> *ASD*: Let's just stay home today. I don't want to go out. Stay with me?

> *NT*: OK.

Is this partner with ASD needy? Clingy? So emotionally bankrupt that she cannot entertain herself for a few hours? Under an experienced ASD psychologist's microscope, we would most likely see a female with ASD who sincerely needs the physical presence of someone she can trust (her partner) in an effort to rebalance herself. Although she is probably too strung out to be able to verbalize it, she is aware on some level that she needs downtime in order to calm her sensory overload. She may not be able to identify it, but probably knows subconsciously that if they stay home, her husband may give her a deep-pressure back rub to relieve sensory overload and do many other things that help her rebalance. Note that the husband does not ask why because he already knows and trusts that his wife has a good reason that is most likely based in ASD-related difficulties. It would be very easy for him to feel controlled or manipulated if he did not understand his wife's intentions.

Codependent people try to monitor and control their partner's activities. In terms of NT codependency, the previous example shows a desire to convince and control. In terms of ASD traits, the previous example shows a partner who is self-monitoring and self-healing. In all aspects, the partner with ASD is trying to be the best partner possible by avoiding further meltdown.

In my initial research into codependency, it occurred to me that perhaps the partner with ASD, due to vastly different neurological wiring, resists some of the poisonous side effects of codependency, not allowing for either partner to overlap in an unhealthy way. Perhaps this is what can turn a normally damaging interaction in an NT marriage into a helpful interaction in an ASD marriage. As one woman stated:

> I used to be so busy with work and family that I could have kept three clones of me busy around the clock. I used to beg, plead, rant, and chastise my husband into helping me but he wouldn't. I used to think my husband was the person who "completed me" and that meant intermeshing my life with his to such a degree that my responsibilities were automatically his also. About a year ago I read a book about codependent relationships. It stated that you should never look to your significant other to complete you in any way. You should be a complete person, able to live happily on your own, who *chooses* to live with a particular person you love. Once I grasped that concept, I consciously fought the urge to ask my husband to "help with this" and "help with that." I learned that if I couldn't do it on my own, maybe I was doing too much. I dropped several volunteer activities, cut back on work hours, and let a few hobbies gather dust. As I drew the line between what was my responsibility and what was his responsibility, it became shockingly clear to me that my husband had simply not allowed me to bring him into my busy little world in a codependent way. He stood his ground because he knew my busy world was a place where he could not live.

Perhaps codependency looks very different and serves a different purpose in an ASD-linked relationship. This is an issue that I hope professionals will research in the future, as we explore the intricacies of building healthy adult ASD-linked relationships.

WHAT IT MAY LOOK LIKE: SHARING INTERESTS

> *"…reduced sharing of interests…"*

> It is the mind which creates the world about us, and even though we stand side by side in the same meadow, my eyes will never see what is beheld by yours, my heart will never stir to the emotions with which yours is touched.
>
> George Gissing, *The Private Papers of Henry Ryecraft*

Let's see what it looks like when someone does not share interests spontaneously:

> Normally, when I'm walking down the street with a friend, we chat about what we did last night, what we've been reading lately, or how things are going at work. We share our interests and our experiences. When I walk with my husband [ASD], we are silent. Sometimes I'll share something interesting with him and he'll always respond pleasantly, but the conversation soon dies out.

Another example:

> He [ASD] so rarely shares his insights into the world that I often assume that he feels no pleasure, no interest, and no satisfaction in his life or in the people around him.

I believe our understanding of this particular aspect of ASD lies in what is called "instrumental" interaction. In the second chapter of his book *Autism/Asperger's: Solving the Relationship Puzzle*, Steven Gutstein (2000) outlines the differences between instrumental interaction, i.e. connecting with someone in order to gain a specific objective, and experience sharing, i.e. connecting with someone for the emotive benefits of human interaction (pp.7–11). Instrumental interactions are the necessary, common exchanges that keep the gears churning in everyday life. The following examples describe instrumental interactions:

He [ASD] knows that if he cleans the dishes, then I will leave him alone for the night. He does them to get me off his back, not because he believes that doing dishes is part of his contribution to running the household or to please me.

Or:

I can't always tell, but I think she [ASD] participates in sex only for the sake of the act itself. There doesn't seem to be an emotional connection. It seems to be a physical, medical need rather than the hugging, talking type of closeness that my previous girlfriends enjoyed.

Or:

He [ASD] buys me chocolates and flowers every Valentine's Day, but it's so strange. He doesn't seem to notice that I enjoy them. One year I told him, "Husbands buy chocolates and flowers for their wives on Valentine's Day." He took it as a rule and doesn't seem to notice my reaction to them.

There are many motivations behind people's actions, but an action is considered instrumental if it fits the five criteria Gutstein (2000, p.9) outlines: the end result is predictable, the partner is not necessary to achieving the goal, the partner is interchangeable, there are scripts for the interaction, and emotional communication is not necessary to achieve the goal.

The third criterion struck me the hardest: that the partner is interchangeable. Perhaps this is why some partners of people with ASD wonder, "Does my partner really need me? Or does he just need someone? A warm body? Would he notice if I left?" Perhaps the level of interaction between the two partners occurs on an instrumental level for such a large portion of the day that the essence of the "interchangeability of partners" begins to seep in on a subconscious level.

All of us engage in instrumental interactions throughout the day. Problems arise when the person with ASD experiences life only on an instrumental level. There is a whole other level of interaction—experience sharing is intentionally interacting with another human being for the sake of interacting, for the sheer joy of social human contact. Due to the wiring of the ASD brain, it is likely that many people with ASD would not use the word "joy" as synonymous to "social human contact." Let's look into what excessive or exclusive instrumental interaction does to a relationship.

Implications and solutions: Sharing interests

> "...reduced sharing of interests..."

When you do not share interests spontaneously and freely with another person, it appears as a deficiency in the relationship. I quickly overlooked this trait, realizing that, yes, my husband does not spontaneously share his interests, but that I did not necessarily need such sharing. Here is an early marriage journal entry when I realized that he was not sharing spontaneously with me:

> It seems like I have to dig for information. I have to dig, prod, and pry, asking just the right question in order to get any information out of him. Sure, he'll give me relevant, timely information, but anything that is not immediately necessary is deemed pointless.

A few years later, I convinced myself that I did not need my partner to share with me spontaneously:

> He still doesn't initiate talking with me, but it doesn't really matter anymore. We don't have much time to talk and, when we do have a spare minute, we are too busy discussing kids, money, or emergencies.

During the busier times in life, casual communication skills did not seem important, but in the back of my mind was a nagging little voice: "You'll want him to learn this now, so that when you're older, you'll be able to enjoy each other's company." Even though I did not have time to think about, or even care about, our more frivolous communications, I looked at it as an insurance policy for our future marital happiness. I kept looking for ways to open up channels of communication between us. Whether by luck or persistence on both our parts, he began communicating for the sake of communicating. A relatively recent journal entry explains:

> Lately, I've been telling him specifically what I need to know about. I can't say, "Talk to me." Instead I have been saying, "Please tell me what you did at work today" (he can almost always talk

about this) or "Did you hear anything interesting on the news?" Somehow, somewhere along the line he finally got the idea that frivolous chitchat can be fun. He'll say, "Guess what?" or "Wanna hear something?" He is *spontaneously sharing*, unprompted and unrehearsed and there appears to be no purpose to it.

I knew that my better half had finally tasted the joys of experience sharing when he started making comments such as, "I miss talking with you," and, "Let's spend some time together." He had come to feel the sweet pleasures of interacting with someone. He did not have a specific goal in mind and he wanted to speak with me, not just anyone.

This particular diagnostic trait, lack of sharing interests, may appear to be a small, frivolous issue, perhaps even nit-picky, but it is the problem that, if unaddressed, leads quickly to a depressing sense of isolation that is common among partners of people with ASD. A large portion of the human experience consists of us sharing with others:

> Memories of shared experiences with a particular person greatly enhance the pleasure of Experience Sharing. Our relationships are strengthened by the perception of a shared past and potential common future. In addition, we learn that partners who are aware of each other's unique ways of relating have an easier time maintaining the relationship. (Gutstein 2000, p.9)

Without spontaneously sharing parts of our lives with each other, one or both partners can sense that they are very much alone in the relationship. One woman married to an ASD husband summed it up as:

> It's not the easiest marriage. Rather lonely...

ISOLATION

> Solitude vivifies; isolation kills.
>> Joseph Roux, *Meditations of a Parish Priest*

Why is it so common for the NT partner to feel isolated? I believe that, in an ASD-linked relationship, isolation comes from various sources, providing a multi-pronged attack on our sense of connection to each other.

The diagnostic criteria show us the first reason for isolation… reduced sharing of interests. When the most significant relationship in your life is enveloped in a relatively silent shell of non-sharing, you may begin to feel emotionally alone, not only in your marital relationship, but in the entire scope of your life. A person's relationship with a significant other tends to set the tone for the household, work life, family life, and so many other areas. It can affect your sense of self. The sense of loneliness between you and your partner may spread to feeling isolated in general.

Second, your partner with ASD probably needs far less social contact than you do and may even be "aggressive in ensuring [his] solitude" (Attwood 1998, p.31). For example, he may have a few hours of social communication during the day and consider it more than enough. One of our sons with ASD, originally diagnosed with High-Functioning Autism, has a black t-shirt that says, "You read my t-shirt. That's enough social interaction for one day" (www.thinkgeek.com). As he progresses through his 20s we talk to him often about how important it is to find a mate who can love him regardless of his need for reduced social contact. The NT partner may wish for a full day's worth of social contact. The differential may cause problems as partners try to align their social needs. The NT partner may end up with fewer friends than she needs in order to stay emotionally healthy. Any imbalance can spiral.

Third, on a functional level, your partner with ASD may actually *require* a socially toned-down environment to keep sensory issues at bay. You may find it nearly impossible to invite friends over for dinner, have social evenings in your own home, or otherwise bring social experiences into your life.

Finally, your partner with ASD may naturally gravitate toward more solitary, isolated activities, as these are the most familiar and most enjoyable for him. For example, he may prefer to spend the day at the library rather than go to a sports event. He may prefer to stay home for lunch rather than go out to lunch with friends.

When you recognize the problems for what they are—a difference in levels of needed socialization—you are on your way to finding solutions. Without the realization of the root causes of the isolation, you may be flooded with resentment so deep and so pervasive that you can only see the darkness around you.

Even with the realization of root causes, you may still have a voice in the back of your mind saying, "Why?" Why does my partner need so much less social interaction than I do? As a counselor for ASD couples explains: "…they seem never to have had any close friends, and do not appear to have really needed any" (Aston 2014, p.21). People with ASD do not have the strong pull that NTs do to socialize and mingle with others. Your partner may not be getting the satisfaction you do from social interaction. No wonder he does not enjoy it—it must be similar to eating without tasting.

INTENTIONAL HURT

Over and over again I read in the literature that, despite appearances, people with ASD do not intend to inflict hurt on others. I latched onto a particularly helpful motto from Liane Holliday Willey (2001, p.91): "I would never intentionally hurt any person I care about. I do not think any decent person would."

There are a few ground rules that should never be broken. One of them is intentionally hurting your partner. If you and your partner are intentionally hurting each other then you probably knew a long time ago that your marriage was doomed—you are just getting up your courage to get out. But beware! A telltale sign of someone with ASD is that he *appears* to be hurting you when it is completely unintentional. As Uta Frith (1991, p.25) stated, "Hurting another person's feelings is a behaviour [sic] that presupposes an active theory of mind, something which autistic people conspicuously lack." It is possible that your partner is *cognitively incapable of hurting you intentionally.* Ironically, he may have learned enough NT behavior to make his actions *appear* obviously intentional. The very behaviors he thought would help him survive in the everyday world are the behaviors that may prohibit long-term intimate relations.

One wife came to an awareness of the importance of weighing intentionality over appearance:

My husband is on the severe side of the Asperger spectrum. People quickly comment, "What's wrong with him?" My husband can't hide it like other AS people can. We've found little in the way of support and no one has been able to address our marital problems. There are so many issues that counselors and doctors don't understand.

The most troublesome problem is how he hurts me; he says horrible things to me, he ignores me, he embarrasses me in public, he shows little to no affection unless I tell him exactly what to do. My marriage has been a painful ordeal.

One Sunday several years ago, I took off in the car, promising myself I'd never go back to him. I spent the day wandering around a lake near where we lived. I finally came up with the one question I needed him to answer once and for all: do you want to hurt me?

I went home and got my husband, and drove back to the lake. I took him to a secluded spot and both of us sat down on two big rocks. Although I know he can't look at me while we are talking, I gently made sure that we were facing each other so at least he was facing my direction. I asked him my question slowly and directly, "I need to know: do you want to hurt me?" He looked at me with a scared and confused expression and said, "Of course not!" I started to cry; he started to cry. It was the turn-around moment in our marriage.

Now, when he says something horrible, I say, "That hurt me. Please say it differently." Often he'll ask why it was hurtful and he'll even ask me what to say specifically. It has become a learning process.

This wife needed to clarify her own personal ground rule: "We will never hurt each other intentionally." Once she recognized and verbalized the ground rules, she was able to respond to her husband cognitively instead of emotionally, a strategy that works well with individuals who have ASD (Asperger 1944, p.47 in Frith 1991). In the past, she responded to his hurtful comments as most people would—by being emotionally hurt. Once she understood that the emotional hurt was not intentional, she went from emotional victim to a supportive partner for her husband, giving him the life lessons he sincerely needed in interpersonal relations.

WHAT IT MAY LOOK LIKE: FAILURE TO INITIATE OR RESPOND TO SOCIAL INTERACTIONS

> *"…failure to initiate or respond to social interactions…"*

There is a certain part of the German folk song "Edelweiss" that strikes a chord for our little family: "Blossom of snow may you bloom and grow…"

The flower edelweiss comes from the smallest speck of a seed that grows under the snow in the Alps. The small seed produces vibrant, strong flowers, even in the most frigid conditions.

My husband often comes across as cold. The first criterion of the diagnosis explains why: he does not see any purpose in sharing his life with others. His words (when we were younger): "Why would I tell you about my day? It happened. So what?" His words and his actions were so cold that I felt a polar chill in our home. As most newlyweds do, I hoped that our relationship would bloom into a long-term, lifelong romance. I quickly realized I needed to respect his need to keep his snowy, chilly ASD homeland. I would not (and could not) transplant him to my world…it would kill him. I felt that if I respected his need to stay in his snowy homeland, he would "bloom and grow." Sure enough, he did.

If we were an NT/NT couple, we would probably both initiate and respond to each other naturally, spontaneously sharing that he received a promotion and me sharing that I landed a new contract. We would see each other grow as adults and as professionals. We would not have to make such a monumental effort to see the blooming process.

If your partner with ASD fits this part of the diagnosis and does not initiate or respond naturally, it may impact on your relationship. What does it look like when a partner does not initiate, or even worse, does not respond?

> He [ASD] will listen to me talk about my day, but he doesn't share anything about himself unless I ask him questions. It's like a kid coming home from school: the mother says, "What did you do at school today?" to which the child says, "Nothing."

Implications and solutions: Failure to initiate or respond to social interactions

> "…failure to initiate or respond to social interactions…"

If we are accustomed to people spontaneously sharing with us and naturally responding to us, we expect it, assuming that if our partner does not speak up, then there is nothing to share, and if a partner does not reply, there is something wrong. We may assume that he is disconnected or deliberately trying to shut out others. The appearance and reality may be opposites. He may appear to be cold when in fact his day was packed with small victories and he has wonderful information that you would be pleased to know. The implications of this lack of sharing are that we cannot recognize our partner's strengths, accomplishments, and struggles if we do not know about them. Without this information, we may assume that our partner is lazy or boring.

Ironically, our partners with ASD have a huge undercurrent of achievements every day: surviving sensory overload, managing a conversation, smiling at a crucial moment even though it feels horribly unnatural, figuring out a new social rule, etc. Perhaps the undercurrent is too large to contemplate. Here is a personal example of what my husband with ASD used to share at the end of the day:

Shares: Today was "fine."

Reality: He went out to lunch with a group from work so he has already had more than enough social contact for the day. He found out that he might receive a significant bonus soon. One of his co-workers pointed out a huge flaw in his work and he will need to work overtime for the next few weeks to fix it. He has been feeling sick to his stomach and may be getting the flu again. On the way home, he managed to avoid hitting a deer (dyspraxia makes this quite a feat).

The difference between what your partner with ASD shares at the end of the day and what really happened during the day may be big enough to cause significant communication problems. With us, it eroded trust. I thought it dishonest for my husband to withhold significant information when, in reality, he never thought to initiate conversation about it. This was one of those crucial areas where an awareness of the ASD diagnosis helped me see past my NT knee-jerk reaction of distrust to the real issue of "…failure to initiate or respond to social interactions."

APPEARANCE OF WITHDRAWAL

The end result of "Persistent deficits in social communication…" is that the person with ASD develops an appearance of withdrawal; he appears to have purposely distanced himself from others. Some may call the person with ASD a loner, outsider, outcast, or foreigner.

The appearance of withdrawal may be just that—an appearance. People with ASD sometimes want to be socially active (Attwood 1998, p.50) but do not know how to get into the inner circle of social acceptance, let alone survive in that inner circle for long. Focusing on the withdrawal shifts our focus away from our partner's strengths and directs our focus to the negative comparisons of how a partner with ASD falls short in the NT world.

When we see the appearance of withdrawal, it is vital that we remember the causes. The causes are found in the diagnostic criteria and in the ASD literature. When we rely on our assumptions, we assume NT reasoning that applies in the NT world. For example: if a person is withdrawn, it is because he wants to be. He is capable of participating, but chooses not to. What a horrible burden to carry! "If only I *tried harder*, I could fit into the group and make lifelong friends…" Even the most conscientious person with ASD may fall prey to these assumptions. The appearance of withdrawal is only an appearance—an appearance based on the NT yardstick of normal human behavior.

WHAT IT MAY LOOK LIKE: EYE CONTACT

"Deficits in…eye contact…"

Have you noticed how people look at each other in the eyes when conversing? Looking away can signal dishonesty, but a gaze that is unflinching can cause tension. There is a fine balance achieved when you gaze into each other's eyes with interest and meaning. Some people with ASD do not do this. Why? Among other reasons, they do not see any reason to give eye contact because they do not gain any information from eye contact.

When I first learned about the eye contact issue, it sounded fishy to me so I asked my husband with ASD:

Me: Why do you look at me?

Him: Because I have to.

Me: You have to? What makes you think you have to?

Him: Because you'll get mad at me if I don't.

Me: Oh.

Later that day I tried again:

Me: What do you see when you look at me?

Him: You.

Me: What about me? What details?

Him: Nothing. Just you.

Me: Come on, you must see something.

Him: Nope. Just you.

I knew he was being honest so I tried to compare it to what I see. When I look at him I see his mouth curved up at the edges, showing his basic optimistic nature, his eyes relaxed and tired, a bit red. I see his deep golden hair a little messy but, oh, so sexy. I see the tan on his skin and the rosy color in his cheeks from going swimming with our children. I see the worry lines carved in his face from the stresses of work and family. I see the two deep wrinkle lines in between his eyebrows that come from furrowing his brow when I confuse him. I see his history contained in the lines and curves of his face.

I tried looking at his face the same way he looks at mine—blank. I could not do it. There is too much detail, too much information in his face to *not* see it all. Using a mirror, I tried looking at my own face the way he sees me. I could not do that either. Through this exercise I gained empathy and a little sorrow for the details he may never see.

I sat down with him and told him what I saw in his face and also told him what he might see if he could see my face as others do. I told him that he would see that my big golden-green eyes widen when I am scared and soften when I am comfortable. He would see sorrow, pain, and wisdom in my eyes, although I cannot tell him logically why those emotions are visible. He would see spontaneity in my mouth curving up, curving down, and constantly wiggling in-between. He would see cheeks that are smooth and rosy, peachy from a healthy childhood. He would see eyebrows raised to show concern or compassion and he would see eager openness in the tilt of my head. Behind my eyes he would see my rock-solid, don't-mess-with-me belief system that tells people I am steady and strong.

When I told him all he could not see, he just said, "Wow." It was a curiously strange human insight he thought was odd, but only vaguely interesting. It is highly likely that he thought I was making it all up. Reading information in a person's eyes and face is as foreign to him as his programming code is to me.

While I have only a smidgeon of hope that my husband will someday see my eyes and face, at least now I realize that he is not receiving the many messages my eyes are sending. I cannot be angry with him for not receiving messages that he cannot see.

Implications and solutions: Eye contact

> *"Deficits in…eye contact…"*

It is written somewhere in the ethereal book of "Codes for Human Conduct" that a person must give specifically choreographed eye contact that is appropriate to the situation. Unfortunate news stories highlight the times that people with ASD are picked up by police as being suspicious because of their darting lack of eye contact. People with ASD may use their peripheral vision to view the world around them rather than looking directly at objects and people (Asperger 1944, pp.42 and 49 in Frith 1991). NTs interpret this type of peripheral glance as disinterest at best, dishonesty at worst.

For many people with ASD, learning to give appropriate eye contact is necessary for social survival. It is a basic skill and it needs to be learned, even if it is only fake eye contact. To learn about eye contact and other human behavior a person with ASD may turn to books, TV, magazines, or other highly fictionalized sources. One woman experienced the following:

> One time, we received in the mail a trashy female magazine with articles such as "How to Seduce Your Lover." Out of curiosity, my husband [ASD] glanced through the magazine, thinking he could learn more about the female mystique and me. One of the many bizarre situations that came from him reading this magazine was that he would stare at me for five full minutes at a time, trying not to blink. An article said that gazing into your partner's eyes heightens the sexual tension. Unfortunately, it was just creepy.

Even if the person with ASD learns to give eye contact and can interpret information from that contact, the visual information may be too much, too fast, too overwhelming. An early marriage journal entry helped me see this issue play out in real life:

> We have been fighting constantly… Last night the power went out. I lit a few candles, but it was a new moon so it was particularly dark. It was one of the most romantic nights we'd had in a long time. We were able to talk, laugh, and play together. Next time we have a long night ahead of us, I plan on faking a power outage by shutting off the power switch on the house's breaker box.

Short of living in a dark house, maybe your partner with ASD can communicate important concepts with his eyes closed. Since eye contact is problematic for many people with an ASD-wired brain, you may want to eliminate the need for it during really important conversations that deal with life-changing situations such as moving, kids, cars, finances, etc. Maybe the following will work:

- Talk by candlelight. If the room is dimly lit, it will be harder for you to read his facial expression and you will be a little closer to having a level playing field.

- Talk by monitor-light. We have found that working on the computers at night, with only the light of the monitors to illuminate the room, creates an atmosphere that is conducive to "chatting" (something I adore).

- Talk while back to back. Lie down with your backs touching. Neither of you can see each other to read facial information but the body positioning may put your partner with ASD at ease.

- Talk while walking. Talk while waiting at a stoplight. Talk while making dinner. If your partner with ASD has an excuse for not looking at you, it will take a little pressure off the conversation. (This only works if your partner with ASD can manage two things at a time.)

- Use asynchronous communication from a distance. Cell phones, e-mail, letters, texts, chats, and other forms of long-distance communication can sometimes work better than in-person communication.

Probably the most important thing you can do is remember that your partner with ASD is not trying to hurt you by the lack of eye contact. For many NTs, eye contact is an affirmation of caring. Recognize that this affirmation is what you are missing, and then find a substitute for it, such as holding hands, touching toes, communicating with little notes, or otherwise connecting on a meaningful level. Brainstorm with your partner for ways he can reaffirm his honest intentions without having to remember to give appropriate eye contact all the time. He should be able to relax around you. Give options.

> Within our family, at least, we Aspies can hopefully be who we need and want to be. (Holliday Willey 2001, p.86)

TRUST

Why is it that so much of our trust is wrapped up in eye contact? Apparently, lack of eye contact is the number one indicator of lying. When police, lawyers, or bosses question you, they are probably watching your eyes, testing if you can maintain casual, honest eye contact. If you cannot, they will probably think you are lying.

If eye contact is overwhelming or painful for the person with ASD, then it will be nearly impossible to maintain honest eye contact for an extended period of time. Even if your partner truly wants to please you, he may or may not be able to give it. You can explain, "It helps me trust you when you look me in the eyes while we're talking," but it may or may not make sense to your partner. You cannot force eye contact, but you can change how you deal with the lack of it.

First, recognize the eye contact for what it is. If you dismiss eye contact as something your partner cannot give and you do not need, you may gloss over the fact that lack of eye contact is digging deep holes in your trust in each other. When you fully recognize eye contact as an important factor, you will be able to assess the problems honestly when they occur. Especially if the ASD traits are mild, you may find yourself saying:

> We have been getting along so well, but for some reason, we don't trust each other—not even a little.

Instead of staying in a world of befuddlement, analyze what is missing and recognize it for what it is. Once you have identified the problem, you will at least be out of the frustrating stage of wondering what is wrong.

Second, find ways to work around the lack of eye contact. Eye contact is a perk that brings you two in sync with each other. Moving in sync with each other is vital and there may be other methods beside eye contact that can provide the same effect:

> To help us communicate better, we work off a strict schedule. We write up what we want to do and when we want to do it so we're working towards a common goal.

Or:

> Instead of eye contact, I ask him [ASD] to put his arm around me whenever he can. For me, it actually communicates far more warmth and closeness than eye contact ever has.

Or:

> So that we don't get "off-beat" with each other, we communicate about every little thing in the most minute detail. We don't assume anything. We talk; we discuss; we agonize over even the simplest matters.

There is something about eye contact that helps two people flow together. If you cannot get that flow through eye contact, try to find it in other actions such as increased communication, touching, or written messages. It takes creativity to find options that work.

As a final suggestion, do not berate yourself for not being able to overlook the lack of eye contact. When we underestimate the power of eye contact, we begin to think, "I shouldn't really need this," placing blame on ourselves when blame is inappropriate.

Despite the work-arounds my husband and I have for the lack of eye contact, I have found that there are certain times when my NT brain needs eye contact. Most often, it occurs when my partner is looking at his computer screen and I am trying to tell him something important. I will ask him to look at me because, "I need to see your eyes." The message usually gets through to him. As long as I present it as my need—which truly it is—then we can work in sync. If I try to force him to give eye contact as NTs do, because it is supposedly good for him, the pressure is too great, and he will turn his head towards me with his eyes still on his trustworthy computer screen. Or worse, he will suffer through real eye contact then meltdown later.

It takes a full realization of the purpose of eye contact for us to identify the origin of our misguided lack of trust. Books such as *Mindblindness* by Simon Baron-Cohen (1995) explain in great detail the technical reasons for eye contact and what it does to human interactions. Perhaps you will need a more in-depth explanation of this phenomenon before you can forgive yourself for your natural NT tendency to need eye contact. If your partner experiences mindblindness, you may need this additional information to build a solid foundation of trust.

WHAT IT MAY LOOK LIKE: BODY LANGUAGE

> *"Deficits in…body language…"*

There are hundreds of complex gestures that humans make to help each other understand their messages. For example, if you are talking to someone and that person opens his eyes a little wider, moves his body a little closer, leans in a bit, puts his hand near you, and stays relatively still, you know that he is listening to you intently. If that same person takes a step back, slits his eyes, crosses his arms, taps his toe, fidgets, and turns his body as if to leave, you know that he is ready to end the conversation.

Body postures can be amazingly complex and explaining them all in their various combinations could fill volumes. Crossing your arms means you are closed off, unfriendly. Crossing your legs in a certain way means you are sexy. Hands on your hips means you are aggressive. Feet spread apart means you are strong. Understanding the language of another person's body posture comes naturally to me; to my husband with ASD, it may as well be Latin.

Without an understanding of body language, your partner may use "inappropriate" body postures, i.e. body postures that communicate an incongruous or inaccurate message to an NT audience. For example:

> When he [ASD] goes for a job interview, he sits far back in the chair with his arms folded, his teeth clenched, his legs tight together, and his eyes downcast. He looks tense and withdrawn. We're working on the appropriate body posture: leaning forward slightly, arms open, eyes up, feet apart, and whole body sitting upright but relaxed.

Or:

> She [ASD] stood so close to her boss that her boss got the idea that she was attracted to him.

Or:

> She [ASD] stood so far away from me that I thought she didn't want to talk.

Or:

> Even when we're in the heat of an argument, he [ASD] looks so relaxed, leaning back on the couch like nothing has happened. It makes me furious!

It is easy to see the number of difficulties that can arise when a person's body posture does not match the situation.

Implications and solutions: Body language

> *"Deficits in…body language…"*

When a person with ASD uses a body language that does not match the situation or is incongruous with what he is trying to communicate, he gets a double-slam. Not only is his message misunderstood, but also he probably does not understand the repercussions of the miscommunication. For example:

ASD: …but I'm trying to talk with you.

NT: You look so angry. Your arms are crossed, your face looks mad. You look like you're about to explode. I can't talk with you until you relax and open up a bit.

ASD: What?

Although body posture seems like a simple part of communication, it can lead to all sorts of trouble. Without an intuitive understanding of body postures, the person with ASD may misread a person's intentions. For example:

We ran into some friends when we were out the other day. They were talkative and wanted to catch up with us, but my husband [ASD] hurried us on our way and rudely cut the conversation short. I asked why and he said, "Because they were carrying heavy bags." He could not see all the other indicators that showed that this couple wanted to talk with us for a minute. I pointed out the indicators: their arms were open, their bodies relaxed, their heads leaned forward slightly, they stood a little closer to us than normal body spacing, and they focused their visual attention on us. I showed my husband the contrast: if they did not want to talk then they would have held their bags in front of their bodies, stood a little further away, turned their bodies slightly away from us in the direction they were headed, and would have looked around anxiously. Once he could see the difference in body postures, he understood that the body posture was a more accurate indicator than the pure logic of his interpretation. True to his engineer-style, he said, "It appears that 89 percent of the indicators pointed to desired conversation, but only 11 percent of the indicators pointed to desired departure."

Body posture communicates volumes and, unless the person with ASD is with someone who truly understands him, any inappropriate body posture will be misinterpreted. Around you and other safe people, your partner with ASD will probably not have to make the extra cognitive and physical effort to calculate appropriate body posture.

Body language is often part of romantic overtones and may or may not have been an issue for you and your partner when you were first getting together. One woman explains:

> When I first met him [ASD], I sent him so many cues. We met in college... I would sit next to him in class and lean ever so gently in his direction, brushing my arm against his. I would always sit a little bit closer to him than I needed to. I would brush my hair to the side in a sexy way. I would do all sorts of things unconsciously and consciously that said, "I'm attracted to you." After about three months of this with no response, I felt rejected. I wondered if he was gay.

If body postures are a problem for your partner with ASD, you may want to give yourself a constant mental reminder that his body postures are not part of the message he intends to send. For example, if he indicates friendly, compassionate feelings, but his body says otherwise, it might be best to trust his words first and disregard the other nonverbal messages he is sending.

Of course, a person can learn about appropriate body postures. Most people know how to read body posture intuitively; a person with ASD can learn to read methodically. As my husband learns about appropriate body postures and the messages they convey, it becomes easier for him to match his body to his words and emotions. Once, when I commented that body posture must be like Latin to him, he said, "It's pig Latin. I don't understand it immediately, but I can figure it out if I want to."

CLUMSINESS
Clumsiness is often associated with ASD (Attwood 1998, p.103; Tantam 1991, pp.162–164). It is often called "global motor delay," indicating that fine motor skills, e.g. small refined movements such as handwriting,

are often as delayed as the large motor skills, e.g. large muscle groups used for running or dancing.

These motor skills are so much more important than they appear to be on the surface. A person's sense of clumsiness, although it is based in a physical dysfunction, can carry over into self-esteem issues. The adult with ASD may withdraw or mask his poor coordination by not participating in athletic activities. For example:

> My husband [ASD] is an expert at sidestepping situations that would showcase his athletic inabilities. He has even been able to portray an image of ability while adeptly avoiding any situation that might reveal his lack of coordination.

A person with ASD may be able to effectively hide the clumsiness from view but nearly all traditional courting requires coordination. Despite best efforts, the lack of coordination may become evident as you two become intimate. For example:

> I adore him [ASD] but he is such an awkward kisser. I wish he could somehow relax.

Or:

> We can't just hold hands—the hands must be interlocked a certain way with a certain tension. He's even picky about the temperature of my hands.

Or:

> I love it when he puts his arm around me but he almost never does it… It's so stressful for him that it isn't worth it.

A person with ASD may have an overreliance on visual information which may contribute to the clumsiness. For example, ask a person with ASD to hop on one leg in a straight line and he may hop just fine, but ask him to hop in a straight line with his eyes closed, and he may not stay standing. Try a few activities with your partner with ASD to see if he relies heavily on visual input. Ask him to walk in a straight line, turn around and walk back, this time with his eyes closed. What happens? Make up a few of your own ideas to see if this is the case. If you find that your partner with ASD relies on visual input, use that information to your advantage. The realization that your partner is a visual thinker may open up your eyes to issues that have previously been problematic. For example:

> I have learned that if I use visuals with my partner, she [ASD] responds so much better. Instead of explaining something to her, I show her what it looks like.

Or:

> Once we started talking about my wife's [ASD] sensory issues, we found that she is deeply affected by visual stimuli. We have spent some time and money making our home visually comforting to her. We had the inside of the house repainted and we took down the bright mauve drapes... It soothes her to have a calm environment.

Or:

> I [ASD] get dizzy easily. Sometimes when I close my eyes, it feels like I'm falling into bottomless black space. I'll keep my eyes open just to keep the dizziness under control. If I can see something solid, it helps reassure me that I'm not really falling.

There are all sorts of compensating measures that a person can take to increase coordination and body awareness: physical therapy, a healthy diet, staying physically fit, or pinpointing the most difficult tasks, then finding exercises that help build muscle and refine coordination. Of course, these may only help, not "cure" the condition and they all require a willing partner and a kindhearted, supportive you. My husband and I are egged on by our children begging us to go swimming, play tennis, ride bikes, go on walks, and other activities that practice coordinated body movement.

People with ASD are typically not athletic while growing up (Attwood 1998, pp.104–105). Maybe your partner with ASD was able to participate in semi-solitary sports, such as karate, gymnastics, skiing, or golf. Team sports, such as football, basketball, soccer, hockey, and baseball, are particularly difficult for a person with ASD because they involve a high level of coordination, plus a high level of communication between team members. Your partner may not have had the same amount of experience, and thus the same amount of hard-earned skill, that you have in being a solid team player. One husband explains:

> I played football in high school. We all had to cooperate as a team or we'd get clobbered. Now that my wife [ASD] and I have kids, I've tried to explain to her that we need to work as a team, but she just doesn't get it. I feel like I'm the quarterback and I'm getting sacked several times a day.

So, maybe the athletic comparisons will not mean much to your partner. It may go in one ear and out the other when you say, "We need to work together," or "We're a team." The concept of teamwork may be something that you build slowly and conscientiously within your relationship.

EXECUTIVE FUNCTION AND DYSPRAXIA

Executive function describes a person's ability to plan and execute tasks. For example:

> During the week he [ASD] has a highly structured work schedule. On the weekends the schedule isn't there and he can't plan the day or even what to do next. If I don't give him a schedule, he goes into zombie mode and doesn't do anything except walk slowly around the house.

Dyspraxia is the impairment of the organization of movement. It affects how the person plans what to do and how to do it. It can be something as simple as getting dressed in the morning to something as difficult as a romantic encounter. Here are two examples:

> My wife [ASD] often spills food on her shirt when she eats. She tries hard, but somehow she can't manage a meal without getting a few stains on her shirt.

Or:

> Have you ever seen a movie that shows two young teenagers kissing for the first time? They try to get close to each other, but their motions are tentative and awkward. That's my boyfriend [ASD]. If I

was not so careful, we'd get knocked teeth or bloody noses from his poorly coordinated kissing.

If your partner has dyspraxia or difficulties with executive function, you may find it is at the base of thousands of misunderstandings. You may wonder why your partner, "doesn't care enough to help you plan the kids' birthday parties," or, "can't clean up after himself." The lack of success with small daily matters may carry over to so many aspects of your lives together that you have a hard time identifying it and can only be angry at the times when the negative consequences flare up in front of you.

Once, based on some poor advice given in a marital book written for NTs, I made a "Won't Do" list. The list contained tasks that my husband would not attempt, even though he knew that I needed his participation. Based on this list, I wondered why I was still married to this man who apparently was not participating in the marriage. Some of the items on the "Won't Do" list were:

- Won't help me figure out the children's schooling issues.

- Won't help with the tougher cleaning tasks.

- Won't help me schedule our work hours around the kids.

- Won't make phone calls or write appointments on the calendar.

This list grew quickly to 40 items. In retrospect, I could see that every item required significant skill in planning and executing tasks. My husband's difficulties with executive function made it nearly impossible for him to attempt such tasks. For example, "Won't help me figure out the children's schooling issues" is a task that takes a tremendous amount of organization, brainstorming, critical thinking, and other skills that he is lacking. He has his unique strengths, but troubleshooting issues such as these is about as complicated as asking him to physically move the children's school closer to our home. It is a fantastical request.

If I were to make a comparable "Will Do" list, it would contain items such as:

- Will keep home computer network functioning.

- Will vacuum the whole house (even the corners) every Saturday.

- Will pay bills on time. Every time. Without fail.

- Will participate in regularly scheduled activities with the children.

The "Will Do" tasks are predictable, linear, and routine—they do not require planning. Knowledge of my partner's strengths (predictability) and weaknesses (novelty) shed light on an otherwise dark, angry part of the marriage.

Personally, I have often wondered if dyspraxia or difficulties with executive function are what cause my husband to slow down and even freeze sometimes. I received much-needed insights from Dr. George T. Lynn's (1999) article, "Five Survival Strategies to Help Children with Asperger's Syndrome Overcome Inertia." When I first saw this article, I nearly hyperventilated at seeing that there might be a reason for my husband's apparent paralysis. It was the first time I had seen Asperger Syndrome (Autism Spectrum Disorder) and inertia in the same sentence. Here are several examples of inertia:

> He is a young, healthy male, but when he is stressed, he climbs the stairs as slowly as a 90-year-old granny with a broken hip. Sometimes I can barely detect movement.

Or:

> If he [ASD] walks past a TV screen, computer monitor, or anything with moving pictures on it, he freezes. He's in a sort of coma until someone can engage him in something else. It's far more than just being a couch potato.

It can actually be dangerous, as in the following scenario:

> The baby was crawling towards the half-dozen electrical cords plugged into the surge protector. He [ASD] was sitting right beside them, but he moved so slowly that his movement to stop the baby couldn't keep up with the clumsy, slow movement of our infant son. He couldn't move fast enough.

Dr Lynn explains the apparent inertia and why it may occur in those with ASD:

This lack of ability to initiate activity probably relates to the fact that kids with ASD may be deeply apraxic when it comes to affective, cognitive, and behavioral tasks. That is, they do not automatically visualize what movements look like, what conversation with others might sound like, or generally what will happen in the future. Having no way of seeing the potential future, the child cannot plan his present action and so does nothing. Normal people continually feed themselves flashes of images of the next movement a split second before the movement happens. The child with ASD may lack this awareness. As a result he is slowed in movement to the point of not moving at all. (Lynn 1999)

THE PARENT–CHILD TRAP

Without several of the crucial elements of basic human social interaction—gestures, body language, facial expressions, eye contact—you may find yourself falling into a nasty trap: you may treat your partner like a child, and/or you may fall into the role of parent or teacher.

You may find yourself saying, "Look at me when I'm talking to you," or, "Sit up straight," or, "Wipe that smile off your face." All of these smack of a parent talking to a naughty child. While we want to do whatever it takes to help our partners to be functional, this is a slippery slope. It appears to be wrapped up in attitude. There is a difference between, "Eat your peas, honey," and helping your partner past the obstacles that often occur at a dinner table. Listen in to one couple's journey through this issue:

> My wife [ASD] hates it when I speak to her like she's a child. It seems like she's always complaining, "Don't talk to me as if I'm two! Just leave me alone." I hear the words, "Leave me alone," several times a day and, to be honest, it does remind me of a child.
>
> She is partly right; I am talking down to her. I don't know how to say what I need to say without it sounding parental. The content of what I'm saying is so elementary. For example, I'll say, "Honey, you really need to put down that spoon and move on to the next thing you want to do tonight." She gets stuck in ruts and needs help going from one thing to the next. She appreciates my

help and doesn't function effectively without it, but she resents the way I give it.

One day she said, "Why don't you treat me like you do all your friends from work?" It occurred to me that I didn't treat her like an adult and maybe I should give it a try. For several days I tried to catch myself before I talked down to her, but I just couldn't do it. She was still doing all the silly things she always does and I responded the same way I always do.

One Sunday she wore a professional looking dress and, for the first time in ages, I found it easy to speak with her eloquently and respectfully. She loved it! I still gave advice, timely nudges, and redirected her efforts but the words had changed. Instead of, "Put down that spoon," it was, "Hey, let's go for a walk."

In hindsight, I realized that I needed a visual. I needed to see her look like an adult before I could treat her like one. It is embarrassing to admit; it seems so shallow. I guess we both have our faults. When I need help treating her like an adult, we go out to dinner at a nice restaurant and she wears a tailored outfit. It works every time.

As we struggle with the difficulties that ASD presents daily, some of us throw tradition to the wind and adopt a "whatever works" attitude. The couple mentioned above found a small but meaningful way to circumvent several significant problems. They managed to achieve the desirable end result—mutual respect without too much personal sacrifice. We all have to resort to odd tactics at times, and if both people are truly committed to the relationship, they will do unusual things to make it work.

WHAT IT MAY LOOK LIKE: GESTURES

"Deficits in…understanding and use of gestures…"

Some people talk with their hands; some people keep them relatively still, but these small gestures create the nuances that change the tone and direction of conversations. Gestures can indicate anger, aggression, pride, friendship, love, and many other emotions nonverbally. One woman shows her husband's use (or lack) of gestures:

> My husband [ASD] is very still. He doesn't fidget and he doesn't move unless he has to. He doesn't do any of the natural wiggly things that many people do. When he is talking about computers to someone, he'll point his fingers in the weirdest way. I've never seen anybody point like that and it's impossible to describe, but several people have commented to me how weird it looks.

Since the gestures do not come naturally, it is possible that a person with ASD may try to imitate the gestures he sees others make. The gestures do not feel natural to him and therefore look odd. To a person with ASD, learning appropriate gestures can equate to learning a foreign language or sport. Liane Holliday Willey (2014), an adult with ASD, explains her own "uncanny…ability to copy accents, vocal inflections, facial expressions, hand movements, gaits, and tiny gestures." Some people with ASD can copy motions as accurately as a trained professional actor, while others can only fake the gestures on an amateur level.

There are two components to this portion of the diagnostic criteria: the person with ASD may not be able to successfully communicate using common gestures and/or may not be able to read the gestures made by another person.

Implications and solutions: Gestures

> *"Deficits in…understanding and use of gestures…"*

Gestures are at the heart of movie-screen romance. Watch any romantic drama and you will notice that gestures are a large part of what leads to the romantic encounter. Of course, there are also the cues from the eyes, the sensual body postures, and the delicately crafted conversation, but the gestures are a vital component. Watch the man's arm go near or gently around the woman's shoulder, or better, her waist. Watch the woman's hand touch her hair or face softly in a come-hither way or both of them make small, smooth, sexy motions with their hands. Birds are not the only ones who do a mating dance.

If your partner with ASD wishes to learn the art of romantic gestures, one easy way is to watch films together. Actors spend many hours learning how to make their gestures communicate particular messages. The hand motions will most likely be well rehearsed and accurate. A full-length film will give your partner a chance to analyze a full range of gestures for one particular character or several characters.

Although your partner with ASD may be able to learn the appropriate gestures for a given situation, it is only speculation that leads us to believe that a person with ASD can put the learned behavior to good use consistently over time. He may use the gestures awkwardly or inappropriately. The gestures may appear practiced or phony. There is also the chance that even though the gestures can be executed correctly and fluidly, they will be performed at inappropriate times: e.g. gestures that indicate flirting performed in front of a boss or co-worker.

It is possible that your partner with ASD does not wish to learn the gestures used by NTs. It may be a language that he does not care to learn. In this case, pointing it out does no good and only increases the obvious distance between you and your partner. Personally, my spouse with ASD does not care to learn appropriate hand gestures. He would rather keep his hands still and not bother with such complicated and frivolous matters. I respect that.

MINDBLINDNESS

Simon Baron-Cohen points out in his intriguing essay *Mindblindness* (1995) that our ability to determine another person's state of mind is crucial to our social success. For example, if approached by a stranger, how do you verify if the stranger is friendly or threatening? There are clues that a person gives and we need to pick up these clues in order to stay safe and move around effectively in our social world.

For NTs, mindreading is as natural as walking or talking. NTs know others have intentions and motivations that are different from their own. We look for clues to tell us whether or not someone is going to be a friend or foe. For example, if a stranger approaches you and your partner with ASD, you may determine that the person is aggressive and harmful by his gestures, speech, physical appearance, and body positioning. Your partner with ASD may not realize that the stranger has harmful intent and therefore may act inappropriately.

One of the first studies done to show mindblindness consisted of telling a child a scenario and seeing if he could correctly interpret it. Researchers quizzed the children about a scenario in which a little girl named Sally places a marble in a covered basket then leaves the room. While Sally is gone from the room, her friend Anne moves the marble from the basket to a covered box nearby. When the children are asked where Sally would look for her marble, even children with intellectual disabilities knew she would expect to find it where she had left it, but some of the brightest children with ASD thought Sally would look in the box where Anne hid the marble. The children with ASD had "mindblindness"; they could not see the world through Sally's eyes.

I tried this experiment with my own children and my husband. I made up an example using their friends' names and the current gadget. If I had used details that were unfamiliar to them, they may not have been able to answer at all. We may not have gotten past the questions of "Who is Sally?" and "Why do you want to know?" and "Why are you asking me?" and "Can I go now?" I have learned that the most successful interactions between us occur when we are discussing specifics from their world.

The example I used was the same as Sally and her marble, but with elements my children and husband could see. I thought that they would easily understand the experiment, but to my surprise they all showed mindblindness in the example of Zach and his cell phone. With each of them, I explained that Zach did not know his cell phone had been moved and they quickly said, "Oh yeah, oh yeah, I know, you just said it wrong." Their frustration with the exercise was apparent. They were conscious of a painful sensation—not being able to read the thoughts and behaviors of other people. They quickly asked for another example and were able to predict the pattern once they had been given the rule: "a person won't see an object being moved if he's out of the room." But knowing the rule to this exercise does not explain away the fact that they could not answer correctly without the rule. Although I tested my children with their various shades of ASD and my husband with ASD separately, they all followed the same pattern—complete disbelief over their inability to understand the problem the first time followed by a desire to master it the second time. Once they had the rule and knew that I was testing them, they were on the defensive and I could not "trick" them anymore. They were still mindblind, but now they were equipped with the rule.

Simon Baron-Cohen completed many other studies showing the inability to read others' intentions. One study showed how people with ASD have a hard time reading facial expressions. Even the most brilliant adults with ASD can be stumped with some of these questions.

In my husband's case, early in his career he was drawn to a project that developed one of the first lip-syncing software packages. Many months of intense study went into calculating the exact positions of different parts of the mouth, eyes, and other facial features to show particular sounds and emotions. It was a clinical, logical, extremely thorough breakdown of the positioning of facial features to indicate human emotion. The entire time he was on this lip-syncing project, he was intrigued by the new revelations of facial expression. He would come home bubbling over with information about the human face. It is rare to see him so enthusiastic about a new discovery. I marveled at his new discovery; he did not seem to notice that other people already knew how to read faces without such intensive study. Because of this experience, my husband can now accurately, albeit clinically, determine the mood of a person by the expression on their face.

For people with ASD who do not have months to dedicate to the intricate study of facial expressions, they may be left out in the cold during times when facial expressions are part of the nonverbal dialogue. If a person with ASD cannot perceive the mental state of another person, he will not be able to show empathy or identify deceit. One example:

> People say I'm gullible. They tell jokes just to laugh at me. They tease, taunt, and torture me because they know that I can't tell the difference between a joke and a factual statement.

It seems cruel to take advantage of someone who cannot perceive these nuances. Maxine Aston, a counselor specializing in ASD couples therapy, elaborates:

> To expect a person with Asperger Syndrome to know what someone is thinking, no matter how intimate they are, would be like expecting a blind person to guess what someone is holding in their hand without giving them any clues. (Aston 2014, p.172)

I realized this aspect of mindblindness in a personal way several months ago when I was limping across the family room in our home. I was carrying several heavy objects and obviously needed help. Typically, my husband does not see me unless I request his attention, but this time he stood in the kitchen, looking at me—just looking. He said, "I can see you but I can't understand it." I know he is making a conscious effort to verbalize what is going on internally. In this situation, he could not figure out a correct reaction, but he could identify that something was wrong. All I had to do was say, "Come here," and a quick solution was put into action, but the situation needed to be recognized for what it was—a cognitive blindness.

READING PEOPLE

There are many crucial elements involved in reading the nonverbal signals that people send. It may help your partner with ASD to study people's nonverbal signals in a clinical, detached manner. A casual, non-confrontational way to explore (and teach) is to spend a lazy afternoon sitting on a park bench, watching people go by. You might say, "I think that couple looks like they are in love. Look at how they are holding hands and walking in sync. Their heads are leaning toward each other." This approach may or may not work, depending on how you and your partner communicate verbally. You may end up arguing over a ridiculously irrelevant point such as, "That man looks stressed."—"No, he just looks concerned…"

An excellent resource for learning to decode human behavior is the book *Reading People: How to Understand People and Predict Their Behavior— Anytime, Anyplace* by Jo-Ellan Dimitrius and Mark Mazzarella (1998). Jo-Ellan Dimitrius explains how, as a lawyer, she had to perfect the art of reading people so that she could effectively choose jurors. For her client, her choice could mean the difference between life and death. She carefully and logically defines human nature and discusses stereotypes. Most people pick up this information naturally and fluidly, but people with ASD may need direct and specific instruction. Studying the basics of human behavior may give a person with ASD a social advantage over those who take this ability for granted.

Appendix B in *Reading People* is particularly helpful because it outlines "Body language and what it reveals." It outlines exactly which body postures are linked to which mental states, such as embarrassment, defensiveness, or romantic interest, explaining exactly what a person's body does to communicate a particular mental state. The person with ASD does not naturally attribute mental states to others (Baron-Cohen 1995) so this direct, explicit information may be highly valuable to a motivated person with ASD who wishes to learn more about which mental states are communicated by certain body language, gestures, and the like.

At times, a person with ASD may strive to define and classify human behaviors in an effort to make their interactions more predictable. While my husband with ASD was reading the book, he grasped many of the rules but he could not grasp the generalities—the generalities frustrated him. He could not understand why a certain body posture could mean 20 different things. He wanted concrete, unchanging rules that applied to all people. On a good day, my husband could skim a few pages of *Reading People*, pick up a few tips and apply them successfully in daily life. On a bad day, he could not even touch the book. He has been most comforted by Liane Holliday Willey's explanation of how to learn NT behavior:

> As difficult as it is for me to interpret NT behaviors when I am on the outside looking in, I have learned that, provided I have enough time, I can usually get to the bottom of the pile when I am trying to figure someone out… I analyze my way through people… I put them under microscopes and take note of the things they do with their hands, their eyes, their legs, their entire body. I listen to their voices for changes in their pitch and tone and cadence. I compare how they are acting to how they have acted under different conditions. I can tell when they are lying by noting changes in these behaviors, even though I won't know why they are lying. (Holliday Willey 2001, p.85)

WHAT IT MAY LOOK LIKE: FACIAL EXPRESSIONS

"Deficits in…facial expressions…"

Studies of the ASD brain have shown that people with ASD use a different part of the brain to interpret faces to that which most people use (Baron-Cohen 1995, pp.90–91). Due to many different factors, people with ASD often misinterpret the standardized, unwritten rules of facial expression.

It may sound like a simple fact that many people with ASD do not interpret facial expressions, but let's not fall prey to underestimating this huge part of human interaction. Facial expressions are a crucial part of communication. There are two parts to this particular difficulty: not seeing and not expressing. The person with ASD may not express appropriate facial expressions himself. In fact, "There may be little facial expression except with strong emotions such as anger or misery" (Wing 1981). The facial expressions are often described as "wooden" or, a more general descriptor, "inappropriate." A few examples:

> We were at our child's school, watching our child receive an award, but my husband [ASD] just clapped. No ear-to-ear smile like other parents showing pride in his child.

Or:

> I can never tell when he's angry or happy. He looks so blank.

Or:

> I fell down the stairs and broke my ankle. I looked up to see that my wife [ASD] was smiling like some devious sort of Cheshire cat.

You will most likely misread your partner if he is showing facial expressions that are mismatched to his feelings. When a person does not show the correct facial expression in relation to the situation, it can lead to all sorts of misunderstandings that can derail even the strongest relationship. For example:

> *NT*: Verbally explaining a serious close-to-the-heart concern.

> *ASD*: A blank facial expression.

> *NT*: Perceives this facial expression as a clear signal of uncaring, perhaps even as an insult.

The second issue is that the person with ASD may misread or not notice the facial expressions of another. For example:

> Our marriage is dead. I've been giving my husband [ASD] icy stares for two decades now and he doesn't even seem to notice.

Implications and solutions: Facial expression

> "Deficits in…facial expressions…"

Not being able to read someone's face can lead to devastating consequences. Facial expressions are a vital part of our communication with one another. You may be giving the facial cues, body language cues, all sorts of nonverbal cues to indicate "I'm mad," "I need help," even "I hate you," and your partner may miss them entirely. Here is an off-the-wall solution that one couple found successful:

> I was desperate last Saturday morning so I told my husband that I was doing an experiment for a project (he didn't question me) and that I needed to explain everything to him throughout the day as if he was blind. I explained, "I'm carrying all the groceries in the house by myself and I need you to carry half the bags into the house with me." Later it was things like, "The garbage is overflowing. Could you take it out?" Later that night, while watching TV, I said, "Please put your arm around me while we watch TV." At first, I felt like I was being bossy, but he appreciated the clear directions. I was so thrilled at his responses that it turned out to be one of the best weekends we'd had together in years. The "experiment" still hasn't stopped.

This woman shifted her nonverbal communication to direct verbal communication and it solved many problems. She stopped assuming her partner with ASD could see things that were obvious to her. It became a marriage-saving habit for her to explain things clearly to her husband.

You may try to show your partner what "happy," "mad," and "loving" look like in pictures from a book or magazine, but he may not equate the frowning face in a book to your frowning face in particular—they are two different faces and he may not extrapolate the similarities. Due to weak central coherence (the inability to relate one concept to another), he may not generalize from the picture to your face. If facial expressions are baffling for your partner with ASD, make absolutely sure he at least learns how to interpret you specifically.

For my husband, I was able to tell him, "This is my mad face. This is my furious face. This is my relaxed face," and so on. That's all he needed to know. For a partner with more severe ASD, you may want to make "face photos" as a visual tool. It may sound silly at first, but it will probably pay off better than you expect. Face photos are simply photos of you making your most common natural facial expressions. You may even want to label the pictures with instructions. For example: Upset—Please talk with me; Angry—Please stay away; Romantic— Please touch me; Furious—Run for cover!

You could post the pictures in a private corner of your closet where no visitors would ever see them. You may be surprised to find your partner referring to the photos and looking at the photos in an effort to decode you. If he can't figure you out, he can always ask for a translation of your facial expression. The only rule is that you need to be 100 percent honest in your expression of emotion.

One woman, whose husband with ASD was a bit too defensive to handle direct information, was able to couch the face photos inconspicuously in a children's book. She had made many small booklets for her children that had photos of grandma and grandpa and other family members in them. She made a booklet titled "Emotions" with photos of her own face and captions. The booklet dealt with 12 of the most common facial expressions along with a few desired reactions: happy, sad, angry, proud, sweet ("Wants a kiss!"), bored, annoyed ("Please stop what you are doing"), in need (say, "Can I help you?"), calm, depressed ("Please hug me"), tired, and confused ("Please try to answer my questions"). She set it out as the bedtime story book for her husband to read to the children every night before bed. Interestingly, after making the booklet, she noticed her husband giving more eye contact—staring into her face as if searching for meaning. He was finally learning to decode her.

FACEBLINDNESS

If your partner with ASD has extreme difficulties with facial expression, it may be based in a neurological condition known as prosopagnosia (PPG), or "faceblindness," where the person has difficulties differentiating one face from another.

Faceblindness is a condition that I easily dismissed as too abnormal for our little family to experience, but as I learned about it, I realized a mild form of faceblindness had prevented both my husband and my son from recognizing other people. My first realization with faceblindness was when I noticed that my pre-teen son still was not drawing faces on people. If I required him to, he would draw dots for eyes, a smudge of a nose and a U for a smile. All of his natural drawings contained no faces, just a round, blank circle for a head. A child typically learns how to draw faces accurately between the ages of four and six. My pre-teen son still was not showing any facial features that would differentiate certain people from others. The blank heads were haunting to me but were a natural part of his perception. He saw no reason to draw in a face because it was a meaningless element to him.

Armed with this knowledge, I approached my husband to see if he experienced anything similar. Through his life he has learned, in a clinical manner, to recognize and read faces. He suspects that this information did not come naturally to him but, through diligent study, he can usually distinguish Bob from Joe and Sally from Sue. He has become skilled enough to have only minor difficulties in this area, but not be classified as faceblind.

Although a person with faceblindness may have learned to compensate and is probably blending into the population just like the rest of us, true faceblindness can lead to all sorts of difficulties at work, home, and in any setting where people are involved. For example:

I hate going to office parties because I can never remember who is who, no matter how hard I try.

Or:

I'll make a friend, but then the next time I see that person, I fail to recognize her and she is offended.

Or:

I've seen that person dozens of times, but I still don't recognize him when I see him. He has to introduce himself first.

Or:

I recognize people by the types of clothes they wear. I can recognize people at work during the day, but when they change clothes the next day, I have to start over re-identifying them.

As with many other areas of Asperger Syndrome (Autism Spectrum Disorder), the person with ASD may or may not be aware of the cause of confusion. If the faceblindness is the only experience he has had, then he may not know of any other way of seeing people around him. The realization that most people intrinsically understand the complexities and nuances in the human face may be quite depressing.

WHAT IT MAY LOOK LIKE: RELATIONSHIPS

> *"Deficits in developing, maintaining
> and understanding relationships…"*

Although it is possible, it is unlikely that your partner with ASD has formed many solid friendships in his life (Attwood 1998, pp.50–51). One or more of the following scenarios may sound familiar:

> He [ASD] has one friend on the east coast that he talks to once or twice a year, and he says that's plenty.

Or:

> On one of the Asperger Syndrome questionnaires, he [ASD] responded that yes, he has friends. I asked him about it and found that he thinks that mere acquaintances are his friends. Everyone he has ever met (and not offended) qualifies as a friend.

Or:

> He [ASD] doesn't have any friends of his own and doesn't see why I should have any. Even having one of *my* friends over to the house for dinner is distressing for him.

Or:

> Whenever someone tries to get close to her [ASD], she has a misunderstanding with the person and any chance for friendship is cut off. I don't think she's ever actually had a "friend" in the traditional sense of the word for more than a few weeks at a time.

Or:

> She [ASD] has used the moms of our children's friends as her source for making friends. I don't think they are genuine friends since they

only arrange play-dates and occasionally chat about the children, but it's the only source of friendship that she has found as an adult.

Or:

I don't think she [ASD] likes having or maintaining friends at all. It seems more like a burden or a chore. To survive as a socially acceptable creature at work and in the neighborhood, she picks someone who is socially well placed and does the friendship dance as a matter of survival.

It seems as if every person with ASD has a different approach to friendship. Author Liane Holliday Willey (2014) appreciated her few friends over the years as a source of strength. Other people with ASD see friends as a source of confusion. The level of friendship, desire for friendship, and type of friendship are all personal preferences. If your partner with ASD fits this part of the diagnostic criteria, then the general categorization is that relationships are unusually hard to develop, maintain or understand. It is a subjective, fuzzy measurement, but significant nonetheless.

Implications and solutions: Relationships

> *"Deficits in developing, maintaining and understanding relationships…"*

Some people with ASD may not be able to pretend well enough to make and maintain a real friendship. They may want a friendship or notice a need for a friendship, but they may not be able to do the social dance fast enough to make a friend or maintain that friend over time. It is possible that you are your partner's first true, long-term friend.

What if you are the first real friend? From what I have read and observed, the first long-term friendship is the learning friendship, where children learn what friendship is all about: What is allowed? What is not allowed? What makes the other person go away? What makes the other person stick around and/or come back later? Observe young children at play to see the nascent friendship skills emerge. The two children make all sorts of mistakes within their developing friendship until they learn enough lessons to survive each other's company. One will take the other's toy, say something mean, or pull the other's pigtails. A reaction is solicited and both children fight until they find a common ground. Watching two children form their first friendship is akin to watching puppies rumbling and tumbling together. They tug on each other, make each other mad and (usually) forgive quickly and get back to playing.

If you are your partner's first long-term friend, you may find both you and your partner with ASD are constantly at odds. Perhaps it may help to recognize the differential between you two; you have probably had a hundred gratifying friendships over the years, while your partner has had only a few, or perhaps none. Your partner with ASD is at a distinct disadvantage.

Why is friendship so important in a marriage? Because the rules of friendship provide a phenomenally solid foundation for marriages and long-term relationships. Unless the person with ASD has learned and practiced the rules of friendship, he can't be expected to know them naturally, especially in a complex relationship. As a child, the rules of friendship are: "Don't take people's toys," "Don't hit," "Share secrets," and other simple friendship rules that you learned in your backyard, on the playground, and during sleepovers. The same rules apply for marriage, but on a much more sophisticated level: "Respect privacy and personal space," "Comfort her when she is hurt," "Share your deepest thoughts and aspirations," etc. These rules are decidedly more complex than they appear to be, especially for someone whose main source of confusion is interpersonal relations.

The starting point appears to be recognition of the friendship differential between you and your partner—only then can appropriate compensation strategies be applied. Typically, a person with ASD will respond well to reasonable, logical, clear, and consistent rules (Asperger 1944, p.58). Lay out the rules of the relationship and you may have conquered a significant portion of your marital problems. For example:

> I told him [ASD], "In this marriage we do not hit. You hit me once, even a tap, and I will divorce you immediately." He hasn't hit me since.

Or, a less severe example:

> She [ASD] doesn't talk to me unless I initiate the conversation, so I told her that she needs to tell me at least three things about her day

before we go to bed at night. I don't care what she tells me about, as long as I feel like she's making an effort to connect.

This book can only give a glimpse into the complexity and depth of friendship skills needed to maintain a healthy adult relationship. I have one simple solution that works for us: when I can identify that the current problem between my husband and me is due to a lack of understanding about the basic rules of friendship, then I take a step back, remember what it was like on the playground and say, "Honey, you're pulling my pigtails again." I grin, he grins, and the root of the problem is recognized.

BULLYING/TEASING

A bully is someone who:

- shows malicious intent in either words or actions

- is more powerful than the victim

- hurts the victim, whether it is felt immediately or not.

People with ASD are more likely than any other children to be bullied in their younger years (Tantam 2000, p.393). Why? Because they miss the social cues that lead up to the bullying. They don't know how to deflect the teasing and may unwittingly inflame the situation. On all fronts, a person with ASD is an easy target, an easy victim.

It is very important to stress that although individuals with ASD often present with maladaptive and disruptive behaviors in social settings, these are often a result of their narrow and overly concrete understanding of social phenomena, and the resultant overwhelming puzzlement they experience when required to meet the demands of interpersonal life. Therefore, the social problems exhibited by individuals with ASD should be addressed in the context of a thoughtful and comprehensive intervention needed to address their social disability...rather than punishable, willful behavior deserving...reprimands that in fact mean very little to them, and only exacerbate their already poor self-esteem. (Klin and Volkmar 2014)

What does bullying do to the person with ASD? The person with ASD may become distrusting of other people. Without the ability to escape the bullying, the person with ASD learns that others act irrationally, cruelly, and without respect. The person with ASD either lashes out or retreats. This behavior may become so frequent and the distrust so widespread that the person with ASD becomes suspicious and fearful of people in general (Aston 2014, pp.65–66).

Bullies can smell fear. They are drawn to victims who are alone, on the social periphery—people with ASD. The adult with ASD may find bullies in managerial positions at work, as colleagues, or as neighbors. The more sophisticated adult bullying can be verbal, physical, or written, appearing as gossip, setting someone up, excluding someone, making personal information public, or as direct, cutting comments.

It may be helpful for your partner with ASD to pick up a copy of the book *Adult Bullying: Perpetrators and Victims* by Peter Randell (1997) and study the bullying phenomenon from a safe armchair. Being able to study bullying behavior objectively may give your partner with ASD the background knowledge he needs to stand up for himself or otherwise put an end to bullying behavior he may be experiencing at work or elsewhere. In our experience, my husband with ASD cannot read these books himself—the information is too raw and personal to see visually. Instead, I read the books when I have time and I sift out the important information for him.

My husband with ASD was also the perfect victim, but he managed to learn and even master some of the most important protection and avoidance techniques. His most successful technique was to align himself with one of the popular kids who wouldn't force him into the spotlight, but would allow him entrance into the safe periphery of the crowd of accepted people. As long as he had good alliances within the social sphere of the school, he was relatively safe. He also developed a type of persona that faked bullies into believing he was more able than he really was. Despite my husband's best techniques, he still did not escape episodes of bullying. To this day, his only nightmare is "the bully nightmare" where he is running away from the big, bad bully but never quite escaping. In his chosen profession, he still consciously aligns himself with the "cool guys," i.e. the people who will respect and shelter him.

According to the literature, it is highly likely that your partner with ASD has also experienced bullying growing up (Bashe and Kirby 2001, pp.338–341). It seems to come with the diagnosis and is an unfortunate part of life with an ASD-wired brain. Because your partner has experienced bullying, he may be hypersensitive to it. For example:

> No matter what I say, no matter what I do, he thinks that I'm attacking him. Even a polite little comment is a "stab." He says it's like I'm stabbing him with a dagger. How can "Please take out the trash" be an attack?

One gift you can give your partner with ASD is the vocabulary to help you recognize anything that may bring up memories or feelings associated with bullying. Perhaps phrases such as, "I need you to stop," or, "That hurts," can signal that old, familiar feelings are welling up. You probably won't be able to see when your partner is feeling bullied and probably won't be able to see when he's withdrawing from you. You also won't be able to identify the bullying since, to your ears, your comments sound like neutral remarks. For example:

> My wife [ASD] is hypersensitive to the nth degree about teasing. She thinks I'm the world's biggest teaser and I think she's hypersensitive. One day, we decided that she would tell me directly when she felt teased. For the next few days, she said, "Stop teasing me" at least 20 times a day, several times an hour. Nearly everything I said sounded like a tease to her. No wonder she was defensive! I slowly eliminated most of the teasing, but she still interpreted my comments as teasing. We talked about it and she was finally able to see that I was just being funny and light-hearted. I changed my speech; she changed her attitude.

Developing a defensive nature appears to be a common side effect of ASD. As a counselor specializing in ASD explained:

> The bullying was probably quite severe, and so, as an adult, they may be very sensitive to any form of perceived ridicule or put-down, especially from you. This could instantly anger them and they may react to the situation as if they were suddenly back in the playground, placing you on the outside, as an enemy. (Aston 2014, pp.65–66)

The defensiveness grows in the fertile soil of social confusion for a person who has no language or skills to act as armor against the bully. For example:

> One time my husband [ASD] opened up to me about the bullies he had dealt with in his high school days. They sounded horrific. They blindfolded him and made him do embarrassing things, took his clothes while he was in gym, taped him to the flag pole, everything. After he finished explaining to me some of the horrible things they did, I asked him how he responded to it. (I know that I would have done something about it. I would have sought protection.) He looked confused and said, "What do you mean?" Apparently, he never thought to get help. It all just compounded inside him so that now he's permanently on the defensive, always on the lookout for anything that even vaguely resembles bully-like behavior. He's paranoid about it.

Defensiveness may be on overdrive from a lifetime of believing that others are out to get him, trick him, tease him, make fun of him, and make him look stupid. The defensiveness comes from "a lack of an insider's view into the surrounding social world [which] makes that world quite inaccessible and sometimes hostile" (Klin *et al.* 2000, p.10). Bullying makes a permanent impression on a child and the impression may not only be remembered, but may greatly affect his personality and future life choices.

There is also a possibility that your partner with ASD, in an effort to master this aspect of human interaction, has become a teaser or bully himself. He may fall into the natural human tendency to imitate human behaviors he sees around him in an effort to master a behavior that he may perceive as acceptable. He may not realize that teasing is a behavior that should not be imitated. If a person with ASD does attempt to master the skill of teasing and bullying, it may be done poorly, on an immature, childlike level. For example:

> My husband [ASD] tries to tease me, but it comes out as a juvenile jab. It reminds me so much of fourth grade that I just laugh… If he were good at teasing it would hurt, but he's not.

There is a possibility that in his naïve social innocence, he may be led to believe that bullying is an acceptable behavior and that the bigger, cooler kids do it. He may have actually missed the point that bullying is an intentionally hurtful act. As you and your partner try to end the cycle of teasing and hurt, you may run into a circular argument of, "That hurts my feelings," and, "Why? I didn't mean to hurt your feelings." Due to theory of mind issues, your partner with ASD may not understand the difference in intent. If your partner with ASD tries to tease or bully you, it may be helpful to look at the logic and reasoning behind it to see why your partner is doing something that appears, in the NT realm, to be deliberately hurtful.

BONDING

This particular section of the diagnosis explores the "failure to develop peer relationships." Common sense dictates: if my partner with ASD never learned to develop deep, meaningful relationships with a friend in the past, how could he develop one now, in his adult years, especially within the bonds of a relationship so highly emotive as a marriage? You may find moments in your life together that are reminiscent of children or awkward teenagers learning how to interact with each other. One woman explains:

> It's like we're starting from scratch. He's learning the basics of making a friendship. I've been his "first" in so many areas... I'm his first real friend.

Although my husband and I were able to form a friendship, I often worried that he was not as bonded to me as married couples should be. I thought of bonding as an emotional connection and an intricate union that linked us together as one. I looked at other couples for this role model and our marriage did not seem to fit. This notion came from the lack of communication that to my NT mind indicated commitment.

His way of experiencing life together with me was on a different level. I began to see what this was like for him when I read the following: "Once a child realizes that people have their own minds—containing unique thoughts, impressions and viewpoints—he understands that sharing physical proximity is not the same as sharing his experiences with them" (Gutstein 2000, p.28). Perhaps my husband sees commitment as just "being there" and sharing a house. He does not show his commitment through words. He shows it through actions. Perhaps our different forms of dedication to each other balance out.

Perhaps people with ASD experience bonding in a different sort of way than NTs do. For NTs, bonding in a marriage or long-term relationship means shared experiences, shared insights, and soft, tender moments that are remembered for a lifetime. Perhaps your partner with ASD sees bonding differently.

In my own experience, I also found that my spouse was extremely committed to our relationship. Many times, I have been ready to throw in the towel, call it quits, and give up on it all. Every time, I have been pleasantly surprised to find that he is far more dedicated to the marriage than I have ever been. Experts say that people with ASD are often capable of being extremely loyal and I found that to be true. I found that he has bonded to me in his ASD way, not in the normal, recognizable way, but in his own way that I will probably still be seeking to understand for many years to come.

WHAT IT MAY LOOK LIKE: SHARING ENJOYMENT

> *"...difficulties in sharing imaginative play..."*

Before we delve into the different types of non-sharing, let's look at the overall "...difficulties in sharing imaginative play..." Note that children are the ones most often diagnosed with Autism, usually when the first unique traits become obvious during a doctor check-up during preschool years. If the child is higher functioning or has less obvious physical symptoms, the ASD diagnosis may not be given until they reach school and their different ways of learning are discovered in the NT-oriented school environment.

The diagnosis for ASD is generally used for younger people. To make this particular criterion of the diagnosis better fit our understanding of how adults typically interact we need to make an adjustment in semantics by using "imaginative play" and "enjoyment" as well as "interests" interchangeably. For example, a child may share imaginative play with another child by moving little toy cars around the floor while making vroom, vroom noises. We would refer to this as play. An adult may play a racing video game, with the game making the satisfying vroom, vroom noise. Or perhaps the adult achieves financial success, purchases a Lamborghini or Ferrari and makes the vroom, vroom noises with a high-octane engine. We probably would not refer to this as play. Instead we may call it an intense interest, hobby, or happy diversion.

NTs tend to point out objects of interest, sharing their observations with others: "Hey, did you see that guy with the green hair?" or "Did you see how slowly that car is driving?" The partner with ASD may or may not spontaneously share observations such as this. If the NT partner points out objects of interest and the partner with ASD does not point out objects of interest, there is a significant discrepancy. For example, if the partner with ASD and the NT partner spend the day together and the partner with ASD is quiet all day while the NT partner talks about what she sees and hears, the day will end with a long one-sided conversation hanging in the air. One-sided conversations may or may not be all that bad, but what if resentment starts to sink in? From the NT partner's point of view, it has been an emotionally blank day with little to no contribution from the partner with ASD. As one adult with ASD said:

Why speak unless something needs to be said?

From the silent partner's point of view, the NT partner has babbled all day long. Some people with ASD find it enjoyable to have a verbal partner; some don't. Some people with ASD hear the chattering as unnecessary and sometimes insulting. On a subconscious level they may be thinking, "Duh, I can see that the sky is clear today. Do you think I'm blind?" They see no need to state the obvious. They may receive no pleasure from the mere act of speaking and responding. To them, spontaneously sharing an observation may appear as an insult to their intelligence.

See how this simple trait can affect relationships? This sneaky little discrepancy may push us down the path which leads directly to defensiveness, injured feelings, and eventually, the divorce lawyer's office.

Implications and solutions: Sharing enjoyment

"...difficulties in sharing imaginative play..."

The person with ASD may not spontaneously share insights on the things they enjoy, expressing appreciation and friendship. This missing desire can lead to endless misunderstandings. Here are a few examples:

Every Sunday night, we go on a walk as a family. My children point out the bugs on the sidewalk, the birds in the sky, and the warmth of the breeze. I chatter about the fun things we did during the day, what I'd like to do tomorrow, and what I'd like to make for dinner. My husband [ASD] walks in silence. For some reason, he doesn't share anything unless he is asked a direct question.

Or:

Since we both work, we take turns making dinner. I always call everybody to the table when dinner is ready. When she [ASD] makes dinner, she will sometimes just sit down and eat, forgetting to share it with the rest of the family. We'll wander in and she'll remember the scripted behavior: "Call everybody to dinner when it is ready." It just doesn't come naturally to her to think of sharing it with us.

Or:

Sometimes I wish he [ASD] would talk with me about what he likes, the pleasures of his day, but he doesn't. He answers my questions, but he doesn't instinctively share.

If the partner with ASD does not spontaneously share, the NT partner can easily misinterpret the lack of sharing as a lack of caring. For example:

I am always telling him [ASD] about my day but he never responds in kind. I often wonder if he cares enough about me to let me into his world a bit. How hard is it to say what you did during the day?

There may also be the assumption that if a person with ASD does not spontaneously share, there is no enjoyment. The NT logic goes like this—without verbalizing or otherwise giving recognition to the enjoyment, there is no enjoyment. Yet the ASD-wired brain does not conform to this logic. A person with ASD may experience a range of enjoyment—it simply stays internal to the person's mind. For example:

When he [ASD] makes dinner, we all compliment him on how wonderful it tastes and we make a big deal over him having cooked for us. When I make dinner, he just eats it and the kids follow suit. I know he enjoys it because when I ask him directly, he'll tell me exactly how well he liked it, but he won't offer a compliment and he doesn't understand why he should.

Or:

> Every now and then I make an attempt to please him, but he rarely ever gives me any reaction as to whether he likes it or not. How am I supposed to know if he appreciates my efforts?

Solutions? It seems obvious: ask. Ask your partner, "Did you like dinner?" "Did you like the movie?" "Did you enjoy the walk?" Blatant honesty is a common trait for people with ASD (Attwood 1998, p.32). Accessing the truth may be as simple as asking straightforward questions, then encouraging your partner to expand on the one-word answers.

SEX

Although sex is a delicate and controversial topic, it must at least be mentioned in a book about long-term relationships. Note that there is more information about building a mutually fulfilling sexual relationship later in this book under the section titled 'Sensory pleasure as a crucial part of relationships'. Also, there is more information in another book I wrote titled *Troubleshooting Relationships on the Autism Spectrum* (2013).

None of the ASD diagnostic scales discuss matters of sexuality, but an awareness of the ASD traits (sensory dysfunction, lack of emotional sharing, etc.) may enlighten us in our own relations with our partners with ASD. Comments about sex in an ASD-linked relationship can range from:

> The rest of our lives are falling apart, but our sex life is fantastic.

To:

> We haven't been physically intimate in years. He [ASD] doesn't like it when I touch him. I can't even remember how long it has been since the last time.

The variety is enormous and no generalizations can be drawn, but an awareness of ASD traits may lead us to a personalized understanding of why our partner with ASD perceives sex in the particular way he does. For example, if a person with ASD does not read body language or value the emotional (and illogical) aspects, then the act of sex may be more utilitarian to him. He may completely miss the romantic aspects of the act. For example:

> Whenever I tell him [ASD] that I am too tired for an "encounter," he tries to convince me that I don't need to do anything. He says, "You can even go to sleep," as if that would make it easier. Usually I'm too tired to explain to him why this reasoning makes me sick to my stomach.

There is also the tendency to view sex as a disconnected act, as something that is entirely separate from other events of the day. This is due to "weak central coherence" (not seeing things as interconnected) and a tendency to misunderstand body language. A common example:

> *NT female*: Angry over comment or action from earlier in the day.
>
> *ASD male*: Initiating sex but not getting anywhere and not understanding why.

If the NT partner sees life as interconnected, then issues from earlier in the day will carry over into the bedroom. If the partner with ASD sees portions of the day as disconnected, he will see sex as an entirely separate act and may not even respond to explanations or reasoning (NT reasoning) why one issue affects another.

A solid understanding of how your partner presents the various ASD traits will most likely help you understand and solve potential problems related to this vital area of a long-term relationship. Of course, this is an issue that is most appropriately dealt with through a doctor, therapist, counselor, or other ASD-aware professional if help is needed.

BABIES

For a person with ASD whose difficulties lie in strict routines, bonding with others, and sensory difficulties, a baby may be an unwelcome addition. A baby can be a highly emotional and unpredictable little bundle. Your partner may respond to the birth of a baby inappropriately:

> I was in labor... He [ASD] dropped me off at the hospital and told me to call him when I wanted to be picked up.

Or:

> While I was giving birth, he [ASD] talked with the doctor about sports scores and wouldn't stop talking about it even though the doctor told him to shut up.

Or:

> At least he [ASD] stayed for the birth, but I doubt he'll ever stop telling me how disgusting it was (the blood, the meconium, the afterbirth, etc.).

It may help to focus on minimizing the difficulties related to ASD. One woman explains how she restructured the experience as much as possible to allow her husband with ASD to be physically and emotionally present at the birth:

> The birth of our first child was horrible because we were still unaware of my husband's Asperger Syndrome. I didn't know better and scheduled the birth for a large hospital and allowed family and friends to come. My husband was a detached outsider, extremely uncomfortable, and was on maximum overload the entire time. For the birth of our second child, I knew better. I went to a small hospital, scheduled us for late at night when the hospital would be dark and quiet (they made an exception for us based on my husband's disability). Only my husband and I went. We didn't inform anyone else except the babysitter that we were leaving for delivery, so no one could possibly come and visit us. For good measure, we also told the nurse to disallow visitors under any circumstances. The birth was quiet (I had asked for extra painkillers) and my husband was gently at my side the entire time. In the dim quiet of our room, he was able to keep the overload at bay and experience the birth with me. When he saw his son being born, he was open to the impact of the miracle of birth. He cried (I had never seen him cry before). It was the beautiful experience that I'd always dreamed of and we had it because we structured it around our understanding of his AS needs.

Of course, the birthing experience is a highly unpredictable event and you may prefer to rely on the back-up support of a doula, midwife, etc. As in other aspects of adult life, we can make as many accommodations as possible that allow both partners to enjoy the experience.

CHILDREN

Sometimes parents with ASD bond beautifully with their children and sometimes they don't. Here is our own personal example of a parent with ASD bonding with his children:

> When he [ASD] comes home after a long day of work, he wrestles with the kids. He lets them climb all over him and he particularly loves it when they dog pile on top of him (deep body pressure). He plays games on the computer with them for hours on end. My husband's face is usually expressionless, except for when he sees the kids. Of course, he didn't naturally do this on his own. It took many years of tentative trials, failed attempts, and worthless arguments. We both worked diligently to find ways around the big problems such as noise level, touching, and energy level.

I suspect that without intense efforts from all parties, the parent with ASD may have a difficult time bonding with children at their many phases of development. For example:

> Nope. He [ASD] doesn't have any sort of working relationship with the kids. They don't talk and they don't do anything together. They'll sit at the same table for dinner and, of course, we all share the same house, but that's it.

Or:

> I don't think he has ever actually played with the children.

Or:

> I see other dads have such a natural, carefree relationship with their kids. They hoist their toddler on their shoulders, give piggyback rides, talk, and play. My husband's [ASD] relationship with the children seems stilted and practiced, almost staged.

Researchers have noted that "imaginative pretend play is noticeably absent" in people with ASD (Frith 1991, p.3). Perhaps this is a big strike against the parent with ASD. To bond with a newborn, a parent must spontaneously talk with the baby, pretending the baby can talk back in order to keep the conversation going. To bond with a toddler, the parent must pretend that inanimate objects have live properties, e.g. a puppet can talk. To bond with a school-age child, the parent must put into motion a whimsical sort of imagination that can soar through the solar system and dig for dinosaur bones. To bond with an older child, the parent must have a more sophisticated level of imagination that can enter into the capricious emotional life of a teenager. Without the ability to pretend play, the parent with ASD may be at a distinct disadvantage.

As with nearly all other ASD traits, there are ways to train a person how to play with children by providing scripts, guides, instructions, etc. In some situations it may prove impossible if the problems run too deep. In more optimistic situations, there is a chance that a child is the perfect impetus to help your partner with ASD grow into a stronger individual. We have found that our children are my husband's best therapy.

I was thrilled to read Digby Tantam's work "Adolescence and Adulthood of Individuals with Asperger Syndrome" (2000). The best part can be found in the closing paragraph. Others may have stated it before, but this was the first time I had read that being in a long-term adult relationship with a friend/partner may be good for my husband with ASD. Tantam describes how a person with Autism may be able to achieve greater expressiveness, empathy, and intersubjectivity as they age. He makes two particularly interesting points: 1) social contact is assiciated with a good prognosis, and 2) that "a long-standing sexual relationship does reduce impairment."

The children and I are my husband's peers. We are the ones he talks with and interacts with. We are the ones who "make few allowances." Digby Tantam's insights have helped me take some personal joy in my husband's successes; we may have contributed to a better prognosis for him as we encouraged him through his occupational difficulties, sensory obstacles and—in my view the most important issue—his responsibilities as a parent.

I believe the first step in encouraging parenting in an ASD-linked relationship is to be extraordinarily cautious not to correct, put down, or otherwise reject the attempts until we fully understand the ASD dimension of the situation. The following personal story explains how a simple observation can hinder or even halt the delicate bonding process:

> When my husband first started wrestling with the kids, I videotaped them playing because they were so funny. They went at it with all

their energy, throwing each other around, struggling against each other, and otherwise pushing, pulling, and twisting. As I videotaped, I noticed that my husband gave up quickly and lay relatively still, taking their blows, always at the bottom, receiving the bulk of the impact. I worried that the kids were learning to hit their dad and I was standing by encouraging it. I presented my concerns to my husband and he could not explain why he encouraged the wrestling to become one-sided, but he made a token effort to balance it out. Within a few days, he stopped initiating contact with the kids. My small comment was perceived as criticism and shut down the father–child bonding process.

After I read some of Temple Grandin's work and learned about the calming effect of deep body pressure, I looked back at the home videos. My husband was so happy when the kids dog-piled on top of him! He was always in a more good-natured, relaxed, and peaceful mood after the wrestling. I explained to him that what was occurring was a biological, physical reaction to deep body pressure and that his children probably needed it too. This was the logical explanation he needed. Now they take turns in one rolling dog-pile that looks like big puppies at play.

You could also encourage a relationship between your partner with ASD and your children by providing visuals. One wife explains how she encouraged the bond:

I did all sorts of gentle encouragements with him at home to show him how to relate to the kids, how to talk with them, how to care for them, coping skills, etc. but one of the best things I ever did was to make a Daddy Book "for the kids" (it was really for my husband's benefit). I took a few dozen photos of him with the kids and put them together in a little 20-page book with captions like: Daddy takes us to the movies; Daddy plays with us; Daddy puts us to bed at night; Daddy shows us how things work. He read the Daddy Book to the kids and they loved it but he showed only a mild interest in it. (What did I expect? A gushy "Oh how cute!" reaction from him? I don't think so!) He read it to the kids every time they asked for it and it gave my husband the visual images he needed to see that *he is their dad* and to see that he does things for his kids even though at the time it wasn't much. I had to be quick with the camera. I was so proud of myself. I took the small seed of parenthood and planted it. Now it has grown into a loving relationship with his children who are about to enter their teen years… My husband has grown into a stronger man and our children have a father in the home.

As you encourage your partner to develop as a better parent, you will want to consider his parenting abilities within the framework of ASD. What does a person with ASD typically respond to best? Logic. Children are rarely logical creatures (thus the parenting difficulties for a person with ASD), but techniques and strategies for effective parenting can be explained in a linear, logical fashion that will provide a solid lead-in for parenting in an ASD-linked relationship. Books such as *Parenting with Love and Logic* by Foster Cline and Jim Fay (1990) may provide your partner with the foundational knowledge he needs to begin the journey as an active parent. Your partner may also benefit from prepackaged parenting strategies that won't require him to mindread his child. Books such as *Teaching Your Children Responsibility* (1982), along with others in the series by Richard and Linda Eyre, may provide your partner with the unambiguous strategies and explicit details he needs.

5

Diagnostic Criteria B

RESTRICTED, REPETITIVE PATTERNS OF BEHAVIOR

B   Restricted, repetitive patterns of behavior, interests, or activities, as manifested by at least two of the following, currently or by history (examples are illustrative, not exhaustive):

1.   Stereotyped or repetitive motor movements, use of objects, or speech (e.g., simple motor stereotypes, lining up toys or flipping objects, echolalia, idiosyncratic phrases).

2.   Insistence on sameness, inflexible adherence to routines, or ritualized patterns of verbal or nonverbal behavior (e.g., extreme distress at small changes, difficulties with transitions, rigid thinking patterns, greeting rituals, need to take same route or eat same food every day).

3.   Highly restricted, fixated interests that are abnormal in intensity or focus (e.g., strong attachment to or preoccupation with unusual objects, excessively circumscribed or perseverative interests).

4.   Hyper- or hyporeactivity to sensory input or unusual interest in sensory aspects of the environment (e.g., apparent indifference to pain/temperature, adverse response to specific sounds or textures, excessive smelling or touching of objects, visual fascination with lights or movement).

The second part of the diagnostic criteria contains my favorite aspect of ASD—the "…interests that are abnormal in intensity or focus…"

One of the many reasons I fell in love with my husband was that I marveled at his ability to lose himself in his work. Never in my life had I met someone who could focus so intensely on one particular topic of study. Unfortunately, as it is with all human nature, there were plenty of drawbacks to this trait that required work-arounds in order for us to function as a couple and as a family.

WHAT IT MAY LOOK LIKE: REPETITIVE MOVEMENTS

"Stereotyped or repetitive motor movements…"

You don't often see conspicuous restricted and repetitive motor movements (called "stims") in adults. People can be trained out of a stim even if the training is not formal and even if they are not aware they have ASD. For example, a child may perform a certain type of hand flapping but his mother, father, nanny, or teacher forces his hands to remain still by physical constraint. The hand-flapping urge may transfer to foot tapping. The caretaker is less inclined to get down on the floor to constrain the child's feet and the foot tapping meets less resistance. If you want to identify whether or not your partner fits this trait, you may need to talk with your partner's siblings, parents, or childhood friends to see if they can recall any childhood repetitive motor movements.

In my husband's case, he had several small stims as a child, but his mother forced him to control the more obvious ones. Certain hand movements were eliminated but are now manifested in less conspicuous hand movements and eye rubbing. Often, he'll rub his eyes for 15 minutes at a time. The stims are still there but they have morphed to more acceptable forms. In my husband's case, the red eyes that result from rubbing them can be explained away as allergies or perhaps a bit of dust in his eye. To find out if the eye rubbing was a repetitive motor mannerism or just a means of getting something out of his eye, I asked my husband why he does it. He responded, "I don't know." Upon further prodding, I found that it actually hurts his eyes sometimes, but he feels he needs to do it.

What are some other types of stims in adults? Knee bouncing, finger tapping, toe tapping, twisting hair, twisting fingers, forehead hitting, teeth grinding, blinking, twitching, and even complex whole body movements. For example:

She twists her index fingers as if they are locked together.

Or:

He thumps himself on his forehead when he's agitated.

There are many examples of repetitive motor movements. How do they impact a long-term relationship? Read on.

Implications and solutions: Repetitive movements

"Stereotyped or repetitive motor movements…"

Often, by the time a person with ASD is an adult, he has learned to control the stim for a period of time, but as a live-in partner, you will probably have the opportunity to see the stim sooner or later. The ability to control the stim is a skill that can be strengthened with practice. In Echo R. Fling's book, *Eating an Artichoke* (2000), she explains how she taught her young son to control his hand flapping so that he wouldn't embarrass himself in front of his friends. The process she followed was one of kindness and compassion, helping her son gradually learn to control the behavior until he could control it for significant periods of time.

In a long-term relationship, you can't take on the mother/teacher role without serious implications. It may be safest to turn the training over to a professional and give yourself the latitude to be a support person only.

First, determine whether or not the stim is merely a disturbance or if your partner needs to stop it. Of course, this is subjective. My husband's eye rubbing used to make me anxious because I worried it would damage his eyesight. A quick check in a few medical reference books plus a few specific questions to an ophthalmologist revealed that the eye rubbing is doing little harm. Now, when my husband rubs his eyes, I look the other way and comfort myself with the thought that I have better things to worry about.

What if the stims are a disturbance? A person with ASD who experiences multiple repetitive motor movements of a more conspicuous nature may need professional training to rewire his brain for a new pattern of behavior. Your partner can receive help through a physical therapist, occupational therapist, behavioral therapist, psychologist, or other professional who can give ideas for how to minimize the stim with a replacement stim or general behavior.

An adult with ASD has probably already identified the safe places (often home) and the unsafe places (everywhere else) for performing the stim. When the person with ASD returns home after a stressful day on the job, he may "go berserk":

> His stims are toe tapping and knee bouncing. At work his toe taps softly or his knee bounces gently. When he's home, the movements are bigger and his whole body is twitchy.

Or:

> She tugs on her hair a funny way that looks like she's pulling it out, but she can usually resist uprooting it. I noticed the other day that when she's in public, she only twists her hair in a casual sort of way, but when she's home, it's a pulling and tugging.

If you are unfamiliar with ASD you may misinterpret the timing and intensity of the person's behavior because it is the mirror opposite of what you would expect. NTs will act nervous (performing actions that look like stims) while they are in the situation that makes them nervous. People with ASD often learn to suppress their nervous stimming, only to let it out later at home. If you judge a person with ASD using NT rules, you would assume that the person with ASD is more stressed at home (the safe environment) than he is out in public (the unsafe environment). This assumption is yet another example of how inappropriate it is to judge a person with ASD by an NT yardstick.

The stim is affected by stress and can be minimized through certain body stimulation exercises. Through a therapist, you may be able to identify activities that will help the person with ASD release tension and clear the sensory confusion. Our favorite stress release is jumping on a trampoline. If you and your partner have children, you have an automatic excuse to own a trampoline. The physiological reaction of the body to this jumping motion relieves stress quickly and effectively. Whether it is jumping on a trampoline, running, walking the dog, or listening to music with a clearly identifiable beat, the therapist will probably recommend an activity that has a predictable, repetitive pattern to replace the less productive stim.

It is important to first identify the stim and recognize its purpose and second, be open-minded about potential solutions. My partner with ASD originally hated running. In our early years together I would occasionally get him to go on a run with me, but the sensory assault of sun, wind, and sound was so intense that it was never worth it. Later, we recognized that he had a need for the consistent thump, thump full-body reverberation of the trampoline, but we lived in a place where owning a trampoline was not possible. Instead, he tried running, focusing only on the consistent thump, thump. For some reason, this change in perspective realigned his perception of the physical activity. Now he enjoys a 30- to 60-minute run nearly every day. It provides an extreme benefit.

Adults with ASD find their own small stim replacements over the years (behaviors that satisfy the stim, but are less obvious). For example, my husband's stim is rubbing his eyes, but he is aware that he can't do it at work, so he has several stim replacements: chewing on a toothpick, bending paperclips, or playing with small objects. Here are a few stim replacements that work well:

- Small play objects such as a squishy ball, small bean-filled ball, or other hand-sized object that can be twirled, squished, moved from hand to hand, or otherwise manipulated.

- Pliable objects such as putty, clay, or sticky substances such as a small piece of tape.

- Brightly colored objects such as crystals, tinsel, colored paper, shiny rocks, jewelry, pen-sized flashlights, or laser pointers.

- Everyday objects such as pins, paperclips, pencils, toothpicks, or other small objects that can be easily acquired and inconspicuously manipulated.

The person with ASD may never outgrow the need for stims. One couple describe their experience:

My better half [ASD] can play with a child's toy for hours on end. This Christmas we gave up on regular gifts and gave him toys such as spinning tops, crystal gadgets, prisms, and spiral twirling things. He's nearly 50 years old! He's a brilliant engineer with many accolades to his name, yet small, shiny objects entertain him.

While the person's ASD ability to marvel at a crystal may appear juvenile, there is more to it. Digby Tantam explains:

> Repetition seems to be intrinsically attractive to anyone with autism. It has been speculated that this is a consequence of frontal lobe abnormality, but it does not have the character of perseveration. Most people find some satisfaction in regular movement or regular sensory stimulation, for example, that provided by music or dance. The social nature of these activities makes them unappetizing to people with AS, but it may be that they obtain a similar satisfaction from spinning tops and watching the drum of a washing machine, or in other highly predictable pursuits. The more intellectually able a person with AS is, the more likely he or she is to find satisfaction in conceptual repetition (e.g., making lists). (Tantam 2000, p.384)

The repetitive motor mannerism may serve many purposes: the person with ASD may be deep in scientific thought, engaging in a highly effective form of relaxation, or freeing up part of his mind to consider a bigger, more creative solution to an unrelated dilemma. There is no predicting what is going on in a person's mind, but we do know that the ability to discover ingenious new solutions often appears as a simplistic, juvenile quest. Throughout history, great insights have been gained from childish playing with simple objects such as shiny rocks, bits of metal, or cast-off pieces of junk.

> The dynamic principle of phantasy is "play," which belongs also to the child, and as such it appears to be inconsistent with the principle of serious work. But without this playing with phantasy no creative work has ever yet come to birth.
>
> C.G. Jung, *Psychological Types*

WHAT IT MAY LOOK LIKE: ROUTINES

> *"Insistence on sameness, inflexible adherence to routines, or ritualized patterns of verbal or nonverbal behavior..."*

When I first read about ASD, this line of the diagnostic criteria made my brain go numb. Routines? What routines? My husband does not do anything nonfunctional… (denial setting in). I needed to read many examples before I was able to recognize the nonfunctional routines that had gently ensconced themselves in our lives. Here is one example that helped me visualize this particular issue:

> He [ASD] absolutely must eat his meal a certain way. He starts on one side of his plate and works his way around the plate clockwise, eating certain portions of each food item so that he finishes his plate with a perfect amount of each one left for the final bites. If he gets to the end of his dinner and he's somehow mismanaged the portions, he's agitated. There must be exactly enough mashed potatoes to go with the teaspoon of gravy left on the plate.

So what if a person eats funny? It becomes a problem when the routine is inflexible, when doing things differently makes the person nervous or creates anxiety.

Let's break it down: "Insistence on sameness, inflexible adherence…" A lack of flexibility in any shape or form can cause undue stress and strain on a marriage. Marriage and other long-term commitments to another person require a certain degree of flexibility if both partners are going to move in sync with each other. For example:

> When I look at our marriage from a larger viewpoint, I realize that there have been many changes in our lives that my husband [ASD] has not been able to handle because they require him to be flexible—something he's not. We had kids (who needed lots of help). He lost his job (we had to move). I went back to work (shifting the responsibilities of the housework). It's part of human progression for everything to change over time, but I keep getting this feeling like my husband is still standing back in the 1970s with his heels dug in deep, wishing things had never changed. He's holding on to old possessions and old ways of doing things in an effort to stop the changes.

The "inflexible adherence" refers to how a person with ASD will not change the particular behavior in any way, for any reason. For example:

> Whenever we go on vacation, my husband has to pack the car a certain way. It doesn't matter if we're late—he has to do it his way. If I try to do it, he'll find a reason to take everything back out of

the car and repack it. He has to put certain things in certain spots or, well, I don't know what would happen. It just isn't an option to do it any other way.

If you both show inflexibility, you may relate to the following example:

We both have ways of doing things. I have to arrange my books a certain way. He has to keep the computer desk a certain way. If either of us rearranges, even slightly, the other person's stuff, we're both in trouble. Neither of us will back down.

Next: "…ritualized patterns of…behavior…" The word "ritualized" is in this part of the diagnosis for a good reason. There are specific details about the routine that must be followed exactly. For example:

When my boyfriend [ASD] comes home from work, he has to take his coat off (right arm then left arm), put his keys down in a particular way (with the key-chain logo facing up), and do a dozen other things. At first I thought it wasn't that bad, and then I realized that it has to be the exact same way every single time.

The verbal or nonverbal patterns of behavior may be nonfunctional, meaning the behavior does not serve a purpose. For example:

My parents are an ASD/ASD couple. They are amazingly skilled at doing nearly nothing for hours at a time. For example, they have a particular way of doing dishes where they wash off the dish, put it through the dishwasher, and then sometimes wash it again when it comes out. When they go for a drive, they always use a map even though they know how to get there. Something that would take the average person two steps to complete takes seven or eight steps for my parents. If someone questions them on their nonfunctional behavior, they are always dumbfounded: "This is the best way to do it."

Often, a person's efforts to explain the nonfunctional nature of the routine will be met with a quizzical look, a blank response, or maybe defensiveness.

A nonfunctional routine may be as simple as how a person gets ready for bed, sharpens a pencil, arranges the table, or drives the car. When you were first dating, you probably thought your partner's eccentricities were charming, but once you were married, you probably noticed the repercussions that come from the inflexible nature of the routines. For example:

> My [ASD] husband has a bizarre way of putting on his shoes. At first, I thought it was charming. He took such great care to get his shoes on just right, loosening the laces to just the right length, putting his foot in and nudging the shoe here and there, then getting the laces all to the perfect snugness. It never bothered me until, once, we were in a hurry and he couldn't speed up the process. I was fuming. We were late and the least he could do was grab his shoes, get in the car and let us get on the road. But no… he had to do it the way he always does it. Over the years, this bothered me more and more. Once I timed him. Two minutes and 53 seconds just to put on a pair of shoes! This "charming" shoe behavior became a huge source of contention for us. I finally learned to give him a few minutes of time while I cleaned the car, cleaned the garage, or did something to keep myself busy and not think about his ridiculous shoe ritual.

You may notice nonfunctional routines in your partner or not. Sometimes they are conspicuous, sometimes they are not. The varying degrees of traits in a person are what create the beauty and diversity of human nature.

Implications and solutions: Routines

> *"Insistence on sameness, inflexible adherence to routines, or ritualized patterns of verbal or nonverbal behavior…"*

Although I first thought that my husband with ASD was immune to this part of the diagnosis, once I understood it, I discovered several nonfunctional routines that threatened to become part of our lives. For example, every Sunday we teach a group of children at our church. Usually, we use our scanner at home to make photocopies of a coloring sheet from our teacher's manual. Despite the fact that we are often late, our kids need breakfast, and several tasks are screaming for our attention, my husband still must scan the image into a photo-editing program, clean up any flecks on the page, and touch it up so it is perfectly centered, perfectly straight. The copies often look better than the original. Why go to so much effort for something that will be scribbled on by five-year-olds? His answer: "I have to do it this way. I don't know why."

What's the solution? First, identify the routine. If I had been too mentally distracted to notice, I may have overlooked time and time again that my husband was engaged in a specific routine. I would have thought, "What *is* that man doing? Why isn't he helping me?!" Instead, I chose to seek methodically for a reason and observe what was happening week after week. Once I observed the behavior as a "neurological rut," I realized that there was only one potential solution for us: I make the photocopies, which takes me less than a minute and frees up a full 30 to 40 minutes of his time, during which he helps the children with their routine tasks and makes us a delicious breakfast. The solution was simple, but required a little thought. He does not care what the photocopies look like—he simply cannot do the photocopying process any other way.

It would be great if our partners with ASD could simply say, "It isn't a big deal," and move on, but if we underestimate the power of these nonfunctional routines, we fall prey to the damage that may be done by overlooking them. For example:

> One day he [ASD] and I were late for a party. I told him, "Just shave in the car! We have to go!" I grabbed his shaver and went out to the car. He followed in a sort of daze. I drove so he could shave but he didn't start shaving until I complained that he needed to hurry up. The car ride was smooth; in fact, we were stopped in traffic most of the time. He had a towel to protect his clothes from the stubble and it should have been a simple buzz, buzz, buzz, but it wasn't. He has a way of shaving where he uses the mirrors at home. Plus, I think the thought of getting the hair in the car might have been too much for him. By the time we got to the party, he was such a nervous wreck that we had to turn around and go home.

So, a potential solution is to not underestimate the power of the routine in the first place. To accurately weigh the cost, I ask myself, "Do I really want to see the repercussions of this routine gone awry?" This is where the diagnosis comes in handy—if we know it is a nonfunctional routine or ritualized behavior, rather than just a whim, we can deal with it appropriately.

There are ways to train an adult with ASD out of a nonfunctional routine, but these need to be taught by a qualified therapist and they may or may not be effective. Let's be realistic—even if a person with ASD can be trained out of the particular nonfunctional behavior, he may already be so set in his ways that retraining will take a long time or even prove impossible, especially for routines that the person with ASD likes.

The saying "You can't teach an old dog new tricks" takes on new meaning for those in an ASD-linked relationship. First, many people with ASD have identified themselves as cats in a dog-eat-dog world. Their personalities and basic characteristics are more similar to cats (picky, aloof, particular) than to dogs (easy-going, a follower, friendly). So if people with ASD are cats, the appropriate saying would be: "You can't teach an old cat tricks that were intended for dogs in the first place." Perhaps people with ASD, especially ones who are already grown up, may not wish to change their routines even if they are nonfunctional.

Certain routine behaviors may be ignorable while others may depreciate the quality of life for your partner with ASD. For example, hand flapping during a meeting or scratching himself in certain spots may be thoroughly unacceptable. These behaviors need modification in order to help the person with ASD survive on a functional level in public. Apparently, "the repetitive speech and motor habits cannot be extinguished, but with time and patience, they can be modified to make them more useful and socially acceptable" (Wing 1981). Hand flapping could transfer to a toe tapping, knee bouncing, or rocking. A scratching could transfer to hair twisting or the manipulation of a small object such as a squishy ball or a pencil in the person's hands.

Even if the routines are not harmful, what if the routines still bother you? Make allowances for them. Look the other way. Find ways to work around them. If there is one thing I have learned from couples who have been happily married 20 years or longer, it is that they work around each other. Often, when standing in a particularly long line at the store, I'll start up a conversation with the grandma or grandpa in line beside me. They are always glad to share their advice. I have talked to more than a hundred over the years and, from what I can tell from the happily married couples, the advice always boils down to "Learn to live with it." This secret to a happy marriage is often shared with a wink and a twinkle in the eye. I suspect this is a profound wisdom that comes after years of personal experience. "Learn" indicates the active process of seeking out knowledge, an effort to analyze our mistakes and put that knowledge to good use. "Live" indicates an effort to be consciously alive, choosing to work hard and exercise—to open up our physical and emotional lungs and breathe. Learn to live with it.

If you start bemoaning the numerous allowances that you are making for your partner with ASD (especially if your partner has many routine behaviors) it may help to think of the number of allowances that the typical person with ASD has to make every day just to survive in an NT world. Try this exercise: ask your partner, "What specific things do you have to force yourself to do?" If you get an answer, it will probably give you valuable insight into the massive amount of effort your partner is already making just to survive day to day. Your efforts to work around a few nonfunctional routines won't seem quite so daunting.

I tried the above exercise once with my typically quiet husband. He launched into a long list of tasks that he has to do to get by in the world, listing probably 30 details such as "touch dirty things," "look at people," and "move my body." Afterward he was out of breath from the uncharacteristic amount of talking; he looked exhausted. By verbalizing it, he realized how heavy his load was. Over the next few days he thought of other tasks he had to do just to survive. As he shared these with me, I was stunned. I realized that if I were him, I probably wouldn't want to get out of bed in the morning. It helped me see the depth of his tenacity and willpower.

It helps to realize why the routines are important. A person with ASD perceives "…a universe where the sheer amount of noise invading his brain constantly threatens to overwhelm him. He learns to specialize in avoiding chaos, by shutting out and avoiding most elements of variability and novelty. Instead, he focuses on the non-changing aspects of his environment. Elements that remain the same provide him with the greatest experience of meaning and relation" (Gutstein 2000, p.37). The routines may serve a vital role in maintaining your partner's mental health.

A final solution? Look at the big picture. Especially if you are losing your temper, force yourself to look at the big picture. Does the routine or ritual really impact on your lives in such a significant way that you can't function as a couple? In the grand scheme of things are you going to care how he arranges the books on the bookshelf? Is his morning routine really that annoying? If you want to make the effort to overlook it, force yourself to visualize something, anything that will help you get beyond the frustration and inconveniences you may feel in relation to the routines.

I have a visual that works for me when my husband is doing something which I perceive as irrelevant. I think of the man I married. I force myself to see him walking across the university campus and remember the feelings it created in me then. There does not seem to be enough room in my heart to hold both the feelings of current frustration and the feelings I felt as a college girl. The more powerful feeling wins out and the tension is successfully diverted.

One final word of caution about routines in a partner with ASD: researchers often cite that people with ASD latch on to routines or patterns and have unusual difficulty breaking out of them (Aston 2014, pp.102–103). If a pattern such as anger, fighting, or even abuse becomes routinized, realize that your partner with ASD may need more extensive help than an NT would need in order to change the pattern. If you cover up the negative pattern, ignore it, or don't force change, your partner with ASD may interpret your actions as approval of the behavior. For the issues that really matter, you must be clear and unmoving: "Neither of us cheats in a marriage. Ever." People with ASD appreciate the hard, unchanging, immovable rules (Asperger 1944, p.58 in Frith 1991).

Why are the rules and routines so important to the person with ASD? As one insightful adult with ASD explains, "Routines are often the very glue that holds us together... They bring forth the same consequences and the same emotions every time we engage in them, unlike that which happens most every time we try to engage in NT events and situations" (Holliday Willey 2001, p.129). The rules and routines can be comforting. By streamlining the decision-making process, the person with ASD achieves a bit of predictable serenity.

People with ASD deal with complexity by ritualizing it (Tantam 2000, p.393). They cling to structure, routines, and patterns in an effort to stabilize their precariously balanced world. We can use this knowledge to our advantage in our adult relationships, especially in areas such as household chores. Simple chores can be made doable by ritualizing them, finding and building patterns so that the task is linear and predictable. For example:

We both work full-time so we must split the household responsibilities evenly between us so neither one feels overburdened. We have learned that he [ASD] does best with tasks that are the same every time. I do best with tasks that need problem-solving abilities and creative solutions. I cook and he does the dishes. Doing dishes is the same every time: silverware, dishes, and pots. He has order and rhythm while I enjoy the spontaneity of figuring out what to cook.

We can maximize our partner's obsessional tendencies by encouraging him to take on the tasks that are routine and predictable. A quick analysis of each task shows us what is a simple task and what is a multi-layered, decision-laden task. For example, vacuuming is a simple task as long as the coats, toys, and other extras are picked up off the floor. Vacuuming is a multi-layer task if the person vacuuming must pick up each item then decide whether to throw it away, put it away, or set it on a shelf nearby. In our home, we divvy up the tasks based on each other's best skills. Our energetic, ever-running children do best with putting away items that belong in various locations throughout the home. As my husband with ASD vacuums, the children clean up ahead of him. When the children have a question, they ask me, "Where does this belong?" and I problem solve. Since I enjoy creating solutions, I handle the problems that have no precedent. We put our unique strengths to good use.

FLEXIBILITY

Tony Attwood, in his "Workshop for Partners of People with Asperger's Syndrome" class at the May 2000 conference in Coventry, tactfully stated that "…flexibility, spontaneity, may not be their greatest attribute." People with ASD are capable of so much, but flexibility is not on the list. Instead, people with ASD tend to thrive on predictability, a stable environment, and a visible, set schedule (Attwood 1998, pp.99–101). For example:

My wife [ASD] does great with the schedule she has set up for our family but sometimes she breaks down. If the kids have a last minute science project for school or if someone drops by the house unexpectedly, she can't handle it. She's a computer and she writes her own daily code (her schedule). She can't handle many changes in that daily code without crashing.

While flexibility comes naturally to many of us, it may be difficult for a person with ASD. An adult female with ASD explains: "While we sit persistent, NTs walk with cognitive pliability. NTs are more wont to engage in behaviors that stretch even their elasticity to its limits" (Holliday Willey 2001, p.96). Another woman explains her experience when she asked her husband what it was like to be a person with ASD:

> I have unusually thin skin and when I am pregnant, I get painful red stretch marks... I can actually feel the skin ripping... I was asking him [ASD] to help me with "just one more thing" when I knew he was already on overload. He said, "You're giving me psychological stretch marks!" Imagining what that must be like, to have the skin of your psyche ripped by those around you who profess to love you, helped me see how I had pushed him past his limits.

Lack of flexibility is a well-known ASD trait. Here is the common scenario: one partner has ASD, thus has little or no flexibility. The other partner is NT (or maybe mild ASD or other) and is capable of flexibility. Who is going to bend to make difficult situations work? Most likely the person who is capable of flexibility will be the one to compromise, change, bend, or otherwise make the situation work. It is a simple equation. One person can bend; the other one can't. A common complaint:

> Does it always have to be "my way or the highway" for him [ASD]? I'm so flexible that I think I broke my spine, but he never compromises, not one bit.

The upside to this situation is that the partner with ASD may not be as "pig-headed" as he appears to be at first glance. There is a significant possibility that the partner with ASD is not consciously trying to be inflexible. The basic act of give and take—I bend a little, you bend a little—may be a foreign experience. Flexibility comes naturally to NTs when they are young, playing games on the playground or in the neighborhood. They naturally experience the give and take of casual human interaction—it is enjoyable to them. In an ASD brain, the give and take is not natural and may need to be taught directly. If presented right, you may be privileged to see your partner have many "Ah-ha" moments as he realizes exactly how couples compromise with one another. For example:

Every time we see our therapist, the problems always boil down to the issue of compromise. The therapist finally showed us by drawing figures on a piece of paper that show what it looks like to give and take. With a concrete visual that was related directly to our situation and our experiences, we were able to see what compromise looks like. She gave us five situations in which we could practice compromise, scripted the situations for us, and told us to try it. It worked and we both agreed that it had a positive outcome. One more small victory!

It may help to draw a picture, make a diagram, or list the items that are involved in the give-and-take interaction. For example, on a Saturday when there is a mountain of work to be done, I draw a list of chores for the day. Everyone has an equally long list. It takes less than a minute to write it out and post it where everyone can see it. Without this list, my husband and our children with various shades of ASD would be oblivious to the fact that everyone is giving and everyone is benefiting. The entire mood of the Saturday changes when we are all aware of the psychology behind our actions.

Of course, there are times when our best efforts come to a screeching halt. I have found that there are certain factors that trigger an "inflexibility attack." If we have company visiting, if it has been a physically exhausting day, or if there is too much noise in the house, my husband may have an attack of inflexibility where he is not capable of doing things any way other than his own. It is common for people with ASD to respond to certain external factors, causing the ASD traits to appear more visible than they would be on a good day (Attwood 1998). The factors that bring out the inflexibility are as varied as the person's particular personality.

CHANGING

As you learn about ASD, you will find that there are two camps in the field of Autism: one camp encourages the autistic individual to change; the other camp does not wish to change the nature of the autistic individual. Typically these two camps are at odds. As a generalization, people dealing with children are often in the "change" camp while adults with ASD are more solidly in the "let us be" camp—they would rather keep their Aspieness or Autisticness as part of their character. A common view for an adult with ASD:

> If they were to change my sensory issues, my routines, my intense interests, my speech, my tone of voice, the way I deal with people, then who would I be? I surely wouldn't be me.

This is one of the central issues that you will need to ponder and decide on your own position. Do you want your partner with ASD to change or would changing the ASD traits make him an entirely different person? What do you hope for for your partner?

Your partner with ASD will need to ponder it also. Without deciding this issue, the internal conflict will tug in both directions: "Do I try to fit in or do I maintain my current sense of self?" My husband's stance is to seek out niches where he can be most like himself and avoid those situations that crush him. He would suffocate under a mask worn every day, every hour.

NTs can make a change in plans or adopt a change in attitude quickly and easily. It is entirely different for a person with ASD. It took years of questioning to determine how my partner with ASD perceives a change in behavior:

1. I must realize that I need to change.

2. I need to know the exact parameters of what to change.

3. I need to see a logical reason to change. If it is not logical, I won't change.

4. I need to know the specific details of how to make the change.

5. I need to practice the change to make it permanent.

6. Conditions have to be optimal for a change to occur.

Six steps! Compare that to how NTs make an instantaneous judgment, then change—nearly a single-step process. NTs make changes easily and encourage others to change also. How do NTs elicit change in others? Through encouragement, insistence, even emotional prodding. In the past, my chosen method was based on the extinction theory.

The extinction theory states that if you ignore a behavior, the person will stop doing it, thus the behavior becomes extinct. The theory may work well for dogs and rats, but it apparently does not work too well for people with ASD. Ask anyone who has been married to a person with ASD. If you ignore one of your partner's "annoying" behavior, it does not mean that he'll stop doing it. People with ASD don't stop or start behaviors because of how you respond to them. In fact, "the normal person…is influenced by his social experiences, whereas the person with Asperger Syndrome [Autism Spectrum Disorder] seems cut off from the effects of outside contacts" (Wing 1981). You may relate to the following example:

> I believe in turning the other cheek [extinction theory in practice] when someone does something hurtful. When I ignore my wife [ASD], she still keeps doing the inappropriate behavior. She doesn't see that I have cut myself off from her. I ignore her, abandoning her in a world full of hidden meanings.

It seems like the most successful and optimistic approach is to identify your partner's ASD-style decision-making process in all its complexity, then to support his efforts in the changes he desires to make.

WHAT IT MAY LOOK LIKE: FIXATED INTEREST

> *"Highly restricted, fixated interests that are abnormal in intensity or focus…"*

Sometimes, people with ASD make a career out of their intense interest and sometimes it is relegated to a hobby. The difference between the NT man's hobby/job and a hobby/job for a person with ASD is the intensity and focus. We had one incident that I wrote in my journal, long before we knew about ASD:

> We just got back from vacation and the first thing he did was make a beeline for his computer. He sat down at his computer and played for a few hours. He is utterly sleep-deprived but instead of crashing on the bed as any normal person would do, he plays on his computer?

The oddity lay in the fact that he was past the point at which most humans can maintain wakefulness. Over the span of one week, he had slept a total of 17 hours (70 hours is minimum for him). We were driving cross-country and he drove overnight. He did not find significant time to sleep during the day. By any physician's analysis, he should have collapsed on the nearest soft spot. But, to his ASD-wired brain, the computer was calling him so loudly that he responded to it over the most intense physical fatigue he had ever felt.

We have seen this happen in other people with ASD whose intense interest happens to be computers. My husband's colleagues can pull all-nighters, all-weekenders, and other forms of intense non-stop work time. The key difference between someone who is simply working hard toward a deadline and a person with ASD indulging in an intense interest is that the person with ASD enjoys it, engaging in the task for pure involvement. Liane Holliday Willey (2001) explains that when a person has ASD their "…desire to spend time and thought with a favored passion is extremely gratifying. Our obsessions are our enchanters… it can be the closest thing to nirvana we will ever know" (p.122).

When a person with ASD has a "Highly restricted… interest…" it may be severely limited in scope. This refers to the rigidity of the interest. If a person with ASD is interested in trains, he will probably be interested in trains only, not transportation vehicles in general. The interest will be restricted to a specific topic or area of study. Sometimes the interest is obscure, such as fifteenth-century doll making. The interest is "restricted" in that it does not overflow into other areas (Tantam 1991, p.162). For example, if the person with ASD is interested in rare books, he may be interested in collecting them and caring for them but not reading them.

The next part of this portion of the diagnosis says, "…fixated interest…" meaning he may focus on it and nothing else. For example, if the interest is sailboats, he may have one, live on one, build one, work in a factory that makes sailboats, read about sailboats, etc. As long as it falls within the boundaries of his interest then it will encompass many areas of his life: thoughts, speech, and actions.

Finally: "…that are abnormal in either intensity or focus." The interest is not just something the person with ASD is interested in; it appears as an obsession. The person with ASD must study it, learn about it, examine it, and do whatever it takes to satisfy the interest. There are rare news reports about a naïve person with ASD breaking the law or otherwise overstepping social rules in pursuit of the interest. For example, if a person with ASD is interested in staplers, he may collect all the staplers from the office and bring them home to study them. For most people, the laws of acceptable human behavior speak louder than their current interest. For people with ASD, their current interest may speak louder than anything else.

Implications and solutions: Fixated interest

> *"Highly restricted, fixated interests that*
> *are abnormal in intensity or focus…"*

An intense interest can be a blessing in disguise, especially if it can be put to good use in paid employment. Many people with ASD are interested in computers; they make wonderfully dedicated programmers, network analysts, or any other position that focuses on the computer without the emotive element of human interaction. People with ASD may also be drawn to professions in law, accounting, astronomy, mathematics, higher education, or other positions that require sustained periods of intense study.

At first glance, a partner's obsessive interest may lead you or others to believe that he has obsessive compulsive disorder (OCD). Perhaps it is part of the equation, but perhaps the obsessive nature of the interest is based more solidly in the ASD diagnosis. If you have questions in this area, it is important to seek an ASD-aware professional's guidance. The methodologies used to treat an adult with OCD are polar opposites from how a professional handles an adult with ASD who has an obsessive interest. An inappropriate approach could be damaging. For example, OCD patients are often taught to force themselves to do without the obsession. Force an adult with ASD to do without their obsession and you are asking for a meltdown or at least "extreme annoyance" (Frith 1991, p.14). One male with ASD stated:

> Asking me to give this up is asking me to throw away my personality. This is who I am.

One of the big differences between OCD behavior and ASD behavior is motivation and emotive reaction to the behavior. A person with OCD feels anxiety and fear if not engaged in the behavior or thought. The action or thought is continued in an effort to hold the fear and anxiety at bay. In contrast, a person with ASD feels a great sense of satisfaction and pleasure when engaged in the intense interest (Tantam 2000, p.386). Engaging in the activity may even be therapeutic (Attwood 1998, p.99). For example:

> When she [ASD] talks about bugs, her eyes light up. (She's an entomologist.) My ex-wife's eyes lit up like that the day I showed her the huge diamond on the engagement ring I'd bought for her. Some women need diamonds; all my Aspie wife needs is a glimpse at a rare bug and she's on fire…

Or:

> Whenever he [ASD] is stressed out, he plays video games and computer games. It relaxes him.

Another difference between ASD intense interests and OCD is that the person with OCD is aware of the illogical nature of the obsession whereas the person with ASD is not aware that the obsessive activity is anything but logical and fun (Attwood 1998, p.93). If your partner's obsessive interest is toilet bowl brushes or other people's jewelry, you may run into problems and need assistance. If your partner's interest is something inconspicuous that can be put to good use, count your blessings. Listen in to one woman explaining her husband's interest:

> I grew up thinking that work was work, and then I married a guy [ASD] who thinks that work is play. He comes home from a 12-hour work day excited about what he's done. Sometimes he can be talking about what happened at work and not even notice that I've left the room. He just has to tell me (or the wall) all about it. It's such a blessing to have a husband who enjoys what he does.

How do we make the best of this particular ASD trait? We can support and encourage our partners to find or create a job that ties into the intense interest. If your partner can't find a niche in the world of paid employment, there may be a huge price to pay—the intense interest will need to be satisfied after hours, meaning that you will see each other only rarely. These obsessive interests are time-consuming and may leave little room for marital interaction.

There also appears to be another option, but it is a horribly destructive one. Although it appears to be (thankfully) quite rare, it may happen that at times a person diagnosed with ASD focuses on the partner (you) as the object of intense obsession. As one ASD counselor explains: "[The non-ASD partner] eventually realized that *they* were their partner's obsession a little while after they started seeing each other" (Aston 2014, p.49). For example:

> From the minute he comes home until the minute he leaves, he's constantly complaining about every little thing. Everything I do is wrong... He's the drill sergeant and I'm the unwilling recruit. Our home is a boot camp.

Of course, this type of situation needs to be addressed by the most highly qualified therapist you can find. It may be devastating if the intense interest is directed at you personally.

There is another interesting implication: when we see someone deeply consumed in an interest, we know he is capable of great dedication. We expect our partners to be deeply dedicated to us. We hope that they will do whatever it takes to make the relationship work. To our surprise, we may find that our ASD partners are unwilling to do even the perfunctory tasks to hold the relationship together, e.g. discuss personal matters, attend counseling, etc. Hans Asperger (1944) observed that his charges were "...egocentric in the extreme. They follow only their own wishes, interests and spontaneous impulses, without considering restrictions or prescriptions imposed from outside" (Frith 1991, p.81). We see that our partners can dive deep into their interests but won't even consider issues regarding marital relations. This discrepancy looks like a conscious choice.

The rigidity of the interest may appear as obstinacy. Researcher Lorna Wing (1981) observed and described one individual with ASD: "She would do no work in any subject that did not interest her." The person with ASD may see little else in the world that is worth doing besides the particular interest. Personally, I have had a hard time with this issue because I was raised with a strong work ethic, not cringing from unpleasant tasks. The contrast is stark because my partner with ASD will not do things he doesn't like to do. He can be as stubborn as a two-ton mule. Here is how a typical conversation went when we were first married:

Me: I need you to ___ (take out the garbage, help me unpack, etc.).

Him [ASD]: No thank you.

Me: Please do _____.

Him: I'd rather not.

Me: I need you to ___.

Him: (Silence.)

Me: Why won't you do ___?

Him: Because I don't want to.

We were both baffled with the other's point of view. Both of us have made progress over the years; I have learned how to ask less and he has learned either to do it or explain that he can't. He has come to see the trade-off—he wants to have his family by his side and if it means dumping the garbage, so be it.

How do we deal with a partner's apparent lack-of-reciprocity-based obstinacy? I believe the first step is to recognize it for what it is: a simple way of viewing the world through the rose-colored glasses of a person with ASD. Through their glasses, the beauty lies in focusing on one phenomenally intriguing topic at a time and not allowing anything to detract from it. With no thought to the social repercussions, they are able to say, "I don't want to." Compare this to the average person who says yes to nearly everything, is so distracted by so many tasks, never finding time to do the things they love. I'd much rather have my husband's ability to focus and tune out all other distractions. The intense interest may be an ASD-style method for staying strong.

When I was first familiarizing myself with ASD, I met a couple who kindly revealed to me that the husband had ASD. I had always wondered why he disappeared for a half hour at a time while I was visiting. Consistently, the wife tactfully dismissed it as, "Oh, he has something that he has to do." I assumed that he was performing a household chore, but later found out that he was playing games on the computer. This might have been considered rude if he had not been able to hide it. Social situations were painful for him and he needed downtime. The intense interest, whether it is computer games, astronomy, trains, calculating numbers, or watching a trivia show on TV—they all equate to a person's desire to lose oneself in something enjoyable. This is where the ASD and the NT worlds overlap, at least in principle if not in intensity—everyone needs an escape of some sort.

EMPLOYMENT

Ideally, a person with an encompassing interest in a topic will be able to find paid employment that satisfies his interest. Unfortunately, finding the perfect match of employee to employment can be extremely difficult, given the list of limitations that may be present. For example:

> She [ASD] has been out of work for 14 months now. She has so many restrictions. She can't work near fluorescent lights; she can't do presentations; she can't make it through an interview (she runs out of the room); she can't handle the perfumes of other employees; she argues with her co-workers. There are a lot of companies who can't accommodate her.

If your ASD partner has difficulties finding and maintaining employment, you are not alone. The following story is common:

> Over the last five years, he [ASD] has been fired seven times. He just can't seem to keep a job. Finding a new one that fits him is nearly impossible.

Once the person with ASD finds a satisfying job, there is the issue of advancement. The rigidity and strict nature of the interest may limit his abilities to flow with the natural upward progression of the job. For example:

> My husband [ASD] loves to program, but typically programmers advance to "lead programmers" and take on management responsibilities supervising other programmers. At his first job, they gave him management responsibilities and found out what a big mistake that was! He just can't handle people. "They're too unpredictable," he says. He ended up doing the work of five people because he simply could not tell others what they were supposed to do.

This particular problem is more than a lack of people skills; the difficulty lies in the interest being restricted to the act of solitary programming. It does not extend beyond that point, not one iota. The situation is also befuddled by a theory of mind issue (not being able to attribute mental states to others). A person who can't naturally read others' minds is at a great disadvantage in a management position.

A lack of flexibility, rigid focus, or apparent obstinacy may hamper employment. For example:

> She [ASD] creates great advertising layouts, but there are so many things that she lets slip through the cracks. I tell her to edit her text and she doesn't. I tell her to change the color scheme and she doesn't. She just won't do what she doesn't want to do. She's one mistake away from getting fired.

Often, the work of finding appropriate employment is daunting and the efforts to keep the employment are equally troublesome. Employment for people with ASD is such a large issue that it can be covered only superficially here, as it relates directly to the marital situation.

Why is money (employment) at the epicenter of marital eruptions? Because it is at the core of all three of the universally defined human needs: food, shelter, and clothing. They all cost money. By definition, NTs are more flexible and can more easily adjust to the pressures of a tight job market, a difficult work environment, or a changing list of job duties. For a person with ASD, finding and maintaining paid employment may prove to be life's biggest hurdle.

In our experience, our happiest times have come when I have supported my husband's desire to quench his intense interest at work. If he wants to make games for the rest of his life, so be it. It is his life, his choice, and we count our blessings every day that we were born in an era where a person can earn a living developing computer games. The job fits him well. No one cares what he wears or how he looks. There is no pretense and there are few social rules. He is free to be creative. He is allowed to speak without eye contact. In this non-traditional work environment his oddities do not stand out so much. They have toys strewn about their offices, small objects such as bouncy balls, squishy balls, putty, and other small squishable objects that can be used for stims (self-stimulatory or self-soothing actions). He is free to modify his office as needed. No one tells him to clean it up and no one judges him for his messy nesting in his office. There are whiteboards in the conference rooms and in each office so that they can draw instead of speak. There is an atmosphere of creative fun. Despite the incredibly solid fit of person to employment, it is still borderline bearable. As my husband with ASD explains:

> When I'm at work, I have to do junk. This is the perfect job, perfect company with cool people but it still makes me crack.

With this in mind, I remember that his ASDness makes him different from others. He can't just job hunt as others do and he can't just do something else. It does not work like that. His skills are so greatly skewed in relation to the world's view that we need to consider ourselves lucky that he is considered "skilled" at all in today's job market. He has to find the perfect match. He is not a square peg, or a hexagon, or anything else. He's an odd-shaped peg that fits in only a precious few holes on the world's employment board.

WHAT IT MAY LOOK LIKE: SENSORY DYSFUNCTION

> *"Hyper- or hyporeactivity to sensory input or unusual interest in sensory aspects of the environment (e.g., apparent indifference to pain/temperature, adverse response to specific sounds or textures, excessive smelling or touching objects, visual fascination with lights or movement)"*

Sensory malfunction can cause a person to experience severe reactions to stimuli that most people would not even notice.

> Fluorescent lights blind me. High-pitched noises deafen me. A soft touch agitates me...

Although sensory issues are not a necessary part of the ASD diagnosis, they are often a part of life for a person with ASD (Attwood 1998, p.129). Let's look at them one by one.

Touch

I mention this sensory area first because it may be the most important one in an intimate relationship. A person can avoid touch with nearly everyone except the person they have chosen as a long-term companion. How might a touch sensitivity affect your lives?

NT: She always recoils when I touch her.

ASD: Soft touch feels creepy crawly on my skin. A hard touch is much easier to handle.

Sound

When you create a home with someone, sound issues may begin to crop up, especially if you have chosen to have children. Our children were loud toddlers. In order to run off extra energy they would run whooping, hollering, giggling, and shrieking. Their noises could not be confined to any single area of the home. Fortunately, my husband's sound sensitivities are not related to volume—they are related to repetition. He can handle the decibel level that our children and half a dozen of their friends can inflict on our eardrums, but he cannot handle a repetitious chanting such as the same rhyme, jingle, or silly word repeated over and over. For example, when the children would chant "silly sassafrassy pants" with a distinct repetitive rhythm it would drive my husband with ASD to near insanity. Let's look at other sound sensitivities:

He [ASD] cannot hear medium voices well. He can hear soft sounds and loud sounds, but the in-between is an ocean where all the sounds fall apart.

Or:

Anything over a certain decibel level sends me [ASD] running for cover. Anything that pops (even opening a can of soda) is like a firecracker set off in my ear.

Or:

It drives me nuts when someone talks too softly. Quiet sounds are extremely frustrating.

Or:

I can't use a cell phone. I don't think my ears can separate the background noise from the voices.

Sight

Some people with ASD have visual sensitivities. Certain colors or lights may be difficult to handle visually. For example:

> Fluorescent lights make it so I [ASD] can barely see.

Or:

> Blue makes me calm. White makes me freeze. Yellow shuts down my visual abilities. Green makes me nauseous. Red terrifies me.

Smell

Certain smells may overwhelm your partner with ASD even though they seem reasonable to you. For example:

> If he doesn't shower daily, I [ASD] can't get anywhere near him. I am extremely sensitive to body odors.

Or:

> I [ASD] wish that we could outlaw strong perfumes just like we prohibit smoking in public places. Perfume makes me physically ill.

Taste

Sensitivities regarding taste may make home-cooked meals difficult and dinners out nearly impossible. Personally, I gave up cooking with my husband only a few weeks after we married. I realized that he could not identify hunger until a few minutes before it hit, and he needed to eat very shortly after feeling the hunger. Since he is only hungry for one specific food item at the moment of hunger, even a full-time personal chef would have a hard time meeting his culinary needs. Fortunately, he eats a single meal a day which he can usually find at a nearby restaurant, deli, or fast food place. How might taste sensitivities show up in people with ASD? A few examples:

> We have a very limited number of dinner dishes that she [ASD] can eat. It can't be too salty, too sweet, and it must be just the right temperature. Needless to say, she does the cooking.

Or:

> She [ASD] forgets to eat. She'll be busy doing other things and forget to feed the kids too. She says it's because she doesn't enjoy eating and that it's a chore.

Implications and solutions: Sensory dysfunction

> *"Hyper- or hyporeactivity to sensory input or unusual interest in sensory aspects of the environment"*

Touch

The implications almost go without saying. If your partner has sensory dysfunctions, they will impact the physical, intimate moments in your lives together, creating some of the most serious problems mentioned so far. A mild example:

> Cuddling gives me that grounded feeling of knowing that he [ASD] is there for me and can comfort me. I need cuddling in order to feel loved and appreciated. He can't cuddle because it's "too close" for him.

Another example:

> I [ASD] can't stand it when she touches me. I have to be mentally prepared for a touch first. I need to brace for it.

Touch sensitivities may be the number one most important area for an ASD-linked couple as physical touch is so important to the health of an intimate relationship. I believe that Liane Holliday Willey (2001) came up with the ideal mantra for dealing with sensory dysfunction in a relationship: "...work to find a compromise that will harm no one" (p.92). This is a superb mantra for us all.

Sound

Once we identify the sound sensitivities, we can work around them more easily. We can also recognize that voice volume, pitch, or intonation may be perceived as critical or an attack. Sounds may be poorly perceived and your partner with ASD may misinterpret the tone of your voice.

If you are a little annoyed, he may think you are furious, or he may not hear it at all. Your partner with ASD may be functionally deaf to certain sounds. Being aware of the sound dysfunction is the first step in working around it.

A sound dysfunction can impact your relationship by making it difficult for your partner to hear you or, on the other hand, it may be that your partner hears you too well. If your partner has exceptionally sensitive hearing he may be able to hear you when you think he's out of earshot. Also, your partner may be able to hear more than just your words. My husband with ASD has an unusually acute perception of sounds. One example in my husband's past helped us see how his hearing might be a bit out of the ordinary:

> When he was in school as a teen, the class played a game where one person sat in a chair facing away from the chalkboard while the teacher wrote a word on the board. The students facing the board were supposed to give clues to the word. When it was my husband's turn, he guessed the word immediately without any clues. Although the entire class had seen him staring forward while the word was being written on the chalkboard, they were still convinced that he had somehow cheated. He had simply listened to the sound of the chalk as the word was being written and was able to guess the shapes of the letters, therefore the word. All it took was a little concentration, ASD logic, and sensitive hearing.

I am aware of my husband's sound sensitivities and we try to use this knowledge to our advantage. For example, he paid attention to our children's cries when they were little and was able to interpret their cries more accurately than a skilled pediatrician. Since he responded clinically rather than emotionally to the cries he was able to clearly identify and classify each type of cry. This ability improved our quality of life.

Sight
The implications of visual sensory issues can be insidious in their nature. If your partner with ASD cannot identify or explain the visual sensory dysfunctions, they may lead to unnecessary troubles. For example, what if you painted your bedroom a whitish beige but that color shuts down your partner's senses? You may notice that your partner has all of a

sudden shut down whenever you go into the bedroom. You may believe that he has lost interest in you or that there are sexual problems between the two of you. Your partner may not be able to identify or voice the reasons for discomfort without knowledge of the sensory dysfunctions at play. You both may believe that the problems are sexual rather than a simple mistake in home decorating.

Smell

If your partner with ASD has olfactory sensitivities, then being aware of the sensitivity will help both of you identify problems before they get out of hand. Certain smells may set your partner off balance and you may not know why until you identify the root cause. For example:

> Last Monday, he [ASD] came home from work and was an absolute bear. I questioned him extensively about work and nothing unusual had happened. I couldn't figure out why he was being so ornery. He wasn't sick, didn't have a headache—everything should have been fine. It turns out that the new recipe I had tried that day had an odd smell to it that really bothered him. We aired out the house and he was fine.

Taste

The implications of taste sensitivities may spread over a surprisingly large portion of your time together as meals take chunks of time out of the morning, afternoon, and evening of every day. Unfortunately, the only successful solution I have heard of to date is the following, from a family who has learned to work around this issue:

> Mealtimes could rule our family if we let them. My husband [ASD] and my son [ASD] are both so finicky that mealtimes were a trigger point for everyone's temper. We decided that for the good of the family, we wouldn't eat together anymore. We each make our own food. If anybody wants a particular food item, they write it on the grocery list. Groceries are purchased twice a week. People eat when they want to. It took a lot of work to train my son and my husband to make their own meals, but through teaching and practice they have now become self-sufficient (our son is 12 years old and my husband is 39 now). Sometimes we end up eating at the same time

but not always. I don't see it as giving up; I see it as working around an unsolvable problem. Families usually spend quality time together during meals but, because of our family's problems, we couldn't. We just couldn't do it. Instead, we play a game every night or do something fun together. We have to compensate.

SENSORY PLEASURE AS A CRUCIAL PART OF RELATIONSHIPS

One of the many reasons why people marry or otherwise link in long-term relationships is to enjoy physical pleasure. Being in a physically intimate relationship with someone who has ASD may make the relationship more, um, interesting.

With ASD as part of the equation, there are certain aspects that are easier and certain aspects that are more difficult. Perhaps the most important guiding rule is this: find out what feels good to you, then implement.

This section can be helpful to both partners regardless of which partner has ASD and/or sensory issues. Both partners in a relationship need to be aware of what causes physical pleasure. If you have sensory issues, you simply may have to work harder to figure out what feels good. If you have ASD, you may benefit most from the exercise suggested below. If you don't have either ASD or sensory disorder issues, you still need to be aware of your partner's process.

The first step may be difficult. It may be too vague and bewildering for someone with sensory integration issues to find what feels good. Perhaps the following list of rules can give guidelines that will help:

1. Sex is supposed to feel pleasurable.

2. Keep a Pleasure List in a private spot where no one will find it. On the list write what feels pleasurable to you.

3. Throughout the day notice how your body responds to different sensations. Write them down on your list. Note that these pleasurable sensations can be physical, mental, or emotional.

4. Share your list with your partner.

5. Brainstorm for ways to recreate the pleasurable sensations together.

Let's look at each of these individually. First, sex is supposed to feel pleasurable. There is a fairly strict definition of sex in the NT realm: intercourse. But for people with sensory integration issues, intercourse may feel awful, quite awful, unless you figure how to do it in a pleasurable way. If you start with the goal being intercourse, it is highly likely you will not enjoy a fulfilling sex life with a partner who experiences sensory integration issues. If you start with the goal of *mutual pleasure*, you are far more likely to have a fulfilling sex life.

The second step is to keep a Pleasure List. This is more difficult than it sounds. Perhaps the sensation of pleasure is too rare. Perhaps the list will be too hard to make due to embarrassment or worry that the list may be found by someone who will use it to tease or bully you. As one woman stated:

> I made a list but wrote it in code. It was just too scary to think of someone finding it.

By making a list, you bring together all the pleasurable sensations your body is capable of feeling. Orgasm is the combining of many pleasurable sensations at once until the body overloads and releases. That release can be immensely beneficial on a physiological level, releasing serotonin into the bloodstream, helping you feel connected physically when other ways of connecting might not be as successful.

Now the third step. Throughout the day pay attention to how your body responds to different sensations. One person's Pleasure List may contain things like:

- It felt good to be squished in the elevator (or subway, or big crowd).

- The air from the car's air conditioner blowing on my skin felt good.

- It felt good when no one talked to me for a full hour straight.

- When the lights were turned out at night I felt relief wash over me.

- A very hot shower, so hot my skin turns red, felt good.

- It felt good to go swimming.

- It felt good to move slowly, walking slowly to my office.

- Cold rain felt good on my face.

- Hot, spicy food felt good in my stomach.

- When you hugged me tight, I felt a deep sense of relief.

- Scrubbing my legs with a loofah sponge in the shower felt great.

- Rocking in the rocking chair relaxed me.

- Brushing my hair very hard gave me a feeling of euphoria.

- When I hit my leg against the chair by mistake it actually felt good.

If something feels good, do not hesitate to include it on your list. You are not looking for sexual acts, only physical pleasure. Your body is different from anyone else's body so what feels good to you may be entirely different from what would feel good to someone else.

The fourth step. Share the list with your partner. It doesn't matter if your partner is NT or has ASD, ask your partner to meet you in the bedroom at a time when both of you are relaxed and have time to discuss the list.

If your partner does not like eye contact, then sit in a way that means eye contact is not an issue. If your partner likes touch, then lie down side by side with your arms around each other. Find a position where you can both be comfortable. Tell your partner something like: "I have been trying to find out what things feel good to my body. I am hoping that if I can find my own pleasurable sensations we can both experience a better sex life together." Let your partner know that the goal is a mutually satisfying relationship.

It may help to warn your partner that the items on the list are not sexual. They are merely things that felt good to your sensory system.

The final step is to brainstorm for ways to incorporate the good sensations into a physical experience with your partner. Using the previous list as a starting point, here are a few solutions you may come up with during brainstorming:

- It felt good to be squished in the elevator (or subway, or big crowd).
  Ask your partner to be on top during intercourse. Ask for full body contact, aligning chest, legs, and arms.

- The air from the car's air conditioner blowing on my skin felt good.
  Set up a fan in the bedroom and position it in an optimal position. Ask your partner to make sure the fan is not bothersome to her during sex. Who knows? The fan may provide that windblown look that models often have, increasing arousal.

- It felt good when no one talked to me for a full hour straight.
  Before either of you attempt sex, have an hour of silence. Also be silent while intimate. These requests can be sexy if one is in the right mindset.

- When the lights were turned out at night I felt relief wash over me.
  Obviously, turn out the lights! If the other partner needs light for visual pleasure, perhaps try a single candle as this may be perceived as less intense by the person needing dark.

- A very hot shower, so hot my skin turns red, felt good.
  Take a hot shower before trying intimacy.

- It felt good to go swimming.
  Invest in a hot tub (and make sure you have complete privacy!) or perhaps invest in a large bathtub.

- It felt good to move slowly, walking slowly to my office.
  While making love, both partners move slowly, extremely slow, and see if that heightens the pleasurable sensation.

- Cold rain felt good on my face.
  Using a cold, wet towel, have your partner squeeze droplets onto your naked belly or chest. See if this creates the same pleasurable sensation.

- Hot, spicy food felt good in my stomach.
  Have a hot, spicy meal before attempting sex.

- When you hugged me tight, I felt a deep sense of relief.
  Find out what aspect of the hug helped you most. Was it the squeezing of the shoulders? Compression of the chest? A heavy feeling on the shoulders, like a weighted vest? Find ways for your partner to recreate the sensation while naked.

- Scrubbing my legs with a loofah sponge in the shower felt great.
  Ask your partner to shower with you and loofah your legs for you. See if the pleasurable sensation extends towards your partner when he is the one creating the sense of pleasure.

- Rocking in the rocking chair relaxed me.
  While I have not done research in this area, I have heard that there are swings and other apparatus that can be used to create the swinging motion during sex.

- Brushing my hair very hard gave me a feeling of euphoria.
  Ask your partner to brush your hair. If he does not want to, or does not find it pleasurable, brush your own hair before attempting sex.

- When I hit my leg against the chair by mistake it actually felt good.
  Create a similar sensation during sex, probably in sync with the thrusting motion.

In order to experience fulfillment during sex, it helps to combine as many pleasurable sensations as possible. Using the above list as an example, before attempting sex, ensure that the next hour will be silent, eat a hot, spicy dinner, take a hot shower, brush your hair hard and turn off the lights. Fill the bathtub just in case you want to use it, put a cold, wet towel beside the bed, and turn on the fan. While touching each other, guide your partner to do the things that will feel good to you, such as full body pressure and moving slowly.

As you work towards finding your own pleasurable experience, make sure that your partner is also having a good experience. If one of your pleasurable sensations is an unpleasant sensation for your partner, find a solution for both of you. For example, if you like silence and your partner likes noise, wear earplugs. That way your partner can moan loudly, listen to music, whatever, while you have your silence, creating physical satisfaction for both of you.

You both need to tell the other what feels good and what does not. Remember that the end goal is a mutually satisfying physical experience together. Intercourse should not be the goal. Pleasure should be the goal.

MELTDOWNS

In your exploration of ASD, you will undoubtedly come across the term "meltdown." In children, it is similar to a tantrum where the child loses control, screaming, crying, thrashing about on the floor, or punching things near him. A meltdown is more severe than a tantrum in that the child cannot stop it or control it. As the child grows, he encounters parents, teachers, siblings, or others who react to the meltdowns in such a way that it slowly changes the child's behavior. By the time the child is an adult, the meltdowns have probably morphed into another, less recognizable form, but they may be just as destructive as the childhood version of thrashing and crying.

What does a meltdown look like in an adult? It can appear as a burst of anger, an emotional and physical shutdown, obsessive behavior, a vengeful act, out-of-control crying, or any other outlet the person with ASD has found that still releases the stress. A meltdown can appear as a quick burst, but it can also simmer for hours, erupting later at some minor incident. Meltdowns can be tricky and their main identifier is that the person is out of control. For example:

> He [ASD] had a favorite pair of jeans that he had worn since college. They were falling apart so I threw them away. When he found out, he became whiny and irrational. I tried to talk with him, but it just got worse and worse. He lay on the sofa and moaned about it for hours.

Or:

> If she [ASD] misinterprets something I say, she can take the idea and run with it. She obsesses, stresses, cries, and babbles. It doesn't last for long, but it can happen anytime, anyplace. I tease her that she has PPMS (permanent premenstrual syndrome) but of course she doesn't think it's funny.

Meltdowns occur for many reasons, one being that the person with ASD does not have the complex communicative filter the rest of us do. An ASD brain cannot filter out the irrelevant information from the relevant information, thus he is flooded with excessive input. As my children visualize it, "He blows a socket."

Perhaps the way an adult with ASD acts out the meltdown process is influenced by incidents that happened in childhood. For example, if the child had a kicking, screaming meltdown on the floor and a dog came along and licked him/attacked him, the child may have a permanent fear of having a meltdown on the floor. The child then self-adjusts to some sort of standing or running meltdown. Over the years, the person learns what works and what does not. Sometimes the meltdown process is derailed and becomes especially difficult to identify in the adult form. Listen to one person who finally recognized his meltdowns for what they are:

> When I was a little kid, I had meltdowns where I broke things and I hurt myself. One day, when I was six, I had a really bad one. My mom came in my room and lost her temper… I knew that I never wanted that to happen again. I remember the meltdown as if it was a movie in surround sound in my head. Looking back at it I can see that that was the day I started to internalize the pain. Whenever I feel a meltdown welling up, I turn inward and get really quiet and sad. It feels like my soul is breaking.

Meltdowns come in many shapes and sizes. Most experts agree that meltdowns are a necessary part of stress relief (Attwood 1998; Holliday Willey 2001). I like the analogy of meltdowns as storms. They build up when certain factors combine and pressures need to be released. They cannot be turned off—they are a part of nature. I can usually see a storm brewing in my partner with ASD. I know what is going to happen because I have lived with him long enough to know how he reacts to certain things. There will always be occasional storms—some are drizzle and some are lightning. There will always be an end to the storm and there will always be clear skies afterward. I know what precipitates the storms (family reunions, outings, social events) so I can build my own sort of weather forecast.

Here is an optimistic view of a meltdown:

> A meltdown is what happens after I [ASD] have had too much fun! Too much sensory input, too much information, and my brain

goes off in all different directions until I can't even form a coherent thought. For me, it's not dangerous and I can tell when it's coming. It's my overload-meter.

What can we do when our partner has a meltdown? Stay away? Seek professional help? Hide all sharp objects? One wife explains how she helps her husband with ASD:

> My husband is calm, quiet, and kind. He wouldn't hurt a fly, but every now and then he transforms into a monster. He yells, punches holes in the walls, and does everything within his power to keep from hitting me. It only happens once a month or so, and it doesn't last long, but it's awful when it does happen. I have learned to leave the house until he's done. He knows he's out of control. He's embarrassed by it but there doesn't seem to be any way to channel the intensity without it becoming a problem. For a while, I told him that punching holes in the walls was unacceptable and he needed to deal with me directly. Bad idea. Instead of punching a hole in the wall, he'd punch a hole in me. A few bruises later, I went back to letting him release his anger in his own way. A friend told me to go out shopping every time he had a meltdown and that's exactly what I do. On my way out the door, I'll tell him, "This is going to cost you." It sounds silly, but what's important is that at end the day neither of us feels cheated. I feel like I've successfully managed a difficult situation and we are both glad that we've minimized the damage.

Some people with ASD believe that they cannot stop a meltdown once it has started, while some try to stop or minimize the negative effects. If your partner seeks help in dealing with these difficult moments, you can offer ideas for "meltdown management" strategies. Usually a therapist is a wonderful resource for brainstorming for strategies that will help someone deal with a meltdown. For example:

> When he [ASD] has a meltdown, I can't talk with him (I'm usually pretty mad at the time too). Plus, I'm not his therapist—he should be able to figure this out on his own. We wrote out a sheet of things he can do to lessen the meltdown. He sits still for a few minutes, watches TV, drinks a big glass of ice water, works on something in the garage, plays a fighting game on the computer or chooses from a

dozen other options. He has to look at the sheet. He can't remember these things without seeing them in written form.

I learned the hard way the rule that says: once your partner has found a tool that works, let him use it. Here is a journal entry that tells all:

> It seems like every time somebody comes over (especially when family is here) he disappears to the computer room for 15 to 20 minutes at a time. Why is he avoiding us? Are we really that bad? Maybe he's just trying to cope with the stress of the situation. I've forced him to stay with us a few times and the negative energy just oozes out some other way. I always regret it. If I let him disappear for a short while, he comes back rejuvenated, ready to go on pretending to have fun.

One of the most commonly cited strategies that I have read about is to listen to music:

> Whenever she [ASD] is heading for a meltdown, I lead her to her favorite reclining chair, put on a CD of classical music, and gently put the headphones on her head for her. She falls asleep within 10 to 15 minutes and, when she comes to, she's back to her balanced self.

Look for strategies that will help your partner constructively channel the anger, energy, frustration, and other emotions he is feeling away from family members and into an activity with beneficial side effects.

6

Diagnostic Criteria C

SYMPTOMS PRESENT IN EARLY DEVELOPMENT

C Symptoms must be present in the early developmental period (but may not become fully manifest until social demands exceed limited capacities, or may be masked by learned strategies later in life).

Unless your partner with ASD has an exceptionally accurate memory of his childhood, you may want to ask for details about his childhood from his mother, father, and siblings. Diagnosticians often require this information.

Forming a solid relationship with your partner's family is the first step. Asking the right questions is the second step. Getting family members to come to the evaluation session or fill out a questionnaire is ideal but may not be necessary. Of course, documented information such as baby books, the mother's or father's journals, and other written forms of personal history are probably the most accurate.

You may find that parents or other family members recall past events very differently from your partner. One male with ASD explained:

I know that everybody has selective memories of the past, but when you compare my [ASD] views with my parents' views, it's impossible to identify it as the same experience. They'll talk about living on a farm in the countryside. They'll recall happy Saturdays doing projects together, reminiscing about holidays and funny family stories. My memories are different. I recall the pigs and cows being shot and brutally dismembered. I recall the confusion and intense physical pain that accompanied every grueling 5 a.m.

to 9 p.m. Saturday work session. My memories are haunting and chilling; their memories are somehow happy.

Perhaps the difference in viewpoint is due to the fact that the child with ASD is fighting demons that others do not see. In this example, the child was dealing with enormous sensory issues, a lack of downtime, constant socialization for 16 hours a day, and many other issues that required the child to stay strong far beyond a reasonable limit. This child with ASD did not know how to communicate the distress and—since it was present his whole childhood—he considered it part of living. While the parents saw a compliant child, the child was in shutdown mode, scared and unable to voice discomfort.

It is also possible that the person with ASD does not remember much from his past. In our experience, my husband with ASD has so little memory of the past that it borders on amnesia. He can identify photos of himself as a child but often confuses a picture of himself with a picture of his brother. He cannot recall what he did in the houses he grew up in but he can remember the exact street address, zip code, and phone number. He cannot remember anything he ever got for Christmas or birthdays but he can remember all the details relating to when he started building his first computer, even the computer's exact specifications.

At first, I thought his lack of well-rounded, happy memories indicated an unhappy childhood, perhaps even signs of a disturbance or scarring in childhood. The longer I am married to him, the more I observe that his memories are highly selective. He fits the profile of "ASD memories." He remembers objects, not people. He remembers a few select confrontations, not happy times such as holidays and vacations. He remembers small snapshots of things that I would consider irrelevant. Armed with an understanding of ASD and information from his family, I realize that he had a healthy childhood, but that he only remembers the information his brain was wired to remember: computers, numbers, and situations to avoid. He forgot everything about parties, holidays, and other happy occasions that NTs typically reminisce about.

Building a solid, healthy relationship with the family can help the diagnostician fill in the picture of your partner's childhood that may be seemingly skewed in certain directions, based on the way the ASD brain functions.

WHAT IT MAY LOOK LIKE: LANGUAGE THROUGH THE LIFESPAN

> *"Symptoms must be present in the early developmental period…"*

Throughout childhood, a person with ASD may have general language abilities that may or may not send up red flags for the educators, parents, or other adults who are tracking the child's progress. People may notice odd speech, poor pragmatics, incorrect grammar, or atrocious spelling, but the language difficulties may not amount to much. Or there may be no red flags at all. Therein lies the pitfall. The child with ASD may have stilted, pedantic language that leads adults to believe he is precocious. As the child grows into adulthood, the language and communication difficulties may become less obvious while one's inability to interact according to social rules becomes more evident. For example:

> I [ASD] can communicate fine with others at work, in the community, nearly everywhere. No one would ever guess that I have a disability. As someone gets to know me, they perceive something I do as rude or selfish and they are hurt and offended. They can't understand that I have a disability.

The problem with this example is that the person with ASD *did not intend* to offend. There is a world of difference between a person consciously inflicting hurt and a person who cannot anticipate or repair an offense.

As a generalization, we assume that people's abilities are consistent. If they can speak clearly, they must be intelligent. If they are intelligent, they should be able to figure out x, y, and z. But people with ASD have "islands of ability," areas where they show remarkable intelligence. Contrast this to areas where functionality is low enough to classify them as disabled. As Hans Asperger (1944) explained: "Clearly, it is possible to consider such individuals both as child prodigies and as imbeciles with ample justification" (Frith 1991, p.46). It is a matter of extremes— an ability to speak fluently about high-level topics, yet an inability to manage smaller, simple conversations that are intuitive to others. One NT partner explains:

She [ASD] has great verbal abilities with her colleagues, but when we go beyond the standard relay of technical information to more relaxed conversations such as cocktail party chatting or romantic dialogue, she's at a complete loss. She can't form ideas or words around basic, everyday concepts. It is ironic that someone so eloquent when talking about her profession can be so phenomenally amateur at basic speech.

Often, people with ASD will be able to speak about their area of intense interest, whether it is trains or computers or napkin folding, but their ability to hold other types of conversation is limited.

SUCCINCT SPEECH

Although people with ASD can talk endlessly about their current obsession, talking about other topics may be awkward. They may keep their speech succinct and to the point. A common ASD mantra:

I only speak when it's necessary.

From another angle:

I don't speak for the sake of speaking.

Speaking in a succinct manner may not be the most romantic or friendly way to engage in conversation, but it is also highly useful. One woman explains:

My husband [ASD] has mastered the art form of using as few words as possible. I have good English skills and I have analyzed his sentences to see if there is a shorter way to say what he said. Invariably, I will find that he has used the absolute minimum number of words to convey a particular message. I tried learning his succinct speech style because I know there are many skills he can learn from me and many skills I can learn from him. Today a lady from our insurance company called, wanting to know information about a claim that had been made. Instead of talking like I normally do, I used the succinct speech style I was practicing with my husband. It worked wonderfully! What would have normally been a lengthy phone call was over in two minutes. The information was conveyed with precision and clarity. The insurance lady was able to maintain professionalism, get directly to the point, and there was no longer any confusion regarding our insurance claim. I plan on using my husband's speech skills in other appropriate areas. The level of clarity felt so good.

Of course, there are areas where succinct speech may get you into trouble. For example, when you are at a funeral, people expect you to express condolences, no matter how many times they have been said, regardless of whether you feel like expressing them or not. It is a social rule. These are the areas where scripting comes in handy. You can help your partner with ASD through these situations by giving him ideas for what to say or by reminding him that succinct speech will be perceived as rude.

LITTLE PROFESSORS

Children with ASD are often called "little professors" because their speech can be stilted, pedantic, and just plain odd for a child (Asperger 1944, p.39 in Frith 1991). People may assume that the child is highly intelligent because of his speech. While higher than average intelligence often correlates with ASD, the assumption that a person is highly intelligent carries some unwelcome side effects. For example:

> My husband and I met at work… He spoke so eloquently about astronomy. I fell in love with his marvelous ability to put me in a state of awe. We've been together three years now and I'm finding out that he has trouble with nearly every single small task in his daily life. He cannot do laundry. He cannot cook. He cannot deal with anything spur of the moment. How could someone so intelligent, someone who is able to wrap his mind around the wonders of the universe, not figure out how to make macaroni and cheese?

People with ASD grow up with a gap between what is expected and what is possible. If an eight-year-old boy with ASD can talk about electronics on the level of a skilled professional, then he must be brilliant! Hallelujah! The parents rejoice. Their little genius child will afford them a lovely retirement someday. Unfortunately, the parents find out that their prodigy is often bullied, picked on, and may or may not get good grades at school—the indicators of genius are only momentary glimpses. What is wrong?

As the child grows, this annoying gap only widens, heightening the tension between what people think he is capable of and what is within his comfort zone. He may be pushed, pulled, asked to stretch far beyond any abilities he possesses or wishes to possess. Listen in to one mother of a male with ASD talking to her son's wife:

> You know I had his IQ tested when he [ASD] was ten. He's a genius. He can do anything he puts his mind to. He's just so darn stubborn. He'll never amount to much if he doesn't learn to put his talents to good use. I always told him, "You can do anything you put your mind to."

While it is wonderful for parents to have high hopes for their children, it may put an unnecessarily heavy burden on a child who cannot or does not ask for help with his hidden disability. When a child with ASD who interprets things literally is told, "You can do anything," the child believes it 100 percent, no exceptions. The child thinks he can fly if he just tries hard enough when he jumps off the countertop. The child with ASD struggles with the monstrous discrepancy between ability and performance, between brilliance in one area and disability in other areas. One mother of a child with ASD explained her experience:

> Several years ago, before we even heard about Asperger Syndrome, my son's teacher commented on how he struggles in the classroom. She insinuated that he is not too smart, possibly mentally retarded. We finally pushed to have him tested. The tests showed that he is of genius intelligence, super high scores. The teacher's comment: "I didn't know he was smart!"

Assumptions about a person's ASD-impacted abilities may contribute greatly to weak self-worth in the adult years. The following story illustrates the professor-like behavior in action:

> My husband is an Aspie. He can explain the most intricate electronics but can't take out the trash. He just doesn't care about our home, our family, or anything related to us. How can he be so involved in his hobbies yet not find time for us?

The assumptions of aptitude provide the marital partners with a brick wall built of misjudgments, often topped off with dislike, even hatred.

There is a vicious cycle—the person with ASD is highly intelligent, therefore capable of great things. If the person with ASD does not do the basic things to build the foundation of home, he does not care about the home. Ironically, these assumptions go in a direction that is entirely off the map for the person with ASD. If you sit down and have an honest conversation with your partner with ASD, you may reveal workable solutions, as the following couple did:

> I used to make all sorts of assumptions about my husband [ASD]. Now I know better. One day when my back was about to break I asked him straight out, "Why can't you do the simple jobs around the house, but you can do *whatever you want* to do when you want to do it?" I was steaming mad and I persisted until I got some answers. The answers surprised me.
>
> I found out that my husband had never prioritized. He had never thought about why he does what he does. He just does whatever feels right to him at the moment. How had he skipped that important step in becoming an adult?

This woman took the time to draw out how she saw her priorities and how she viewed the natural progression of tasks. She did this while stewing over the situation and ended up doodling pictures by each one: a house, a plate, a child, and a computer. The pictures proved to be an important visual.

Priorities:

1. Clean house

2. Food on the table

3. Kids cared for

4. Hobbies.

This woman continued to explain:

> I dropped the list on his lap and stomped out. I was shocked to see a noticeable, immediate improvement. He simply adopted the same list I had. He now had an order to activities when he came home. He glanced around the house, picked up a few items until it was as clean as he liked it, then he checked to see if anything was

being made for dinner (if I wasn't doing it, he did it himself). Next, he checked on the children and spent some time with them either helping them or playing with them (typically 20 minutes). Finally, he went to relax in front of his computer and shut out the world, as was his habit.

For this particular couple, the adjustment was a marriage-saving improvement. What would their marriage be like today if this woman had let her assumptions fester? The anger at her husband's apparent indifference would probably mount until it became pure hatred. The marriage could have either dissolved or become toxic.

PARROTING/ECHOLALIA

People with ASD may parrot back what is said in an effort to give themselves time to digest the words and to formulate a response. Sometimes, they cannot hear what has been said until they say it themselves. It is as if the response reaction is a rough-starting car engine that needs multiple attempts to get started. For example:

NT: What do you want to do tonight?

ASD: Do tonight?

There is a possibility that the person with ASD has received a few too many negative responses to his echolalia and has replaced it with other dysfluencies. One couple explains:

He [ASD] lets out huge sighs that are embarrassingly long. He says he's thinking.

Or:

In the past, when I asked him [ASD] a question, he would think about it, take his time, and finally answer. I bugged him about it and now when I ask him a question, he knows I want a response in real-time (not ASD-time), so now he gives a thoughtless response so that he can get it out fast enough. I should have been careful what I asked for! I traded one problem for a bigger problem.

Perhaps the parroting has been replaced by sighs, silence, a nonsensical response, or fidgeting. In researching, I did not find a solution to the parroting/echolalia issue except to realize that it serves a purpose for the person with ASD. It is best to allow time for the adult with ASD to compute the information and formulate a response on his own timetable.

"I DON'T KNOW"

What do you want for dinner?

I don't know.

What do you want to do this weekend?

I don't know.

What do you want out of life?

I don't know.

This particular communication pattern occurs often in our home. My husband with ASD can make decisions just fine; it is just that there are far too many decisions to make in the average day. He is usually on decision overload and just shuts down. The "I don't know" response is more a sign of overload than it is a sign of ignorance. Another sign of overload is silence, but unless he is at maximum overload, he can usually muster, "I don't know." It is a sign that he at least has the strength to give a verbal reply, whether it is meaningful or not.

Typically, if a person with ASD does not know what to say, he does not say anything (Attwood 1998). For too many years, I interpreted, "I don't know" (or silence) to mean, "I don't care." In reality, "I don't know" may indicate a tired soul, worn out from the stresses of too many difficulties squeezing into one day. I learned to translate, "I don't know," into, "I'm too tired to know," instead of assuming that his response indicated his level of caring. This proved to be a marriage-saver. It was one of many situations where attributing NT responses to a person with ASD proved to be dead wrong.

METAPHORS, SIMILES, AND OTHER EVILS

Metaphors are non-literal expressions such as "food for thought." Similes are figures of speech such as "sweet as honey." Do you use these in your daily speech? Probably. Often, an NT is not even aware of having used one because it happens naturally as we speak. For example:

> Why can't he understand what I'm going through? I told him to try walking in my shoes for just one day and he just stared at me (and at my shoes).

I have found it useful to use a "metaphor meter" when I am conversing with my husband with ASD. It sounds silly but it is based on the writings of Hans Asperger himself (1944, p.58 in Frith 1991). When I converse with my husband, I mentally turn on a sorting device that separates the facts from the extras (metaphors, similes, hypotheticals, heavy emotional content, poetic phrasing, etc.). With my metaphor meter at maximum power I can sift out the obstacles in a conversation before they spill out of my mouth. What results is clearer communication, more similar to ASD-speak. It is a small price to pay for the ability to converse with my best friend.

HYPOTHETICALS

NTs use hypothetical situations to illustrate a point, to explore possibilities, or for other purposes. Have you noticed that your partner with ASD does not enter into the hypothetical exploration with you?

> *NT*: How would you feel if I had just said that to you?

> *ASD*: But you didn't say it. I did.

Or the hypothetical comment may just send your partner's head spinning.

> *NT*: How would you like it if I did that to you and then you had to clean up this mess?

> *ASD*: I have no idea what you're talking about.

Think back to the last time you used a hypothetical in speech with someone. You probably used it to illustrate a point. Why not skip the hypothetical and get straight to the point? You may not want to make it a habit, but at least it will clear up some communication problems with your partner with ASD. For example, when I try to explain to my husband that we need to update our will, I can use one of the following types of dialogues:

> If we don't update our will then the kids might go to Uncle Joey and he wouldn't be good for them at all. He'd use their inheritance for gambling and would let the kids grow like weeds… Or what if Aunt Sally got them? They would not do well under her care…

Or:

> If we don't have a will, we won't get what we want.

Guess which one my husband with ASD prefers? You guessed it. The direct approach. The hypotheticals are merely detours that his focused ASD brain cannot afford to go down.

UNWRITTEN RULES

When I was 15 years old I traveled to another country to study as an exchange student for a year. It was my first experience of a foreign culture. So many rules: do not put your hands in your lap during meals, be funny, be interesting. The movements, gestures, and body language were all foreign.

Because of this experience I was able, in a small way, to develop empathy for my husband's inability to know the unwritten rules automatically. After all, they are quite puzzling. When I found out about my husband's ASD I did the same thing I did for myself when I was overseas: I wrote down the rules so I could see them, touch them, and realize that they were concrete, real, and definable. I thought this might help my husband since his lack of social graces reminded me of my awkward adjustment to a new culture. In a little journal we passed back and forth to each other during church I wrote: "Don't snore during church." On his "To Do" list at home I wrote: "Hug me when you come home." On his home computer I typed: "Ask the children about what they did at school today." The unwritten rules became written.

I have often wished that I could go to a bookstore and pick up a copy of the "Unwritten Rules of Human Behavior," a 700- to 800-page volume written specifically for people with ASD. I wish that someone else would do this for me, but I have realized that we all make our own rules—especially within a long-term relationship. We define our own rules as a couple. Those who work with children with ASD may be able to teach the rules of acceptable behavior directly, whereas within a marriage it is a mutual definition created one rule at a time.

Implications and solutions: Language through the lifespan

> *"Symptoms must be present in the early developmental period..."*

It is possible that your partner with ASD may be able to mask the communication difficulties from everyone except you. He may appear to be conversationally able in public but, behind closed doors, in your home, he may speak an alien language, if he speaks at all. If this is the case, both of you may be led to believe that the problems lie strictly between you and your partner—when, in reality, the problems lie in a lack of higher-level communication skills.

Intimate relationships require the most elaborate conversational skills of all, discussing everything from the most complex personal negotiations to the softest, most delicate, emotionally charged issues. Communication difficulties in an ASD-linked relationship can create a noticeable coldness between the two partners. I have often marveled at how quickly our conversations can freeze due to the differences in how we communicate. It is frustrating, leaving both of us wondering why we have to work so hard to figure out the day-to-day details of our lives together. Learning how to communicate with my partner sometimes feels like a part-time job, sapping energy out of me when I have already worked a full day. A friend once told me to look at learning to communicate with my partner as learning a new skill. I was taking "night classes from an independent study course in Aspergese." Once I could see it as a learned skill, it helped me realize that I was furthering my education, attaining a valuable new proficiency. Self-pity went flying out the window. I was becoming multi-lingual and it was a respectable, worthwhile goal.

SUCCESSFUL COMMUNICATION

ASD-impacted or not, successful communication is difficult. If it was easy then bookstores' shelves would not be lined with volumes describing how to communicate effectively, seminars would not be focused entirely on the communication process, and universities would not offer courses in communication. I tried all of these resources (books, seminars, courses) and none of them worked for our ASD-linked relationship. I learned how to NT-speak better, but I still could not ASD-speak.

To figure out solid communication skills for an ASD-linked relationship, let's look at the diagnostic criteria once again. What types of obstacles can we overcome simply by our awareness of the standard diagnostic traits? Here is a brief sampling based on particulars from the DSM criteria:

- *DSM-5: A—Social impairment*: Once you know that social situations are difficult, you can work around them by avoiding impromptu social situations, practicing for important social situations, and preparing for the aftermath of social situations.

- *DSM-5: A—Failure to recognize nonverbal language*: If your partner with ASD does not understand nonverbal communication, then don't rely on it. Make sure that your message is communicated in its entirety in verbal or written form. If you inadvertently say, "Come here," with your eyes, try to catch yourself and say it out loud.

- *DSM-5: A—Communication*: As miscommunications erupt, you can more easily trace the problems back to the particulars of ASD-speak (literal speech, logical conclusions, succinct communication, etc.).

- *DSM-5: A—Lack of sharing*: Find ways to encourage your partner to share. Ask pointed questions. Ask questions through e-mail. Communicate appreciation when he does make an effort to share.

- *DSM-5: B—Intense interest*: If your partner is going on and on about his intense interest, have a pre-agreed-upon signal that will pause the communication. For example, if he is droning on about the latest advance in AI (artificial intelligence), tap him on the shoulder until he snaps out of it and explain that you need to take a break but would love to hear more later.

- *DSM-5: B—Routines*: If your partner has established a less-than-appealing communication routine, have a signal to break it. For example, if your dilemma is getting your partner to stop teasing you, keep a small red card in your pocket and hold it up every time he teases you. Agree that the routine (persistent teasing) needs to be stopped for the benefit of you both.

- *DSM-5 C—Persistent symptoms*: Once you know that the ASD-based behaviors have been around since your partner was young, you can better accept them as a part of your partner's personality rather than something that needs to be changed. It relieves some of the pressure.

- *DSM-5 D—Occupational impairments*: When you are aware that your partner with ASD faces large challenges finding and keeping a job, it helps you be more compassionate day after day.

- *DSM-5: E—Not better explained by intellectual disability*: If you know and understand the ASD diagnostic criteria, you can better understand your partner's motives and intentions. For example, if your partner does something that appears nonsensical to you, instead of assuming it means a lack of intelligence, look for a reason that may be related to ASD.

In the ASD literature, you will find several suggestions that are mentioned over and over again: be clear, do not interrupt, and look for alternatives. Let's look at the first of these three—be clear. For example:

I can't say, "It sure is cold out," and expect him to give me his coat. I must say, "Can I borrow your coat?" I must be straightforward and direct.

The second general suggestion—do not interrupt. Why is this an issue? Interruptions are like a break in the train tracks. They cause the ASD-based thought process to derail. Wait patiently. A derailed train is far worse than having to wait for a moment, exercising your patience.

The third general suggestion—look for alternatives. Go with your best understanding of your own needs along with what you have learned about your partner. The answers to our communication problems lie in our abilities to understand the ASD condition and brainstorm for our own best personal solutions. Some of the following solutions have worked for us:

- E-mail or instant message your partner.

- Use a watch that accepts e-mail. The message will be physically attached to your partner.

- Use a cell phone that accepts e-mail. You partner can choose to answer back in cell e-mail or call you directly.

- Write a short note and put it where your partner will see it.

- Make your own list of hand signals. We have secret signals for all sorts of things, especially the "I'm not OK even though I look OK" signal and the "You've pushed me too far" signal. These messages cannot be communicated delicately so the hand signals are valuable when others are present and we have to watch our words carefully.

- Find the repetitive communication patterns and eliminate them. For example, if you say, "Please take out the trash," every night, post a note about it where he will see it and remember to do it, making it a routine, thus alleviating some of the verbal communication overload.

- If your partner with ASD is a visual thinker, draw graphs, charts, or other visual images that explain the concept in fewer words.

- If your partner with ASD is worried about the issue becoming confounded by other topics, set a time limit. Either set a stopwatch or other timing device. Our favorite method is to choose a TV show that puts us both at ease and agree to discuss the particular topic only during the commercial breaks. This confines the conversation to three minutes or less and is not as staged as setting a stopwatch. We can either watch the show or take time to think during the show, preparing for the next commercial break. You can have "Cocoa Talks" where you limit the conversation to the amount of time it takes to make hot cocoa or limit it to the time it takes to reboot your computer—

whatever works. The set time limit will give your partner a sense of predictability.

- Present only one issue at a time. If the problem is bigger than just one issue, write it down for yourself in your relationship journal (see Chapter 3) and then address only one part at a time. You will be able to map out the full topic in your relationship journal and won't lose track of where you are in the discussion. If your partner has weak central coherence, he will only see the bits and pieces of the issue, not the issue as a whole. By writing it down in full, you will be able to work on the issue slowly and methodically, avoiding the feeling that the issue has been dropped or ignored.

Although these are great solutions, I hope you will trust your own instincts. Each couple must find their own solutions because each couple is so phenomenally unique. I will use the e-mail suggestion as an example of how important it is for the ASD-linked couple to go with what works best in their relationship and not consider it a failure if a particular strategy does not work for them.

In the ASD literature, you will read over and over again the recommendation of using e-mail or other electronic communication to talk with your partner with ASD. Using e-mail sounds like the ultimate answer—communication removed from the threatening verbal realm, devoid of body language, eye language, and other nonverbal signals, stripped down to the bare words. It may work wonders for many, but may not work for everyone. Listen to one wife's experience:

> I tried your suggestion of e-mailing my husband [ASD]. He just ignores it like he does every other form of communication. The only way I can communicate with him is when we're lying in bed at night. I guess he needs to be horizontal to be able to talk (and I don't mean that in a rude sexual way). He's not lazy, but he says he needs to have "the gravity off my body." Plus, I'm not looking at his face; I'm tenderly snuggled in his chest. I guess it's the non-threatening nature of our positional relationship to each other that makes conversation possible. When we're standing, walking, sitting at the table, or even in front of his computer monitor, he's incapable of holding a conversation, utterly incapable.

There is also a possibility that e-mail will not work due to the well-earned sense of distrust in interpersonal communication. For example:

> Whenever we have e-mailed each other, it always seems to end with hurt and confusion. My wife [ASD] has gotten so accustomed to hidden messages behind the words that she's paranoid of what might be behind the message.

While working your way to a more successful level of communication, you may be able to learn from your partner with ASD. I believe that certain ASD behaviors can be highly effective in certain situations. For example, when I use the ASD-related traits I have observed in my husband, I:

- listen (although I may only be pretending to listen)

- respond unemotionally (hard for me to do at times)

- am less dependent on what others say or think (your partner with ASD is a great role model for this, if a bit extreme)

- am more centered in self (not too bad if it helps you more accurately identify your needs)

- am concise (excessive frivolous chitchat takes time away from the more important things in life)

- focus on the logic of the message (useful in workplace communications).

BREAKDOWN OF ALL COMMUNICATION

The breakdown of all communication can happen for countless reasons that are directly related to the DSM diagnostic criteria. I will list only a few since the full list I originally composed was more depressing than a funeral dirge.

- *DSM-5: A—Failure to initiate or respond:* The NT partner perceives that the partner with ASD does not want to share any personal, emotional information, therefore assuming dislike or even willfully cold intentions. Communication shuts down.

- *DSM-5: B—Inflexible adherence to routines*: The partner with ASD must stick to a certain script within the conversation (a routine involving communication patterns) and cannot modify the communication pattern to fit the current need. Communication shuts down.

- *DSM-5: B—Sensory issues*: Due to auditory dysfunction, voices that are loud, angry, or have a shrill tone are unintelligible. Without being able to hear the words or read the nonverbal cues, the person with ASD is functionally deaf and blind. Communication is impossible.

- *DSM-5: B—Meltdowns*: Instead of discussing issues ahead of time, issues are dealt with in the heat of the moment when the partner with ASD is in the illogical meltdown state. Communication shuts down.

Enough already! There are so many ways for an ASD/NT conversation to shut down that it is amazing that we are ever able to communicate in the first place. Let's discuss some of the most basic issues that may form a chasm between ASD and NT communication.

One differential may be the purpose of communication. It is possible that your partner with ASD sees communication merely as a tool for getting information. It is possible that your partner "...perceives having a conversation as announcing, informing and questioning; with no idea of the Experience Sharing purpose it serves the rest of us" (Gutstein 2000, p.42). If the purpose of the conversation is merely to get or give information, then conversations will reach a dead-end quickly. You will be left with an empty feeling at the end because your purpose for conversation goes beyond information getting. As my husband and I have learned to share verbally with each other, I have been able to explain that I need three things in a conversation: listen, respond, and share.

For my husband, the listening part was simple. He naturally listens to anyone and anything, logging away details with perfect accuracy. It took several years for the "respond" part to become a habit. We developed strategies that made the responding natural for us both. The final one, the one that we are still working on, is to "share." I have found great relief in hearing detailed responses to: "How was your day?"

Sharing is becoming more natural as we work on it. In order to see the progress, I have referred to my marriage journal many times. I recorded our first efforts as follows:

He'll say something about his work, but it's so boring that I'll interrupt him or somehow cut it short. I can't help it. It's so boring.

I conscientiously trained myself to attend to the conversation even though it was boring. It was important that I support my husband's first efforts at experience sharing. Later journal entries described:

It isn't so boring anymore and the flow is better. He's learning that certain topics are far more interesting than others.

Another potential cause for the breakdown of communication relates to a person's conversational coordination. The autistic person may not know "…how to recognize that the coordination of the activity has been lost, and to perform a type of regulatory or repair activity" (Gutstein 2000, p.20). For example:

NT: Talking about how to raise the children—getting angry and bringing up numerous topics. Conversation is deteriorating rapidly.

ASD: Trying to hold on to a consistent thread in the conversation.

Compared with (if it was an NT/NT conversation):

Other NT: Uses a repair strategy such as, "Hey, I can see this is a hot topic. Let's take a short break and talk about it in a minute."

A repair activity is something a person does to fix a flailing conversation. Here is another example:

NT: Talking about how they should handle a difficult financial situation.

ASD: Doesn't know an answer so stays quiet or walks away.

Compared with (if it was an NT/NT conversation):

Other NT: May try a regulatory approach, keeping his own interest level up to match his partner's interest level: "I'm just as concerned about this as you are, but I have no idea what to do here. What do you think?"

The regulatory and repair strategies may sound easy as you read them on paper, but they are not. They are the diplomatic tactics that push the conversation in a healthy direction. Learning how to repair and regulate a conversation can be taught directly given the motivation and a good therapist. Without regulating a conversation, a person with ASD may plod along, not realizing the damage that his words and actions are causing. For example:

He [ASD] said ____. It hurt my feelings deeply and I told him so, but it didn't do any good. I can be sitting there crying into my hands and he'll still continue drilling in the same argument.

Breakdown may occur if the partner with ASD lacks the ability to see his own fault due to theory of mind issues, e.g. the person with ASD recognizes only his own mind. This is evident in our home at times. You will hear me and others say, "He's always right." He is. Fortunately for him, he has been quite lucky in life and I can recall only a few times over the last 15 years when he has been wrong. One of the times had to do with a particular USA front-line news story. When we met up at the end of the day, I told him the gossipy news. He said, "Nope. Couldn't be." He insisted that my information was incorrect although he had no information to the contrary. I am a news junkie and had heard and read the information verified through several sources. My husband continued to state that I was wrong and the conversation degraded into: "What is reality anyway, other than what you think is real?" While we were discussing the topic, a reputable station confirmed the news story, nearly word for word. We both watched and listened. To my amazement, he remained staunch: "You're wrong." Well, we were all wrong—the reporters, the media, everyone, even me. All I could do was shake my head and marvel at his ability to stick to his beliefs no matter what.

Years later, when I read Liane Holliday Willey's (2001) book, *Asperger Syndrome in the Family*, I realized that our familiar phrase of "He's always right" may have had its basis in his Aspieness. Liane states: "Failure to admit when we are wrong falls into the inflexible range, too. It necessitates the same problem-solving hierarchy that underscores any change in attitude or behavior—the hierarchy we are not wired to turn to" (p.97). I have had to accept the fact that my husband will always be right. The negative side effects are obvious. I doubt that I need to elaborate on what it is like to be married to someone who is always right.

I believe that this inflexibility can, at times, be an asset. Perhaps a person's failure to admit when he is wrong is consistent across the board. Perhaps he will stand up for all his beliefs the same unrelenting way. I have seen my husband stick to a belief that may have been difficult for an NT to hold on to. The one example of this that shines brightest for us at this point in our lives is that my husband has the underlying belief: "I will be there for my children." Time and time again, he has had to leave work early in order to attend a school event, drive the children somewhere, or attend a child's appointment when all his colleagues are still working. Not a single one of his colleagues understands his family life and if my husband did not have ASD, he would have caved into the peer pressure long ago, staying late at work rather than holding to his inflexible, unchanging, die-hard belief: "I will be there for my children."

LITERAL THINKING

It is often said that people with ASD perceive comments literally. A strong example of this comes from Maxine Aston, a counselor in the UK who works with ASD couples.

> Problems with literal…meanings can cause many misunderstandings for those with Asperger Syndrome (Autism Spectrum Disorder), many of whom complain that they wish people would just say what they mean… One woman explained how she had told her Asperger husband she would "kill him" if he forgot to pick up the dry cleaning in his lunch hour. She was going to speak at an important conference and needed the outfit that was at the cleaners for that evening. He forgot to collect it and took her threat to kill him quite seriously, so he was too afraid to go home. She eventually received a call from her sister-in-law to say that he had phoned her because he was concerned that if he returned home he was in danger of losing his life. (Aston 2014, p.35)

Profound confusion can result when a person with ASD perceives comments at face value only. It is likely that you won't notice the impact of your comments unless you work with a therapist or counselor to get to the root of the confusion and track it back to the original source—the literal interpretation of an NT-style statement.

It is also possible that your partner with ASD expects you to live up to your comments in their most literal sense. For example, if you say you're coming home at 5 p.m., you'd better be home at 5 p.m. Although you may have been providing only an estimated time, your partner may interpret your actions as dishonest if you do not follow through on all your comments word for word.

Not only will the comments be perceived in their most literal sense, but they may also be perceived as concrete and unchanging. Forexample:

> When we were first married, I told him that I didn't think I would ever want to have children. He took it as a rule that we would never have children, so when I turned 30 and started getting baby-cravings, he adamantly reminded me of our previous "agreement." He thought I was being dishonest by changing my mind.

Honesty, truth, and trust seem to be big issues in an ASD/NT or ASD/ASD relationship. A person with ASD needs predictability (even in unpredictable situations), literal communication (even in casual conversation), and the simplest form of honesty (even in complex human relations). Perhaps the lack of simple honesty in conversation is what leads many people with ASD to distrust others.

If trust, honesty, and consistency are big issues for you and your partner, you may need to be extra vigilant to keep your everyday actions consistent with your words. For example, if you say, "I'm starving hungry," then do not eat much for dinner, your partner may feel as if you have lied. Another example:

> I told him that I have wanted a pony ever since I was a little girl. He [ASD] figured out a way for us to get a horse on our property… When I explained to him that I didn't want a horse, he couldn't understand it and thought that I had made it all up.

The partner with ASD won't be able to mindread and will take your comments literally, not seeing the implications and insinuations behind the words. For example, I have often used the catchall phrase "I need help" as a blanket statement for dozens of different purposes. Without follow-up information my husband with ASD does not know what to do with this comment. "I need help," is too vague to process and he cannot mindread his way around the request. The following exchange used to occur often in our household:

NT: I need help.

ASD: Yes, you do.

This typically happened when I forgot our newfound ASD communication style and slipped back into old, familiar ways. In my NT language, "I need help," means, "Hey, buddy, can't you see that I need you to carry a few of these bags, give me a smile of encouragement, and recognize my needs before I have to ask?" The simple comment of needing help was supposed to spur on further action from him, but it did not.

We used two helpful strategies to get ourselves beyond this impasse. First, he learned to respond with "What should I do?" It was a prompter that worked in nearly every situation. It triggered our ASD-speak, reminding me in a non-confrontational way that I needed to give further details.

The second strategy was to break the task into subtasks. I learned to word my needs in simple requests containing no more than three items. Tasks that seemed simple to me were actually multi-step tasks for him. For example, "Please get the toy out from under the couch" is a four-step process: 1. Move the couch, 2. Pick up the toy, 3. Put the toy somewhere, and 4. Move the couch back. NTs might perceive this task as a single-step process: "Get the toy." For a person with dyspraxia, it is far more complicated.

I found that, on a bad day, my husband's executive functioning (the ability to execute tasks) would be low, so I would request only one item at a time and I would be explicit in the detail of the request. I would request, "Please move the couch three feet to the left." I would help him through the day the same way I would if he had the flu or a cold. Everything was foggy in his mind and he needed a flashlight to get through it all. The flashlight was the direct and clear instruction that helped him see just one step in front of him—enough to make it through the day.

Part of literal thinking is believing that a comment, once made, will stay constant over time. For this reason, your partner with ASD may tell you, "I love you," once and not tell you again. Why say it again? From the NT perspective, you may feel that one simple expression of love is not quite enough to last a lifetime. From the ASD perspective, there is no reason to repeat a phrase that has not been successfully refuted. Here is where we need to brainstorm for creative, unusual ways to meet the needs of both partners. In my case, I was able to say, "I need to hear 'I love you' at least twice a day." That was sufficient. I hear it a dozen times a day because he is playing it safe. For others, a request stated as a rule may be met with opposition, manifest in comments such as, "I already told you I loved you. Don't force me." In this case, other methods of love-representation work better: e-mails, notes, a special hand sign, a touch that is unique to the two of you, a secret word, roses once a month, cooking dinner, rubbing your back, anything that would be a good substitute for an affirmation of love.

WORDING CRITICISM

Since your partner with ASD looks like most other adults, you may voice opinions such as: "How could you think something like that?" "Didn't you hear a word I just said?" "Don't you get it?" Comments such as these, although justified, are the marital equivalent of a parent ranting at a child: "How many times do I have to tell you?" These comments are pure poison, not only to you and your partner, but to others (children) who are within earshot.

The person with ASD is already aware that he does not "get it." The person with ASD is probably trying hard to ignore the comments or deny their reality. Voicing the opinion reinforces the fear that the person with ASD is an outcast, incapable of understanding what most people understand naturally. Your partner with ASD may be able to weather it for a while, but it is most likely that he will find a way to protect himself. As one male with ASD explained to his wife:

> You know that game…[favorite multi-player computer game]? Well, my character wears a thick plate of armor made of…[technically detailed description of armor]. He's nearly invincible, but if you stab him in certain spots, you kill him. When you say certain things, it feels like I'm being stabbed. I can take a certain number of hits like this before it kills me.

When faced with criticism he cannot refute, he may build a wall, refuse to listen anymore, leave, or develop evasive tactics to save himself from the destruction that you are inadvertently dishing out. Even if you did not intend to criticize, your partner may perceive it as criticism and remember it long term. One comment like, "You're not too smart, are you?" back in the fourth grade may still hurt. The difference between a person with ASD and an NT's perception of a criticism is that an NT may be able to mentally refute the criticism, realizing that his status as a PhD or fiscally successful adult far outweighs the comments of his fourth-grade peers. By contrast, the person with ASD may not generalize current successes to past comments (Frith 1991, p.16). The comments of the cruel fourth graders may still be considered valid in the mind of the person with ASD—they may be unchangeable. Likewise, your comments of, "I'm sorry," or, "I didn't mean it," may prove ineffective in wiping out past hurts. Comments that you make within your adult relationship may be officially logged onto his mental files for permanent storage.

So, now that we know how destructive criticism can be to a person with ASD, what do we do? Do we just shut off all criticism? Do we repress? Not if we want a healthy long-term relationship. There must be other options.

First, look at the criticism. What is it really? I see it as having two parts: one helpful, one hurtful. We can dissect the criticism, maximizing the good and minimizing the bad. For example, imagine that my partner with ASD lost his job. Upon hearing about it, I might say, "What? I can't believe you lost your job. We'd better tighten up finances immediately." There are two important messages here: 1. anger at the situation and 2. an explanation of what I believe should happen.

I have found it most successful to first deal with my anger. If I really need to let off steam, I use a healthy method (leave the room, stomp my foot, whatever works at the moment). I believe it is healthiest to channel anger away from my partner.

The second part of the NT anger response is the statement of the anticipated reaction: "We'd better tighten up finances immediately." This is the action part of the response—the part my partner with ASD is looking for. If I can state my reaction in the form of a desired response only, I am at peace with the fact that I have tried my best. I pat myself on the back that I have pulled myself out of the situation without criticizing my partner or demoralizing both of us.

Why is it so important to separate the emotion from the fact? Because a person with ASD is more likely to understand the factual side of the comments first. People with ASD do experience emotion, but they experience it differently from the way NTs do (Grandin 1995, pp.82–95). Approaching a problem from the emotional vantage point first is most likely to cause confusion since you are both on different wavelengths emotionally. Your interactions are more likely to be meaningful and successful if they are based on facts and logic—it may help to siphon off the high-octane NT emotions before sending the message in your partner's direction. Listen to how my husband with ASD explains the dichotomy:

> I don't see why you're mad about it. It happened. So what. The fact and the emotion are two different things.

NTs tend to mix emotion and fact as quickly and as easily as we mix verbs and adverbs—they go together naturally and easily. Separating these two is only a minor adjustment in how you vocalize your anger to your partner with ASD. You may find that it is healthier to be more careful in your expressions of anger. At least, it is worth a try to avoid all the anguish that accompanies the criticism. Criticism is not only bad for your partner with ASD, but it hurts you as well.

Lest we think that criticism is a simple issue, let's explore why it may go a few steps further for your particular partner with ASD. There is a possibility that criticism is cutting a far deeper wound than you ever intended. You may find that your partner is hypersensitive to criticism, to the point of irrationality. For example:

> No matter what I say, he [ASD] thinks I'm being critical. I can't open my mouth without him automatically judging my comments as criticism.

Lorna Wing (1981) supports this concept: "The tendency found in people with Asperger Syndrome to sensitivity and overgeneralization of the fact that they are criticized and made fun of may, if present in marked form, be mistaken for a paranoid psychosis." Perhaps even the slightest hint of a criticism may lead you to a life where all communication shuts down. For example:

Even the simplest observation such as, "The butter is too soft," is taken personally. She [ASD] gets angry that the butter is too soft, thinks I'm blaming her for making the butter too soft... It is pure hysteria.

The hypersensitivity to criticism may come from previous societal interaction. A person with ASD may grow up with the belief that others are out to trick him and make him look stupid. Over time, he may develop an ingrained hypersensitivity to anything that may possibly be a criticism. The person with ASD does not have the natural ability to perceive the nuances between criticism and comments, let alone the differences between constructive criticism and hurtful criticism.

It would not be fair to mention only the one-way direction of criticism (the NT partner criticizing the partner with ASD). It may easily go both ways, but of course the dynamics are different.

The partner with ASD may criticize the NT partner. For example:

She [ASD] is always pointing out what a slob I am and how I can never pick up after myself.

Or:

He [ASD] is constantly criticizing me that I don't cook properly.

Or:

Why should I listen to him [ASD] criticize me about every little thing? When he is home, he's constantly pointing out how I'm doing everything "wrong."

Perhaps, upon further investigation, you may find that the criticisms are actually intended as logical, helpful comments. Even the comment, "No thinking individual would ever do it the way you just did," may actually have no malicious intent behind it. It may be extremely difficult to accept the fact that most people with ASD are not the manipulative, controlling, critical creatures they appear to be when they are offering insights that they believe will be helpful. The person with ASD who complains about messiness may simply be trying to satisfy a sensory need for order in his surroundings. The partner who complains about cooking may simply be making an observation. The person with ASD who points out all the mistakes of his partner may be trying to improve his partner. It may come across as inappropriate, tactless, and rude, but perhaps the intentions are good.

It may take immense courage to open yourself up to the possibility that the apparently critical comments may not be intended to hurt as deeply as they do. Especially if you have been together for a while, it may be extremely difficult to get past the patterns of criticism that have sunk their roots into your relationship. Despite the difficulties, the easiest way to determine your partner's intentions is by simply asking. I have learned to ask, "Did you mean to hurt me?" Every single time, without exception, my partner with ASD has been baffled that hurt was perceived on my part.

Of course, if the criticism is intentionally hurtful, then it is a matter that needs to be dealt with by a trained, qualified couples therapist. If your partner is excessively hurtful it may be a more severe psychological condition such as oppositional defiant disorder (ODD). A person with ODD is characteristically argumentative, defiant, and hypersensitive. He may actively seek revenge, throw temper tantrums, or stage deliberate attempts to annoy you. A medical professional can deal with this condition.

Somewhere in the distance between the partner with ASD and the NT partner there is a miscommunication—a comment that was benign becomes malignant as it travels through the air from one partner to the other. It is a sort of infectious miscommunication. Let's look at a few remedies:

> When he [ASD] criticizes me, I take a step back mentally before I respond to him and think, "If he wasn't trying to hurt me, how would I interpret what he just said?" It allows me to see past the obviously hurtful parts of the comment and interpret the comment *as he intended it.*

Here is another example from a woman who was desperate to find a way to counteract the criticism that was slipping out of her mouth on a minute-by-minute basis:

> I need to undo the damage of my repetitive "I hate you" messages, but how? This morning, I set a goal to not criticize him [ASD] for an entire day. By 8 a.m. I had already failed miserably. I just couldn't bite my tongue that hard. I couldn't give so much of myself. So, I

decided to write it down. I wrote a long letter to him. He read it, but I don't think he understood it. The words probably floated off the page into the realm of mushy, meaningless love-talk for him.

Since his visual perception is much stronger than his auditory perception, the message should be written—he'll have to see it. I'll post the message where he can see it so it can sink in and counteract the damage of my critical comments. It has to be a logical message. Words like "love," "feel," and "affection" will make the message fuzzy.

[Several weeks later.] When he left for his business trip, I slipped a few 3×5 handwritten love notes in his suitcase like I always do. The notes contained messages such as "Miss you!" or "We love you!" Silly messages that have never made much of an impact but, this time, one of the notes somehow found its way up onto a shelf in the closet. The note said, "We couldn't ask for a better Dad. Be safe." It was clear, logical, direct, and it contained no fuzzy love-talk. I posted it where he'll see it daily. *Voilà*. A message that can help him through the tough times when my critical comments slip out.

COUPLES COMMUNICATION AS A LEARNED SKILL

Couples therapy contains two basic elements: talking and emotion. Neither of these are appropriate for my partner with ASD, so we must use other methodologies. These "other methodologies" may not look even vaguely similar to standard couples therapy.

- *Focus on cognitive analysis rather than emotional analysis.* For example, instead of, "Why do you feel this way?" it might be more effective to say, "Let's dissect this issue in the format of a written list."

- *Take it step-by-step.* Do not expect to create successfully a year-long financial budget when you cannot agree how much to spend on dinner.

- *Deal with one issue at a time.* It may be a bit more difficult for you (NT), since you can see how topics are interrelated, but your partner with ASD may not see the interrelated nature of things the same way you do. Mixing topics only confuses the matter. Work with one issue at a time and interrelate them on your own later.

- *Reading books from the management/business section of your library or bookstore might help.* Learning how to negotiate professionally, how to deal with difficult people, or how to logically state your position may be far more effective than reading emotion-charged marriage self-help books. Perhaps the logic behind management-style negotiations will be more effective for your particular situation than the standard marital relations advice.

- *You may need to be forceful.* For example, if your partner does not refer to your face, tone of voice, or other indicators while arguing, you will have to show your point in explicit, unquestionable detail. Without a knowledge of ASD, you may communicate "Hey, the fight is over" by snuggling up to your partner, smiling, softening your eyes, touching his shoulder, and saying something gentle. Instead, perhaps you can vocalize, "The fight is over. I'd like to relax with you now," and ask point-blank if your partner has also given up the fight.

- *Talk through issues in explicit detail.* The true source of the problems probably will not be revealed until after a significant amount of worthless conversation, when all of a sudden a small, seemingly irrelevant detail is unearthed as an answer to your problems. For example, one day we were arguing over why my husband does not help the children with their school projects. We argued over his role with the children, and how he shows his caring towards them. We argued about nearly every aspect of parenting until finally it was revealed that he could not help the children with their school projects because on this particular day they both had literary assignments requiring a high level of skill with poetic wording. He is a literal thinker, not a literary thinker, and knew that his interpretation of non-literal text would be inaccurate. A minor detail, but it was the root of the problem and we never would have discovered it without half an hour of probing. Without diligence, our conversation would have ended on the dual notes of, "You don't care," and, "You don't understand."

- *Be literal.* Your partner with ASD will interpret your message literally. Be careful not to use metaphors, similes, generalizations, sarcasm, or complex humor in your messages.

- *Wait until your partner is calm, relaxed, and at ease.* It is not worth approaching your partner when he is already on overload. He will not be able to hear you. I consider my partner to be virtually "deaf" during certain portions of the day and this changes my behavior—I would not become angry with a deaf person for not being able to hear me.

- *End the conversation quickly by leaving the room or by giving a quick reassurance and moving on to something else* if the conversation turns from talking to arguing.

- *Do not promise or threaten anything unless you mean it long term.* Your partner with ASD will not understand that words said in an argument have less meaning than words said at other times. He will take the threat at face value and remember it, possibly even creating his own long-standing threat as a defensive retaliation.

Please take these suggestions with a grain of salt. They represent what works in my home and for other couples in similar situations. Every couple must find their own solutions based on their own unique relationship.

There is one rule that I would venture to say covers every situation: the differences between ASD and NT communication *must be recognized.* People with ASD are cognitively different from NTs, just as NTs are cognitively different from people with ASD. I was thrilled to read Liane Holliday Willey's (2001, p.97) description of this difference because it helped me understand what may be going on in my husband's head when I try to talk with him as an NT.

> These words do little to melt us. They become drums drowning out the tiny voice in the ASD heart that tries so desperately to reach the mind. Neurotypicals do not have tiny voices. They have strong, clear, multi-lingual voices that can be heard above the roar of the entire jungle... That mindset requires a cognitive flexibility we typically lack.

If NTs have such strong voices, then why is it so difficult for a person with ASD to communicate with one? Shouldn't the NT be able to adapt immediately to the communication style of the person with ASD? Not necessarily. It just means that successful couples communication is so difficult that it requires a professional level of interpersonal communication skills along with a Gandhi-level of self-control. If NTs have a hard time with it, then people with ASD must truly struggle with it, maybe even despise it.

Compared to NTs who use all their modalities to communicate, a person with ASD may have a much more narrow receptor for communication. For example, when you send a message, your partner with ASD:

- may not hear the message at all if it is given through a modality he does not read, such as body language

- may hear the message and not understand it; i.e. it may be illogical or metaphorical or contain generalizations

- may hear the message and remember it forever.

I titled this section "Couples communication as a learned skill" because I believe that it must be *learned*. I do not believe that it comes naturally to NTs to communicate with someone as logical, literal, and honest as a person with ASD. I also do not believe that couples relations come naturally to people with ASD. Learning to work together, communicate, and successfully form a mutually beneficial union may be a monumental effort, but the necessary skills can be learned.

THE RULE BOOK

I have often wished that my husband had come with his own rule book, user manual, or some sort of guide that would help me understand his unique ASD wiring. Personal life stories by various ASD authors have given me a glimpse into their own individual rule books and from them I can infer what my husband's might be like. I can also look at the research and infer general rules, but I often wish for a more personalized resource that would make our life together easier.

On the flip side, people with ASD are also confused by the NT codes of conduct. They also wish for some sort of definitive work where they could look up the signs of predictable human behavior and learn to interpret them more readily. Plenty of books have been written to define human behavior: body language books, eye language books, books about motivation and intentionality of behavior. These books have been written for the NT mind—they contain generalities and hypotheses that are not concrete enough for an ASD mind, which craves concrete details. A definitive book has not been written because it cannot be written. Human behavior cannot be defined so simply. Perhaps we could define behavior for one individual at a time, but not for the human race as a whole.

Given the understanding that both my husband and I work from different mindsets and that the difference in our thinking is profound, we often comment that access to each other's personal rule books would make life infinitely easier. Every now and then, we joke, "Hey, that's against the rules" or "That's not how it is in my rule book." We work with the recognition that our mindsets are based on entirely different assumptions and we both construe meaning from the world differently.

Here is an example where I misinterpreted my husband's actions. This is a summary of several journal entries contrasting pre-ASD understanding to post-ASD understanding.

Here were my assumptions:

- My husband is angry with me over certain things, just like I am angry with him over certain things.

- My husband sees and feels the emotional iceberg between us.

- If I am too nice to my husband, he will see it as a weakness and be even more mean.

Here is what I found:

- Just because I have an emotion does not mean he will respond in kind—he does not engage in this level of emotional reciprocity. Also, he is rarely angry about anything. Anger is a rare emotion for him. I have misinterpreted his quietness for a cold shoulder when it really was just quietness.

- My husband does not know what an emotional iceberg looks like. I am the only one who can see the icebergs and the cold shoulders.

- My husband does not intend to inflict hurt; he just does not think in terms of reciprocity the way I do. He relishes all the nice things we both do for each other and he is not keeping score like I am.

It takes a lot of work and some introspection to figure out these matters. We have different neurological wiring; different operating systems run in our brains. With a little troubleshooting, a lot of patience, and an awareness of how we are programmed differently, we can begin to decode each other and write our own personal user manuals. Maybe someday we will even have tech support (appropriate couples counseling).

7

Diagnostic Criteria D

CLINICALLY SIGNIFICANT IMPAIRMENT

> D Symptoms cause clinically significant impairment in social, occupational, or other important areas of current functioning.

This part of the diagnosis is so broad that it is difficult to pin down— it covers everything from job difficulties to how well a person with ASD can function at a social gathering. Let's break this part of the diagnosis into three simple sections: social, occupational, and other, i.e. the slippery issues that often dance around the edges of ASD.

WHAT IT MAY LOOK LIKE: SOCIAL

"Symptoms cause clinically significant impairment in social...functioning"

The social functioning of an adult with ASD may look like this:

> We were at a party the other night and I just sat back and watched. He [ASD] can't seem to join in the conversation. He tried once but he could only talk about computers and when he did talk about them, he droned on and on.

But it can also look like this:

> She [ASD] just stands near the wall, with her body turned so that everyone will think she's uninterested in participating.

The social functioning of an adult with ASD cannot be classified as one type. There are many ways to "malfunction" in society. The only specification the diagnosis can give regarding ASD social functioning is that the person with ASD experiences unusually poor social interaction. Here is one family's example that shows a lack of social functioning within the family structure:

> Since my husband [ASD] acts a lot like my friend's husbands, I forget that he can't take care of the children. I'll ask him to bathe the baby and he'll put the baby in scalding hot water because he can't sense temperature well. Or I'll ask him to help the kids with their homework. He'll just sit beside them because he doesn't know what to do. Sooner or later, he'll wander off after not helping the kids at all. I'll ask him to help me figure out finances or scheduling issues and he gives me a blank stare in return.

The social impairment may be easily visible in how a parent with ASD bonds with his children. For instance, the parent with ASD may not hug, kiss, or otherwise show affection. For example:

> When the children touch me [ASD] lightly it all feels like spiders crawling on my skin.

Sensory issues may dictate the level of interaction and type of play the parent with ASD can engage in with his children. There also may be few displays of affection as evidenced in this surprisingly common ASD-style expression:

> I [ASD] already told you I love you. Why would I tell you again?

There is also a possibility that the "social functioning impairment" may be evidenced in relations with the extended family:

> Could it be common for people with ASD not to relate normally with their parents or siblings? Even though his family was wonderfully loving, they still never developed strong familial relations. My husband [ASD] has never reached out to his birth family even though they are a normal, loving family. I was the one encouraging (forcing) the family to get together, but he never initiated it and only occasionally enjoyed contact with his parents and siblings.

Now that we are all thoroughly depressed about the impairment in social functioning both in and out of the home, let's look at some implications and potential solutions.

Implications and solutions: Social

> *"Symptoms cause clinically significant impairment in social...functioning"*

To understand how social functioning is impaired in people with ASD, we must look at the underlying reasons. There is a fundamental difference between how ASD and NT individuals approach social situations. Here is a good example:

NT: Looks forward to a party, enjoys it, and is rewarded by the human interaction. Is emotionally filled by a social event.

ASD: Dreads a party, shows anxiety, lack of social skill, and may try to avoid social interaction rather than seek it out. Is emotionally depleted by a social event.

Both my husband and I have searched for answers to this tricky dilemma. We have found that if we managed a few social gatherings well, it led to increased confidence, which is something we desperately needed as a couple.

Chess, the classic board game, led us to the answers to our social functioning issues. In chess, when presented with a difficult situation such as "check," you have three basic choices: retreat (avoid the situation), block (control the situation), or attack (anticipate the situation). Here is an example of each:

- *Retreat (avoid the social situation)*: If the social event is not too important, we opt out of it. We are creative people and can find just as much enjoyment elsewhere. The retreat option is almost always my husband's first choice.

- *Block (control the social situation)*: If we must go to the social event, we consciously control as much of it as we can. We agree to arrive late and/or leave early, thus setting a predictable schedule. If a social event occurs spontaneously, such as seeing a friend in public, we have pre-agreed-upon rules such as the "Five-Minute Max Rule" and the "Wander Rule" (it is OK if he wanders off when I can't keep conversations to less than five minutes). These give my husband with ASD a sense of control over situations that would otherwise appear out of control to him.

- *Attack (anticipate the social situation)*: Before we go to a social event, we take a strong preemptive strike against the foreseeable problems. If it is a social gathering, we script the important dialogues with the key people who will be there. We deal with sensory issues ahead of time, making sure that he is well rested and has an escape plan. We discuss and even practice portions of the event before we go so he will be prepared. We aggressively attack the problems before they occur.

But, as in the game of chess, even with the best strategies we still may lose the King.

WHAT IT MAY LOOK LIKE: OCCUPATIONAL

> *"The disturbance causes clinically significant impairment in...occupational...functioning"*

This disturbance will probably be one of the most obvious—since our careers occupy the majority of our waking hours. The occupational impairment can occur on many levels. For example:

> On one hand, he [ASD] earns a fine living. We're fed and clothed and we've never gone without. On the other hand, he'll never advance. He has absolutely no motivation to climb any social ladders at his work.

Or:

> She [ASD] was fired more than two years ago and hasn't been able to find a job since.

Occupational difficulties lie first in the interview process; an extremely difficult procedure for a person with ASD. One woman explained:

He [ASD] doesn't interview well, so finding a new job is going to be very difficult. One night, we role-played what he would say in an interview. I said, "Do you know many computer languages?" He said, "Yes." I prompted him that he should then list which ones he knows, selling himself to the employer. He couldn't spontaneously offer information so I asked him, "Do you know C++?" He said, "A little." I couldn't stifle the "*What?*" He's one of the best and most efficient C++ programmers in the field and he says "a little"?

Occupational troubles can range from unusual difficulty attaining appropriate employment to difficulties maintaining employment. If your partner suffers from difficulties finding appropriate employment, you will need to seek professional guidance. As Temple Grandin (1999) points out: "A person with Asperger's syndrome or autism has to compensate for poor social skills by making themselves so good in a specialized field that people will be willing to 'buy' their skill even though social skills are poor."

Implications and solutions: Occupational

> *"The disturbance causes clinically significant impairment in…occupational…functioning"*

The person with ASD may have an extraordinarily difficult task in finding appropriate employment. This is a serious issue and all I can offer here are a few anecdotal solutions. One solution that has worked for some people with ASD is to retreat to a comfortable home office. Nearly all the features of the office can be modified to fit the person's ideal comfort level: temperature, sound, color of the surroundings, everything can be modified without input from a boss or colleagues. It can be a workable solution for someone who needs significant modifications. For example:

I can't seem to work in an office. It makes me so nervous to see all the walls and people. I found out about this inability when I first started interviewing for jobs when I graduated from college. I only went to four interviews before I realized that it was useless. Finding the office, going up the elevator, winding my way through the maze-like offices was all too much, far too much. In nearly every interview, I had trouble breathing, let alone thinking clearly! I knew I'd never be one of the guinea pigs in an office, or worse, a cubicle.

So, now I'm a successful freelance technical writer and editor. I have my own home office that fits me perfectly. Every now and then I'll meet with a client in their office, but I'm only there for a short period of time. I think the interviews were so difficult because I knew that a job would lead me through that awful guinea pig maze every day.

Thankfully, telecommuting is becoming more and more acceptable and may be a solution that allows the person with ASD to reduce human contact to a more palatable, manageable level.

Another solution is to find the ideal niche job. Easier said than done! For example, if your partner with ASD enjoys programming but you think he should be in a more upwardly mobile position, don't encourage him to do something he won't enjoy. The repercussions might be far more devastating than our NT expectations dictate. Encourage your partner with ASD to choose his interest, then go with it.

Finding just the right job is not easy. It may take hundreds of résumés, countless hours of agony, and far too much emotional energy. As an initial step, the résumé should be reviewed by a professional résumé writing service. A poor résumé can cause undue rejection:

> My husband [ASD] sent out over a hundred résumés with no response. He was a fresh college grad with ridiculously high scores. Who wouldn't want to hire him? Once I looked at his résumé, I understood why. The qualifications, as great as they were, were muddled underneath horrible grammar and inappropriate details. I gently told him that it might need some work and within half an hour, I had redone it. The next batch of résumés got a fantastic response.

Once the résumé is decent, then interviewing abilities may be addressed. This is how one couple worked through the interviewing process.

> Every time my husband [ASD] goes out to an interview, we role-play the interview. I learned that he *has* to do this in order to survive the interview. Now I know that it's called "scripting." I tell him exactly what to say when a particular question is asked. If we go over enough questions, he can make it through most of the interview. If

the interviewer asks him a question that we haven't reviewed, he'll say, "I don't know," even if he does have an idea of an answer. He just can't think of answers on the spot and he can't give a partial answer. He has either practiced the answer ahead of time or he can't give an answer at all.

Books such as Roger Meyer's (2001) *Asperger Syndrome Employment Workbook: An Employment Workbook for Adults with Asperger Syndrome* and a book I wrote, Ashley Stanford (2011) *Business for Aspies: 42 Best Practices for Using Asperger Syndrome Traits at Work Successfully* may prove valuable to your partner with ASD as he searches for appropriate employment.

8

||||||||||||||||||||||||||||||||||||||||||||||||||||||||||||||||||||||||||||||||||||||||||||||||||||||||||||||||||||||||

Diagnostic Criteria E

NOT BETTER EXPLAINED BY
INTELLECTUAL DISABILITY

E   These disturbances are not better explained by intellectual disability (intellectual development disorder) or global development delay. Intellectual disability and autism spectrum disorder frequently co-occur; to make comorbid diagnoses of autism spectrum disorder and intellectual disability, social communication should be below that expected for general developmental level.

Despite our best intentions, we all enter relationships with expectations. Just as we expect the sun to rise each day, we expect our partner to act and think a certain way. When our partner shows no significant signs of intellectual disability, and in fact shows signs of intellectual skill, we may be fooled into thinking our unanalyzed NT expectations will be met.

Although everyone experiences expectation letdown in a relationship, in an ASD/NT relationship it is a double whammy. There appear to be two levels of expectations: 1. personal expectations, things we hope for individually, and 2. things that are generally expected on a societal level. Of course, the first set of expectations is often disappointed in any relationship because nobody is a perfect match for another's set of personal expectations (also referred to as a hidden agenda). What makes an ASD-linked relationship doubly difficult is that the second set of expectations also goes unmet. The partner with ASD does not intrinsically know the rules of behavior in general society, let alone the rules of a long-term relationship. One woman explains her full-blown realization of her expectations:

> I expected that he [ASD] would want to have kids and raise a family but he can't stand too much motion or noise. Our first child was so much work for him that it stretched him to the breaking point, turning a gentle man into an angry, frustrated ball of stress. Our second child broke him over and over again. They are beautiful children and he's healed, but having a family was a painful ordeal for him. He knows that the experiences of parenting helped his soul grow, but he's constantly trying to clam back up into his little world that does not involve kids' sports and family dinners.
>
> I expected that he would be romantic. It was my young idiocy that made me think that all men should be romantic. My husband wasn't romantic before we were married and he was even less romantic afterward…he still needs clues and cues from me.
>
> I expected that he would be an equal partner in housework. I had no idea that his sensory dysfunctions would keep him from household chores such as vacuuming and dusting. He's dedicated enough to do several predefined household chores, but when he does, he grits his teeth, ducks his head and tenses his whole body. He does it, but it's an ordeal.
>
> I expected that he would support my work both inside and outside the home. He's tried his best to support my work in thought and in action, but he really does not care what I do. He can't see why I would push myself to strive for bigger, better things. He wants everything to stay the same, stay small.
>
> I expected that he would have a strong religious faith in our church but he does not like to think about it. I suspect that he has a strong personal faith, but he can't stand the amount of socialization that is involved in our church activity. Going to church on Sunday wipes him out—just sitting in a pew is exhausting for him.
>
> Those were my five big expectations: family, romance, house, career, and spirituality. They were all broken. I don't know what possessed me to expect these things when, if I'd had any knowledge of him at all, I knew they wouldn't be met. Here is the key: I thought that since my husband was brilliant, he would naturally be brilliant in all areas of life. His academic and professional success blinded

me to the fact that he had many weak areas. Isn't that the typical post-honeymoon complaint? I did not know he had so many faults.

Once you recognize the expectations for what they are, you can begin adjusting your expectations to be more in line with the current reality. A solid realization of how ASD affects your relationship can help you build for the future. Healthy optimism is always based in reality.

WHAT IT MAY LOOK LIKE: COGNITIVE DEVELOPMENT

"...not better explained by intellectual disability..."

Part of the ASD criteria is that the person with ASD experiences normal cognitive development. Unfortunately, "normal" cognitive development does not assure academic or job success. There are extreme variations from academic excellence to abysmal failure. Whatever the case, it is likely that your partner with ASD has experienced the "genius syndrome" to some degree. The person with ASD may swing wildly between the "genius" and the "syndrome." One minute, his brilliant intellect is recognized—accolades to the genius! The next moment he cannot add one plus one to equal two in a relationship—he is left isolated. The stark contrast is worth noting. Read on.

Implications and solutions: Cognitive development

"...not better explained by intellectual disability..."

At first blush, you may think that the term "genius syndrome" applies only to those people with ASD who are of vastly superior intelligence. Not so. People with ASD often give off the air of genius (Asperger 1944, p.74 in Frith 1991) regardless of their intellectual prowess. They often present a sense of aloofness (lack of eye contact), or they act as if they are right (theory of mind issues). Some people with ASD speak in a pedantic style, sounding phenomenally intelligent to the point of being noticeably different. For example, instead of saying, "Let's go out to lunch," he may say, "It appears to be the hour in which our bodies require nourishment."

Being able to appear highly intelligent is a mixed blessing. If your partner with ASD has managed to achieve a genius persona, it may serve him well in employment or in social settings. People make allowances for geniuses that they would not make for the average Joe. But on the home front, the genius approach does not provide many benefits. Within the home, couples discuss intimate matters, working as a team, adjusting to accommodate other family members.

The genius appearance may end up being a root cause for depression. The person with ASD may succeed in life only to find that the apparent fundamental joys of life are missing (friendships, sensory balance, inner peace, carefree flexibility, etc.). Like a king who can "have it all," the person with ASD may find that the things he desires most cannot be bought, learned, or appreciated. He may curse the knowledge he has gained if he realizes all that he has been missing.

CREATIVITY

What we lack in common sense, we make up for in creativity.

(Adult with ASD)

Researchers and laymen sometimes diagnose at a distance some of the highly creative and prominent geniuses: Bill Gates, Albert Einstein, Glenn Gould, Sherlock Holmes, Bobby Fischer, and many others have been said to have Asperger Syndrome. The book *Diagnosing Jefferson* by Norm Ledgin (2000) shows us an extensive review of the diagnosis of the American president Thomas Jefferson.

There are many aspects of ASD that tend toward high creativity: the ability to disregard society's rules, the unusual viewing of objects as animated and people as objects (Tantam 2000, p.383), the ability to disregard portions of communication, the ability to see a hand waving as multiple frames rather than a sentimental wave goodbye, the ability to separate emotion from fact, etc. People with ASD also have excellent skills on embedded figures tests, e.g. identifying a picture within a picture that may be difficult to see without analyzing it. Researcher Simon Baron-Cohen describes the people he tested:

I was impressed by the degree of talent…many are super fast at spotting details. You hardly have time to get the experimental materials out on the table before they've spotted the target. You've hardly managed to get the stopwatch going. The normal brain, as it were, takes much longer. (Baron-Cohen 2001b, p.186)

This ability may help your partner with ASD solve problems in your relationship—the overall picture will not distract him, allowing him to focus on the smaller details. For example:

> My side of the family was having a bit of in-fighting—sisters arguing with my brother and parents siding with one of my sisters. It was getting ugly. I asked my wife [ASD] how I should deal with it and she stated the answer in one single, simple sentence. She could only see the simple, initial facts and wasn't distracted by emotion or tangents—the perfect solution to a disastrous situation.

There are many potential benefits to ASD-thinking. This creativity, or the potential for it, may be one of the unexpected blessings hidden under the more obvious disadvantageous ASD traits.

UNIMODAL BEHAVIOR

In the NT world we often equate intelligence with the ability to get a lot of things done at once. Ask your partner with ASD: do you become frustrated when asked to do two things at once? Do you have difficulty writing and talking at the same time? If so, your partner may be showing signs of unimodal behavior. Unimodal means that a person's brain can function effectively through only one modality (sight/written, sound/aural, touch, smell, taste) at a time. For example:

> In college, I couldn't take notes while listening to the professor. I could either listen or write—one or the other, not both.

The implications of unimodal behavior can be enormous for a married person with ASD trying to raise a family. Imagine for a moment the typical evening at my home. I am making dinner while talking to a client or a friend on the phone, while helping my son with his homework by writing notes on his paper, while feeding the baby with one hand, while monitoring the food cooking in the background, etc. I must have all senses on overdrive in order to function effectively in the evenings. My husband with ASD is able to pick one of these tasks and perform it effectively. For example, if I ask him to clean the bathroom sink while watching the children in the bathtub, I can be guaranteed that one or the other will go undone. He can focus on one at a time. He may be able to bounce back and forth between the tasks with much distress but he cannot perform them concurrently. Here are a few other examples from the ASD-based perspective:

> She called me on the phone while I was on my way to work. I was trying to do four things at once: 1. press "Talk" on the cell, 2. turn down the radio, 3. shift gears and 4. put on my sunglasses. Instead, I dropped my sunglasses, pulled the cell phone earpiece out of my ear, turned the radio off, and then shifted gears correctly. At least I got one out of four correct!

Or:

> If someone asks me to do too much, I just shut down. I can't do anything.

Or:

> If she asks me to do two things at once, I can only hear part of it. I can do the dishes or take out the trash, but not both. And I need some breathing time in between. I can't be go-go-go. I need time to consciously switch from one task to the next.

WHAT IT MAY LOOK LIKE: SELF-HELP SKILLS/ADAPTIVE BEHAVIOR

> *"…Intellectual disability and autism spectrum disorder frequently co-occur…"*

As the person with ASD grows into adulthood, some people (usually parents) worry that the person with ASD may not be able to take care of himself on his own. Self-sufficiency is the hallmark of adulthood and there are many layers of skills needed. The term "self-help skills" refers to a person's ability to feed himself, shower, brush teeth, get dressed, and otherwise do daily tasks. As an independent adult these tasks expand to caring for a home, acquiring a job, navigating transportation needs, keeping food in the home, and so many more. It is no wonder that parents worry about their children's ability to function at 20, 30,

40, 50 years old and beyond. If the person with ASD also has an IQ low enough to qualify as an intellectual disability, then self-help skills are the first and foremost skills to teach.

Beyond the basic adult self-help skills, when the adult with ASD is married or otherwise linked to a long-term companion, the demand for skills may be stretched to an impossible length. The self-help skills now require coordination with another person. For example, something as simple as brushing teeth in the morning will now require the person with ASD to maneuver around someone else's toiletries, possibly even timing the tooth brushing around that of the partner. Sounds simple, but it could be a significant source of stress.

However, a partner who understands ASD may be able to provide much-needed support and make adult living even easier. It depends on the partner's understanding of the situation and willingness to assist. It also depends on whether or not the partner with ASD can successfully request and receive assistance.

Everyday living skills such as walking around an obstacle, putting on sunglasses on a sunny day or writing "milk" on the grocery list are considered adaptive behaviors. They are the skills that a person learns in order to adapt to the world around him. Adaptive skills are considered developmental, i.e. the skills develop progressively as a person ages and knowledge grows (Attwood 1998, p.176). A person's adaptive behaviors are usually graded on an age-equivalent score. For example, a four-year-old child would be expected to have adaptive behaviors similar to those of other four-year-old children.

Implications and solutions:
Self-help skills/adaptive behavior

> "…Intellectual disability and autism
> spectrum disorder frequently co-occur…"

Self-help skills and adaptive behaviors may be mastered as a person with ASD grows and achieves adulthood. If the person with ASD chooses to enter into a long-term relationship, the necessary skills and behaviors jump quickly to a new level. Even the smaller daily tasks such as cooking meals and sleeping at night may reach a new level of complexity.

Beyond the day-to-day tasks are the big issues: jobs, babies, house moves, sickness, money, and extended family relations. These are big issues that cause many marriages, ASD or not, to break up. Let's talk about a few of them and how they are impacted by ASD.

AVAILABILITY TO HELP

One of the fundamental aspects of a relationship is "being there" for your partner. The general NT consensus is that "being there" for your partner is as simple as a hug, spending time together, comforting each other, or some other simple act. Ironically, knowing how to comfort another individual is a highly complex process involving many steps and requiring the ability to mindread in order to determine what type of comfort the other person requires. Does she need a hug? A drink of water? Do I give her extra space? The myriad of options can all but freeze a partner with ASD who literally cannot mindread and therefore is playing a random guessing game trying to determine his partner's needs.

My husband with ASD, as brilliant as he is, often cannot identify my needs. For example, I have had many back injuries and am not supposed to carry heavy objects. One day my husband saw me carrying several heavy objects in my arms. In an effort to be helpful he said, "I can see that you are limping and that you are carrying heavy things, but I don't know what to do about it." It is rare for him to be able to verbalize his thought processes so clearly, but I appreciated the effort and told him exactly how he could help. In this situation, I was not hurt badly and was able to communicate my needs clearly. Another woman explains her experience:

> Once, I broke my ankle, was five months pregnant and had a torn rotator cuff [a part of the shoulder] so I couldn't use crutches. Instead of helping me keep the household functioning, he [ASD] would trip on me as I crawled on hands and (sometimes bloody) knees to do the household chores necessary to keep life going for our kids. Completely oblivious to what was needed.

In an NT relationship, if a partner does not know what to do for the other, he will seek out answers, try something that may or may not work, but will somehow make an effort. In an ASD relationship, if the person with ASD does not know exactly what to do, he will typically do nothing (Attwood 1998). One woman related:

> I thought my body was aborting our baby. It was our first child. I was devastated. The intense stress was making my body reject my baby and I desperately needed comfort. I was bleeding... During the ordeal, my husband [ASD] sat on the bed, working on his laptop... He didn't know what to do, so he did nothing.

If the person with ASD does not do anything in the face of a difficult situation, it can be misconstrued as many things: a lack of caring, disinterest, a rebuff, or many other unappealing, even sinister, motivations. Whatever the intent, the NT partner knows on some deep level that her partner with ASD may not be available in times of great need. One woman revealed the depth of her concern over this issue:

> I have a recurring nightmare. It starts with me in some type of danger. The worst one is that I am swimming in a large, open lake when something from underneath starts pulling me under. I'm drowning but I manage to fight my way to the surface a few times to gasp for air and scream for help. I can see my husband [ASD] standing on the water only ten feet away. He stands there staring at me. He stands there until I stop coming up for air, then he walks away. When I wake up I'm usually filled with such intense despair that it takes days to pull out of the depression. Sometimes in the nightmare I'm in a burning car, sometimes I'm being eaten by wild animals. There are many different variations to the nightmare but he always stands exactly ten feet away staring at me with a deathly blank stare. I awake in a sweat, shaking and sobbing. Sometimes my husband holds me until I stop crying, but it's little relief for what keeps happening in my nightmares.

This woman's nightmares reveal that she is aware that her husband cannot spontaneously reach out to her on an emotional level and fears that her husband would not be able to help her on a physical level if she ever needed help. Her fear is that even if it came to a matter of life or death, her husband with ASD would not be able to help her.

Unfortunately, she may be right. People with ASD typically respond best to set schedules, predictable routines, and calm support people. Throw in an unexpected tragedy or two and your partner may tailspin into a meltdown or simply not enter into the situation to help you. There is also the possibility that a person with ASD will respond to an emergency situation exceptionally well, due to his ability to react logically and unemotionally.

REACTIONS TO PHYSICAL DANGER

One sign of intellect is a person's ability to self-protect in dangerous situations. One sign of an adult's social intellect is the ability to protect *others* in dangerous situations.

It appears ASD may help a person respond particularly well to dangerous situations that require a logical response. In the face of danger, the person with ASD may be calculating the long list of logical possibilities while the NT is hopelessly thinking, "Help!" Following are two personal experiences with contrasting outcomes. The first shows how my husband with ASD was able to respond successfully to a physically dangerous situation that required a higher level of thinking than is possible for most people:

> One foggy December night, we were on the freeway when we hit several patches of ice. The freeway was busy and there were at least a dozen cars within our view. Some of them started skidding out of control. My ever-logical husband was able to track all the cars in front of us, beside us, and behind us, somehow avoiding them all. I was amazed at his ability to drive out of danger.

In contrast, look at an emergency situation that happened to us where logic did not help my mate with ASD respond appropriately:

> We were watching our son's soccer game when our son was run over by another, bigger kid. I jumped up and ran alongside the coach to go pick up our little boy and carry him off the field. After everything calmed down I realized that my husband hadn't budged from his foldout chair on the sidelines. He had sat there the entire time, staring at us. I asked him later, when my temper calmed down, why ("Why?!") hadn't he come to help his hurt son? He responded, "I didn't know what to do."

One solution may be to offer a quick suggestion either verbally or physically, if at all possible. In the above example, I could have quickly grabbed my husband's hand, encouraging him to run with me out onto the field to get our son—a form of physical scripting. Even if he had not known instinctively what to do, at least he would have gone through the motions of acting like a caring father, resulting in me not being quite as frustrated with the situation. As this sort of response becomes more commonplace for my husband, he is learning how to respond appropriately. He is learning to jump up when his child is in distress. Although it may not be natural at first, it can become a learned habit.

Another solution is to recognize how and why your partner acts the way he does. One enlightening description is given by Gisela Slater-Walker (2002) in *An Asperger Marriage* as she explains how her husband with Asperger Syndrome, Chris, would react to physical danger: "What would he worry about if he found me in the kitchen having cut myself very badly? Chris replied that it would be whether he would do things right, not whether I would be all right" (p.53). An awareness of how a person reacts to a certain situation is the first step to finding a solution.

Another strategy is to help your partner learn to care for you. If you and your partner with ASD have open lines of communication, teaching him how to care for you could easily slide into your regular interaction patterns. For example:

> I'd like it if my husband [ASD] could help me in my old age, so, for now, I'm building his confidence by asking him to help with small things. I sometimes ask him to get my vitamins for me if he's near the cupboard. If I cut myself shaving, I ask him to get a bandage for me. I play tennis and sometimes twist an ankle so I'll ask him to get me an ice pack. I think that if he gets used to helping me with the little things, he'll be better prepared to help me if something really awful happens.

Another potential improvement is to analyze what it is about the situation that sends your partner off balance, then deal with this through a psychotherapist. One wife gave an example of how she helped her husband through a life-changing event that is a standard life event for most people, but was particularly difficult for him:

> I spent eight years preparing my husband for a baby before I threw out the birth control pills. It took eight long years. He needed to

overcome so many things first. He needed to overcome his fear of noise, his distaste for getting up in the middle of the night, his obsession with smells, along with so many other quirks. We did a lot of therapy (well, I went to therapy and brought the ideas home to him) and I had to be ridiculously patient, but now we have a beautiful baby boy and I see my husband growing every day alongside our son. It's beautiful. Without all the therapy and preparatory work, I think it would have been disastrous. It would have been the end of our marriage.

When it comes to life-changing events such as physical injury and dangerous situations, there are no easy answers. The advice "Be strong" does not apply—nobody is always strong and perfectly healthy. If the injury or danger requires a logical response, it is highly likely that your partner with ASD will be able to respond better than most people. If the dangerous situation is unpredictable and emotional, it is more likely that the NT partner will be the one to come to the rescue. Whatever the case, remember that your partner's reaction to severe physical danger may be different, and even the strongest NT may not be able to help you in emergencies.

REACTIONS TO GRIEF
It has been said that people with ASD tend to respond inappropriately to grief. They may laugh, snicker, or smile at an inappropriate time (Attwood 1998, p.159; Tantam 1991, p.176). One husband explained how his wife with ASD dealt with grief:

When we went to her grandmother's funeral last year, something really strange happened. She loved her grandmother dearly but hadn't mourned her death yet. I thought my wife would begin the grieving at the funeral when she saw her grandmother in the open casket but when she saw "Nana" in the casket, she touched her hand, muttered, "Oh gross," and casually walked away. It's been a year now and my wife still hasn't grieved. I keep waiting for the other shoe to drop, but I am beginning to think that there is no other shoe. Maybe this is a good thing and I should take the sigh of relief I've been waiting to take.

Another family explained the following:

> Our neighbor's house burned down and we took them in. The wife
> was sitting at our kitchen table crying. She had just lost everything...
> He walked into the room and with sparkling eyes and a chirpy tone
> exclaimed, "This is so exciting!"

It is no surprise that periods of grief are different for a person with ASD.
If by chance your partner with ASD is able to pull out of the grieving
period more quickly than you, you can count your blessings that at least
one of you is strong during a difficult time. Your partner's ability to skip
past the steps of grief without repercussion may be a benefit, if offense
can be avoided.

ENDGAME IMPLICATIONS AND SOLUTIONS

Although the ASD diagnosis says that the disturbances are not better
explained by intellectual disability you may feel inclined to pencil
in "disturbances in every area of life!" In a clinical, analytical setting
it may be easy to narrow down your partner's difficulties to only a
few diagnostic criteria, but in real life the problems may appear all-
encompassing, covering all areas of daily functioning. You may doubt
whether or not you can help your partner with this heavy load. You
may look at your life one day and realize that you have inadvertently
become—gasp—a support person.

AM I A SUPPORT PERSON?

As you search for answers, you become your own researcher, your own
therapist, and your own best solution. You will spend hours researching,
evaluating, contemplating, brainstorming, and finally trying new
techniques that could possibly improve your marital relations. The fact
that you have read this far in this book indicates that you are probably
already deeply entrenched in the role of support person. An example of
one woman's realization:

> One day when he [ASD] was leaving for work, I had to remind
> him to get his briefcase, to go back and shave, to remember to eat
> breakfast, and to tuck in his shirt. As he left, I realized that he was
> just one of the children to me.

How could this type of relationship occur between two intelligent people? ASD researcher Digby Tantam (2000, p.396) points out that we easily fall into the supporting role "because the adult with ASD seems so indifferent to his or her own best interests…" He calls this "enmeshment" and points out that becoming overinvolved in helping our partner function is the quickest way to burn out.

As we morph into a support person for our partners, the traits we develop and strengthen through daily practice may become part of our character, to the point that we become a support person for others also. While many traits of the support person are good (compassionate, generous, etc.), many of them are detrimental (martyr, failing to meet your own needs, etc.) As one woman explains:

> I determined that I would do everything I could do to build him [ASD]. A-ha! The "savior" syndrome!

As you become an all-encompassing support person for your partner, the tendency to support others may overflow into other areas of life. You may end up being the quintessential support person for everyone around you, as the following woman explains:

> One night I dreamed that I was hiking through a dry mountainous area with about 20 friends and family members. At one point there was a large chasm in the mountain that was wide enough for people to jump across, but nobody wanted to. I went to the front, lay down with my feet digging into one side of the chasm and my fingernails gripping the earth on the other side, staring down into the endless abyss beneath me while people walked across my back. I woke up in a sweat, angry and confused. It was exceedingly clear that I was consciously carrying other people's burdens… Not only my husband's burdens, but everyone's.

Ironically, you may need relief more than your partner with ASD does. You may need to seek out support to fill in some specific needs that are not being met by your partner. You may need to brainstorm for ways to fill some of those voids so that the relationship does not flounder under the weight of your burnout.

One woman explains how her wishes to help her partner contrast with how much help she can actually give:

I wish for a miraculous pill
That will cure my partner's sensitivities.
I wish for a magical potion
That will give him the Tin Man's heart.
I wish for a marital therapy
That will teach him to talk with me as others do.
I wish for a panacea
That he may be released from his social pain.
But
This is his journey, not mine.
I cannot claim it.
I can walk beside him, but not for him.
I can comfort him…sometimes.
I can observe and identify
But I cannot feel his pain.

Unless there is a cut-off point where the NT partner recognizes that her efforts are enough, then the NT partner may fall, without restraint, into the all-encompassing role of full-time support person. More often than not, the supporting partner will resent the responsibility of caring for someone with a diagnosis. Where does the resentment stem from? Usually it stems from a perceived imbalance of one person giving more than the other. Let's look at the imbalance and see it for what it really is.

IMBALANCE

When we enter a relationship, we expect it to be equal, with both partners contributing in their own way. But how many relationships have broken up because one partner perceives a distinct imbalance, usually, "I'm giving everything I can and he just does not care"? This is a common problem, but in an ASD/NT relationship the perceived imbalance may appear more severe. For example:

Right after we were married I realized that I was probably going to end up doing the majority of the work in our marriage. He wouldn't join me in tasks that are typically shared by a couple.

If the imbalance is not perceived immediately, then it may be perceived later, as an optimistic partner holds on to the belief that all people grow and improve, all people adjust naturally. ASD is a developmental disorder, meaning that a person's abilities will develop and improve as the person ages (Frith 1991, p.2). However, the improvements will not appear in the format that the uninformed NT partner is looking for. The improvement will most likely go entirely unnoticed.

One flaw in expecting a balanced, equal relationship is that we expect an eye for an eye and a tooth for a tooth, but unless we married a mirror image of ourselves we will not be able to get an eye for an eye. The reciprocity will not be balanced according to our immediate perception. If we can open our minds to the bigger picture, we may be able to see that an eye for an eye is a raw deal. The issue of gift-giving lends itself as a good example of easily perceived imbalance:

> Birthday presents have been one huge source of grief for me. For my first birthday after we were together, he [ASD] gave me a blender. (He had no idea that he was communicating a Donna Reed stay-in-the-kitchen message to me—I got angry.) The second year, he gave me nothing. (He was still scared from the first year.) The third year, he gave me a new computer (something *he* wanted—I got angry). The fourth year, he "forgot" again. Every year, I've given him a thoughtful present, something he really wanted and needed. He's always been appreciative, but he does not know how to do the same for me.

The wife was expecting that her husband had as much common sense in the arena of gift-giving as she did. Perhaps the balance in this situation lies in a distinct imbalance between two different areas—the gift-giving dilemmas are balanced out by other actions. For example:

> I can never remember when to take my car in for maintenance, get the tabs renewed, change the oil, or all the other things that keep my car running smoothly. He [ASD] manages it all.

The imbalance in one area is measured against the imbalance in another area as both partners contribute in ways that utilize their own unique strengths.

If we expect an across-the-board equality with our partners, we will be disappointed—people with ASD have highly skewed abilities (Attwood 1998). We need to look hard, think outside the box and realize the balance may be hidden. For example:

> I always wanted my husband [ASD] to love the arts as much as I do. I love going to the theater and I adore ritzy social gatherings. My husband enjoys none of these and I often think that my sophistication is lost on him. There appears to be a severe imbalance between us… One night he got out his telescope and set it up on the back porch. I wandered out and we looked at the stars. We saw Jupiter and tracked it across the sky. We talked about our galaxy, our significance in the grand scheme of things, and we talked about eternity: "The length of time I wish to be with you." It was the first time I had a glimpse into the depth of his soul. Since then, I have found many venues through which we can bond as soulmates. I've seen the sophisticated side of him and that's the side I choose to love.

This particular husband with ASD could not possibly equal his wife's social aptitude, but he could definitely equal her level of sophistication. They both had to be patient for the equality to be revealed.

Perhaps your balance is found in your opposing strengths. For example:

> He [ASD] is the strong, silent type who does not get emotionally entangled in difficult situations. He can see them logically. I am vivacious, energetic, and I run on high-power emotions. We balance each other out.

Or:

> I'm the one who brings spontaneity and life to the relationship. He [ASD] is the predictable one who always knows where the car keys are.

A FRAMEWORK

I have found it extremely difficult to differentiate between acts that qualify as supportive acts and those that place me in the role of overworked, underpaid saint (i.e. martyr). I have yet to find a resource (book, counselor, or other) that addresses this issue to an extent that allows me to define my role on a daily, decision-by-decision basis. I developed a visual framework within which I could differentiate between the types of support I can and cannot render effectively to my partner with ASD.

Intense interest   My support   Irrelevance

All the interactions we have as a couple fall somewhere along this spectrum. On one end of the spectrum is my husband's intense interest mode: the particular areas over which he wants total control, and I give it to him gladly. For example, his computer room and work habits, his routines and rituals, his collections and his personal items are all on the intense interest end of the spectrum. I am safer traveling into a war zone than I am intruding into his intense interests.

On the other end of the spectrum are all the issues that he considers irrelevant: being socially active in the neighborhood, bonding with extended family, taking vacations, dinners with friends, and going to reunions. These are the no-man's-land issues that he will not and cannot address. For me to travel into this area, I will travel alone. At times, I may be able to drag him there, but I will be dragging a shell of a man behind me.

In between these two extremes lies the area where my husband and I work together. Within this area, he accepts and even requests my support. This is the area of relaxed weekends together, mutually agreeable decisions, and tender give-and-take interactions. This middle area is safely distanced from his fanatical interests, but it is still relevant and meaningful to him.

All of our meaningful interactions lie in the middle: both the pleasant and the unpleasant ones, such as finding clothes that look good together or surviving a "public performance," i.e. attending a luncheon. In these situations, he wants and needs me by his side and gladly accepts my support. Within this small window, I am his support person, confidante, and friend.

When I can identify a situation and where it lies on this spectrum, I can better identify whether or not my efforts will do any good. Too far to the left and I am walking into the war zone. Too far to the right and I am walking alone. In the past, I intruded into the left and I pushed him to the right, all in the name of supporting a partner with a "disability." Without this particular ASD-related visual for me, the majority of our interactions were negative. I was overextending, covering the spectrum, doing far more than my share of work as an all-encompassing support person because I thought it would be good to support him in every issue all the time, as NT couples strive to do. In my ASD-linked relationship, my work was much more narrowly defined. I did not need to worry about the left or the right—I only needed a small safe ground where we could meet and interact.

ANGER—WHY?

Please note that this section only deals with how the NT partner deals with anger. I do not discuss ASD anger because it is a variable trait, i.e. the diagnosis does not dictate how a person with ASD expresses anger. The only DSM-5 related information we can address is how certain ASD behaviors prompt anger in a partner.

If our partner with ASD is not intentionally trying to cause problems then why are some NT partners so angry? Why does this anger well up so quickly and consistently at things our partners with ASD do or do not do? I have found that living with a person who has ASD can be frustrating, irritating, and tests my temper to its limits. Anger management seems to be a common issue for the NT partner (Aston 2014, p.43, pp.49–51; Attwood 1998, p.167).

In our early marriage years, before we knew about my husband's ASD and before we had learned how to live with each other, I found that nearly every weekend, when we spent significant time together, I would end up becoming furious, enraged with out-of-control anger. For years I thought it was my fault. My husband was calm, cool, and collected (even cold) while I had steam coming out of my ears.

It appeared that I had a significant anger management problem, but in my gut I knew the burden was not all mine. I only had anger management problems with him—all my other relationships were healthy. There were specific things that he was doing (or not doing) to prompt my anger. His peculiarities seemed tame…he made inappropriate comments and ignored verbal and nonverbal cues. Although these are typical ASD behaviors, I needed a strong, fast solution that would help me maintain composure during our time together. This ASD-invoked anger had me blowing up every weekend and I was beginning to hate myself for what I was becoming.

On a typical weekend, here is how I dealt with it:

- Muttered under my breath, "What a jerk."

- Gave him icy stares.

- Grew in anger until I erupted and he begged for understanding.

Here is how he reacted:

- He could not understand my muttering so he ignored it: "To whom is she speaking?"

- He literally could not see my icy stares. He has learned to give eye contact but it is fake. He looks, but he does not see.

- He had no idea that my anger was growing throughout the day. He could not see my body language cues and my cutting verbal remarks went right over his head. When I did erupt, it blindsided him and he was utterly clueless as to what was happening.

Through several marriage self-help books and a few anger management books, I learned how *I* needed to deal with our problem. I learned that I needed to let off steam so I would not boil over. If I could let off steam periodically, I would be able to overlook the minor problems that occurred throughout the day, allowing me to be cool and collected for the bigger problems. Even though it was not an ideal solution, it was a way of limping through the weekend instead of looking for a divorce attorney every Monday.

The marriage self-help books only helped *me*. They could not help my husband because he did not want help. Plus, all the advice was contrary to his way of being. I read, highlighted, and even quoted passages to him from most of the self-help/marriage books I had in my ever-growing library, but none of these books addressed how the ASD mind works. Most marriage books tell you to state how you feel ("What?"), explore your feelings together ("Feelings? Let's not go there!"), and build your therapy on a foundation of emotion and illogical sentiment. This did not work for us. I had to break it down—take it one detail at a time.

- *Question 1.* Can I communicate with him as I communicate with others?

  No, I cannot communicate with him as I do with others. He still needs to learn the basics of common conversation and I am not his teacher—I am his wife. He still needs to learn that when I say something, he is supposed to think of a response. We need to work at a more primal level of survival for now.

- *Question 2.* What do I want to communicate to my partner?

  Honestly, I want to communicate my love and commitment to him. When I am angry it is almost impossible to force myself to say something nice, but I found that I could manage sarcasm. I could let "I love you too" slide off my tongue in a sarcastic, "Yeah, right" sort of way.

Here is the pattern: he would do something that appeared mean-spirited and his actions would say to me, "I don't care enough about you to pick my dirty old socks up off the floor. You do it." His actions showed that not only did he not care, but he despised me. I desperately wanted to respond with, "I hate you! I really, really hate you!" I tried responding with my true feelings but it provoked no response from him and just made the anger hotter. Sarcasm was the key. Whenever his actions said, "I don't care about you. I despise you," I responded with, "I love you too."

The first time I tried it, my husband turned around and hugged me with sweet, sincere affection and a bit of relief. My sarcastic jab had been dripping with hatred because it was a particularly difficult Saturday. But he had no clue that I was communicating anything other than a genuine, "I love you."

At first I felt like such a fake. Everything I had read screamed in my mind, "Stop it! You're lying!" I had to hold the strong memory in my mind of why I was doing this. In the deep, strong part of my soul I wanted to tell him I loved him. It was one of those "the mind is willing but the flesh is weak" type of things. I did not want to become a bitter old wife, incapable of seeing her husband for the sweet soulmate he really is. Each time I managed to say, "I love you too," sarcastic or not, I grew more proud of myself. I was conquering my own rage in the heat of the moment and gaining back my self-respect.

Before I made this "I love you too" comment a habit, I looked into any possible damage it could do. My husband is a brilliant man, capable of so many things, but he does not pick up on the tone of voice and has one telltale ASD sign: he is literal—he perceives comments at face value only. I also looked into the possibility that I was giving him positive reinforcement at times when he was doing something I did not like. But I was not training him to do things that made me mad, because his memory from one incident to another is so poor that I cannot train him to do anything. Pavlov has nothing on this guy.

Now our weekends are full of affirmations of love. On a particularly bad day I tell him I love him dozens of times. He hugs me, kisses me, and makes all the stress and anger melt away. It is unconventional, but it has saved us.

Note   Only try this technique if you are sure that your partner has a weak perception of sarcasm, does not interpret tone of voice and has little recall of what triggers a positive reaction in you. Sarcasm is a cutting and destructive element of poor marriages and will do severe harm if used inappropriately. Some people with ASD respond to sarcasm, some do not. The main purpose of this passage is to encourage readers to think outside the box to find strategies that effectively relieve stress and tension in unusual relationships.

Whatever the reason for the NT partner's anger, it must be dealt with for the sake of everyone in the home. My favorite technique is to disappear to a quiet spot to relax. Listen in to one woman's experience with anger management:

Most of the time I'm able to enjoy my husband's [ASD] presence, but not always. Sometimes I get so frustrated at our differences (the fact that we're from such different worlds) that I start in a downward spiral of criticism and even hatred. I learned from a parenting book many years ago that I could send my children to a time-out to cool down. One day, my kids said, "Mommy, you need a time-out!" So I took it. It was the first of many mommy time-outs.

Now I give myself time-outs from my husband. I rarely need more than 10 to 15 minutes to relax, do yoga, practice deep breathing, or go out for a short walk before I can get back into the vibe of enjoying each other again. My husband has learned to say,

"You need a time-out," when he senses I am being critical (the first sign of me sinking into pessimism). I always take it, even if I slam the door on the way. I know that it is an internal fight inside me and me only, to overcome the powerful pessimism that tells me that my husband is a freak and our marriage will never get better. When pessimism overcomes me, I need to get out of the room, regroup, reflect, and realize that I will go nowhere with a bad attitude.

There are plenty of books that deal with anger management. One best-selling favorite for women is *The Dance of Anger* by Harriet Lerner (1985). Look for anger management books that will help you manage your own anger without blaming your partner. Books that focus on your partner's role in your anger may prove ineffective unless they are written by someone who understands the ASD condition.

This section would not be complete without mentioning the theory that a person with ASD may purposely provoke you to a higher level of anger than is necessary for a given situation because the heightened anger/rage is easier to predict than the more fuzzy, option-riddled emotion of being merely annoyed. Digby Tantam (2000) explains it as: "Reactions to extremes are easier to predict…because there is less room for individual variation… Outrageous actions include transparent lies, provocative aggression…any simple action likely to produce an extreme, and therefore predictable, response" (p.390). We can use this knowledge to our advantage by identifying our partner's motivation behind the provocation. If my partner with ASD is provoking me, I know it is because he is confused. He is searching for a predictable, previously scripted resolution to the current confusion and is using a cattle prod on my emotions in order to find it. If we both have the strength, we can revert back to logic, and reason our way through the issues rather than allowing the rage to take its course.

9

||||||||||||||||||||||||||||||||||||||||||||||||||||||||||||||||||||||||||||||||||||||||||||||||

The ASD-Linked
Long-Term Relationship

There is plenty of research about marriage and even more about divorce, but there is scant research available to help ASD-linked couples. Although the prognosis is bleak, I hold strongly to the belief that there are solutions that can help us build successful lifetime relationships with partners who have ASD. I believe that finding these solutions takes an uncommon level of dedication.

WHY DID WE MARRY?

The one question that baffles even the most intelligent NT is: "Why did I marry him?" People with ASD can hide so many of their deficiencies so well that in retrospect it may seem like you barely knew each other before tying the knot. For example:

> When I first met her [ASD], she was so appealing. She was a bit secretive and that's sexy in a woman, especially since we met in the 1960s when most girls were letting it all hang out. She was intensely interested in medicine, particularly in developing new vaccines. She knew what she wanted to do with her life and was very focused.
>
> Once we married, I found that she was focused to a fault. She had no friends, no social life, and seemed to be incapable of holding a conversation about anything other than her work. We had had a long-distance courtship but I thought I knew her. I found that she suffered from depression and was riddled with anxiety.

Under the direction of a skilled counselor who is familiar with ASD you may want to explore how both you and your partner view your relationship. You may find it shocking:

He [ASD] actually said that he married me "because I do dishes."

According to the dictates of logic and reason, your partner may consider the number one factor for marriage to be "the availability of sex" or "someone to pay the bills and wash the clothes." You may be shocked at the apparently crass nature of your partner's views.

Here is where the ASD trait of "brutal honesty" comes into play. The partner with ASD may recognize only the functional aspects of marriage: sex, household chores, financial gain, or social status (escaping the stigma of being single). Although these things are all logical aspects of marriage, the brutal honesty of being told that they are the reasons for your union may cut deep.

Romance and honesty can be counterproductive. For example, if your partner tells you that you need to lose another ten pounds, while it may be the truth, the verbal reminder may squash any desire for romantic physical contact in the near future. Honesty (hardcore ASD honesty) involves facts, logic, and truth. Romance (perfected by NTs) involves flowers, kissing, and chocolates. People with ASD may not recognize the sensual value of romance:

Why would you get me flowers? They just die.

Or:

I hate kissing. It's an aggressive form of germ transfer.

Or:

Chocolates? Sugar, wax, and cocoa bean. Why?

All of these are honest, logical responses to a romantic gesture. A relationship needs a tactful balance of romance and honesty in order to survive. One woman explains:

There was no romance in our marriage until I explained to my husband of 11 years that "Romance means telling me I look 'good' without objectively quantifying the word 'good.' " And that "You compliment me ten times for every one criticism." Once I explained some of the rules of marriage, he began to act like a husband and, once he could act appropriately, he began to feel married too. Even though he can't quantify it, he can now recognize what it's like to *want* someone beside him and, better yet, to *want* to make me happy.

You may find yourself reviewing your reasons for marriage. You may wonder about the future health of your relationship. I wish that I had known about ASD before marrying. I still would have married him—he is my best friend—but I would have had much better understanding. I wish I could have read Liane Holliday Willey's version of "Aspie Wedding Vows" ahead of time:

> To my mate… I want to tell you I think you are a nice person. I will not be telling you that too often because I just did… I promise I will not ask you to change who you are and I ask you to let me stay who I am. I promise I will be a dependable, loyal, stable and honest partner…I would not have joined you in marriage if I did not love you and want you in my life. (Holliday Willey 2001, p.88)

WHEN THE VEIL COMES OFF

> It doesn't much signify whom one marries, for one is sure to find next morning that it was someone else.
>
> Samuel Rogers, *Table Talk*

A person with ASD may learn at an early age that many of the ASD traits get him into trouble. Over the years, he may become a master of pretending, hiding, and avoiding. When the adult with ASD marries, both partners may be unaware that the partner with ASD has successfully hidden his true nature from view. Even the person with ASD may not be aware of the false nature of hiding inborn traits. I asked my own husband if this was the case for us. With a laugh and an honest wink, he stated:

> Sure, I pulled a few stunts to get you to marry me, but you didn't expect me to keep it up forever did you?

It is possible (and logical) that the person with ASD views courting as a form of acting, where he must say certain things, perform certain actions, and give an impression of social and romantic aptitude in order to attract you. It is possible that the person with ASD honestly sees this as a reasonable, even expected, act in one of the many games people play.

When you discover that the dating and engagement phase of your lives was a well-maintained act, you may feel betrayed. While most married people complain of their partner's misrepresentation at least once post-marriage, it may actually be a real phenomenon for ASD-linked partners. It appears as a true betrayal or a well-crafted deception.

It is vital to note that people with ASD are not deceptive by nature. In fact, due to theory of mind issues, they may not be capable of deception (Baron-Cohen 1995, pp.7–78). Deception is a higher-level skill that is probably out of reach for your partner with ASD. To our immediate perception, a person's false act is outright deception, but when we look at the *intentions* we may find that it was an honest, but very poorly executed, attempt at social interaction.

ACQUIRED ASPERGER SYNDROME (AUTISM SPECTRUM DISORDER)

As you bend and flow with your partner with ASD, you may take on ASD traits by habit, finding they rub off on you to the point that you appear ASD also. For example:

> One of my husband's [ASD] most endearing traits is his candid honesty. I've learned how to be much more honest too.

Or:

> Over the years I have stopped caring so much about what other people think of me… I had always admired my husband's [ASD] ability to not care so much about other people's opinions.

Developing Acquired ASD could have a downside. For example:

> As he [ASD] refuses to compromise, so do I. I used to be a happy-go-lucky girl, going with the flow of life, but since we've been married I've become stiff.

Or:

> Since he [ASD] never talks to me about anything, I have stopped talking to him about much either. Actually, I've become much less talkative and less friendly in general.

The goal is to let the beneficial ASD traits rub off on you and disregard the unattractive traits. As a tool for insight into your own personal growth, you may want to read books such as *Shadow Syndromes: Recognizing and Coping with the Hidden Psychological Disorders That Can*

Influence Your Behavior and Silently Determine the Course of Your Life (Ratey and Johnson 1997). As you discover more about ASD and how the neurological functioning influences your partner's behavior, you may forget to focus on your own personal development. Reading books such as *Shadow Syndromes* may help you attain better self-awareness.

THE CAUSTIC MATE VERSUS THE HEALING MATE

A healing mate is a partner whose focus is the common good of both parties in the relationship—someone who can find solutions and can create a healing balm for a weary or wounded partner. Let's first examine what a healing mate with ASD may look like:

> Some days when I come home after a long day at work, I just want to cry, but I know that it doesn't do any good (I obsess over the day's problems). So, I ask my partner [ASD] to give me "the works": a back rub, foot rub, neck massage, and everything else I need to relax and wind down after a long day at work—no questions asked. Voicing my worries just makes them worse and my husband is the only one I can trust to not intrude on my worries.

A solid focus on the ASD particular strengths may bring out the picture of a healing mate. One woman chimes in with her optimistic view of her husband with ASD:

> I am so glad for the years we've had together. I've learned so much about myself, about him [ASD]… As for me, personally? Well, there are definitely good reasons I married him, and a lot of good I see in him. I am so proud of him and all he can do… He loves his children so very much, and they love him. Spiritually, he is very, very insightful, and often says things that I know are inspired. He makes me laugh.

This woman made the clear choice of focusing on her partner's strengths over his disabilities. By magnifying his strengths, she reflects back to her partner a sense of confidence and pride. It is in an atmosphere such as this that a person with ASD has a chance at success.

On the other side of the aisle, the NT partner can also be a healing mate. It is all too easy to think of examples for this since there are so many specific things you can do to support your partner with ASD. Let's look at only one:

> There are times when he [ASD] sinks into depression. I always see it coming. He gets listless or he lashes out irrationally. When this happens, I do everything in my power to clear the path for him. I'm like one of those big snow trucks clearing the road, cleaning away everything from his environment that could agitate him further.

While we all wish for a healing mate, many relationships involve a caustic mate. The caustic mate is one that erodes self-respect and dignity. Here is an example where both mates have become caustic:

> I have finally given in to the constant criticism. He [ASD] criticizes my every move, saying I am illogical and stupid. I'm sick of it. I have learned to criticize back... The children are stuck in the middle of our battle and are learning to be vicious.

The toxicity can get so high that it poisons everyone within reach. A toxic relationship may not necessarily be the direct fault of either party, but it is a situation that desperately needs remediation by an ASD-qualified professional.

DIVORCE

In our early marriage years I read many books on divorce. Nearly every book I read painted a portrait of my marriage as an ideal case for divorce. Several books listed "stonewalling" as an indicator of a dead relationship. My husband with ASD could be a poster-boy for stonewalling— he can maintain a stony expression no matter what I throw his way (tears, rage—nothing phases him). Typically he responds only to direct interrogation-style questions and then only gives a one-word answer. His stonewalling abilities would put a good lawyer to shame.

Other indicators of divorce include defensiveness, contempt, and blaming, all of which may come prepackaged with the ASD condition. Defensiveness is a common ASD trait with its origins in the childhood of the person with ASD when he did not yet have social scripts to help him get by. Contempt may be shown by a sneer (inappropriate facial expressions), put-downs (logical comments that are indelicately worded), or a lack of outward empathy. Blaming comes into play when a person with weak central coherence has difficulties identifying the correct origin of a problem.

The diagnostic criteria for ASD dictate that certain skills are lacking: i.e. higher-level communication skills, empathy, emotional reciprocity, and many other skills needed for a successful intimate relationship. Despite the apparently daunting difficulties, measures can be taken to improve our chances of creating a happy relationship. I believe the most effective approach is to work on making ourselves better, more knowledgeable, and more caring people. Even if the marriage eventually ends in divorce, if your focus is self-improvement (learning from the experience) then you will be a better person in the end.

One woman explained how she craved divorce, but realized that she did not want an actual separation from her partner with ASD. She dreamed of shedding the world's stereotypical version of marriage. She wanted to divorce herself from the back-breaking and unnecessary efforts being made to achieve "normalcy" in an "abnormal" marriage. As she tells it:

> I had a telling dream once about divorcing my husband [ASD]. I dreamed that we were finally divorcing (relief!) but I told the lawyer to write up the divorce papers so that we could still live together, raise the children together, etc. The divorce contract had to ensure that nothing would change and I'd still get to live with him. When I got the divorce papers successfully signed, I felt a huge, cleansing sense of liberation. I was finally free! And I still had my best friend!
>
> I interpreted the dream as meaning that I felt trapped by all the details of marriage (acting like a couple, having friends over for dinner, having a husband who volunteered at the kids' school, etc.). We were having so many troubles with standard marital relations that I felt crushed by them and I desperately wanted to throw the burden off my back.
>
> After the dream, I started consciously getting rid of activities we were doing simply because "Married couples do this." We hired out household chores, we stopped inviting friends over to our house, we did not plan any more family vacations, and we managed to back out of all sorts of extraneous responsibilities. As I was able to throw off more and more of the standard marital expectations, I was able

to relax more, enjoy more, and see more of the wonderful things my husband with ASD did to strengthen our family.

Perhaps ASD-linked relationships can be successful when partners work diligently towards creating a structure that works for them. A successfully married female with ASD put it succinctly: "Create your own kind of marriage. Try to relinquish the traditional roles and invent new ones..." (Holliday Willey 2001, p.94) The ability to be creative in your marriage may serve you well.

This section on divorce is noticeably short. There are plenty of people who are arguing for the incompatibility of ASD/NT relationships as well as ASD/NT relationships, plenty who say it is "impossible," "not worth it," "dysfunctional" by nature, and some who even say that people with ASD "cannot" or "should not" marry. To me, those are ridiculous ideas—as ridiculous as telling Rosa Parks to go to the back of the bus. People with ASD need understanding, awareness, and support for making and maintaining long-term relationships if they wish to do so.

Please note that this book does not address issues of adultery, abuse, or other pernicious behaviors that are reasonable grounds for divorce. These issues are not ASD-related and therefore are irrelevant to this book. If you are currently dealing with such issues as adultery or abuse, please find help through a competent counselor, therapist, or lawyer.

BREATHING LIFE INTO THE RELATIONSHIP

If you have been together with your partner for a while or if your marriage is struggling, there is a good chance one or both of you will wish to breathe life into your relationship. The typical relationship renewal activities are to renew your vows (why?), try something new (no!), or to go on a romantic faraway vacation (oh, the sensory chaos!). In an ASD-linked relationship the typical strategies are often counterproductive. But we still may wish to breathe life into the more advanced ASD-linked relationship. How?

When NTs think about revitalizing their relationship, they think in idealistic terms: a second honeymoon in Tahiti, an expensive anniversary ring, a romantic candlelit dinner on a boat in the middle of the lake, or other top-of-the-wish-list ideas. But in relationships where we are dealing with aspects of a disability on a daily basis we may lower our expectations, thinking we cannot have the best. The tendency to lower expectations when dealing with a disability is a common knee-jerk reaction that I have seen happen far too many times with children in school.

What if we did not lower our expectations? What if we just shifted our focus? If we shift our focus to fit the two people we are dealing with (you and your partner with ASD) then maybe, just maybe, you can breathe life into your relationship just as effectively as the couple who spends three delightfully invigorating weeks in Tahiti.

With a solid understanding of ASD and all its implications, you can begin to think of what would achieve the ideal end goal for you and your partner. For example, my husband's ideal revitalization includes: 1. something at home, 2. something involving computers, 3. something that allows him to sit still for long periods of time. My ideal revitalization involves: 1. travel, 2. good food, 3. art museums. In the world's view, these wish lists dictate a wife pitifully alone on vacation and a husband in a dark room, frozen in front of a glowing screen as his beard grows—nothing you would ever see in a travel brochure.

If we are to stick to our end goal of breathing life into our relationship, we must pick the items that are at the top of our lists and not compromise our way down the wish list to the point that both of us are only semi-happy with the arrangements. We have tried picking the top items off our own wish lists several times and when we link up after the revitalization, we are both so eager to be back with each other that we feel like we have had the second, third, and fourth honeymoons already.

As a comparison, what would we do if we followed the world's view of revitalization? The world's view dictates that we would 1. spend time together, 2. go somewhere mutually agreeable, and 3. visit socially acceptable places. All of these would turn my husband into a beastie. He would be miserable from the sensory overload, the change in schedule, and the too-intense amount of socialization. We've tried this before and we have always regretted it.

If you truly want to revitalize your relationship with your significant other, try making a list of the top three wish-list items that would make you happy and have your partner with ASD do the same. When all is said and done, a happy partner makes for a successful relationship.

THE IDEAL MATE

In *An Asperger Marriage*, Chris Slater-Walker, a happily married adult male with Asperger Syndrome, describes what he wanted in a mate:

> I wanted as far as possible to establish a lasting relationship with someone who was my intellectual equal, who would be able to hold her own in most situations and who would be a good listener and a friendly adviser…who would be intelligent and reasonable… (Slater-Walker 2002, p.19)

Your particular partner may have been attracted to you because of the following traits:

- self-sufficient
- kind-hearted
- strong support system already in place
- religious beliefs to rely on
- solid sense of self
- naturally compassionate
- can reach out to multiple systems of comfort
- gentle and nurturing
- strong self-control
- excellent flexibility with communication skills.

Along with some traits to form the bridge between the two of you:

- logical
- able to analyze a difficult situation
- able to forgo emotional reactions at times
- honest
- dedicated.

When dating, everyone looks for certain characteristics, consciously or not. Your partner with ASD probably exhibited characteristics that were highly appealing to you. Of course, there are exceptions to every rule but, typically, people with ASD are said to have the following traits:

- loyal

- kind

- hard-working

- faithful

- intelligent

- reliable

- capable of seeing the world differently

- detail-oriented

- exceptional memory

- practical.

There may also be some concrete reasons why you need your partner's innate ASD characteristics. For example:

[Details of a difficult childhood]… in order to grow as a person I either needed to be with an emotionally detached partner or on my own. I enjoyed the friendship of my boyfriend who has Asperger Syndrome and we moved in together. Over the years, I have been able to exorcise the demons of my childhood. Through it all, he stood by my side and has slowly grown into our relationship also.

To sum it all up, the following poem describes how my relationship with a person with ASD has made me a better person:

I asked God for a companion.
I was given an odd soul that I might develop a stronger self.

I asked for help. I got confusion,
That I could further refine my needs and wants.

I asked for love. I got silence,
That in the silence I would hear the beating of my own heart.

I asked for companionship. I got cold indifference,
That in the frozen night I would find myself
as my surest source of warmth.

I asked for a friend. I got someone who did not know friendship,
That I could relearn the true nature of reaching out to others.

I asked for a partner. I got a distant roommate,
That I could set my own rules and live by my own standards.

I asked for honesty. I got brutal honesty,
That I could develop a spine strong enough to withstand the truth.

I asked for hope. I got a blank stare,
That I would look for faith within my own soul.

I asked for answers. I heard the hush of a man
who did not know how to answer,
That in the void I would learn to turn to Thee.

My prayers were answered.
I received nothing I asked for, but everything
I needed to build a stronger soul.

Now I am strong.
I can see my partner's strengths: honesty, integrity, and loyalty.
I can feel my mate's love: companionship, closeness, and comfort.
I can see a kind friend reaching out to me with a hand I used to rebuff.

My companion was there all along.

10

Help! Where to Look

BOOKS

The first step in improving an ASD-linked relationship is to understand the intricacies of ASD. The following books are recommended reading for building a solid knowledge base of ASD. Please note that many excellent books that become available after the publication of this book can be found at www.jkp.com (Jessica Kingsley Publishers).

Aston, M. (2014) *The Other Half of Asperger Syndrome (Autism Spectrum Disorder): A Guide to Living in an Intimate Relationship with a Partner who is on the Autism Spectrum.* London: Jessica Kingsley Publishers. First published 2001.

Attwood, T. (1998) *Asperger's Syndrome: A Guide for Parents and Professionals.* London: Jessica Kingsley Publishers.

Baron-Cohen, S. (1995) *Mindblindness: An Essay on Autism and Theory of Mind.* Cambridge, MA: The MIT Press.

Bashe, P. and Kirby, B. (2001) *The OASIS Guide to Asperger Syndrome: Advice, Support, Insight, and Inspiration.* New York: Crown.

Frith, U. (1989) *Autism: Explaining the Enigma.* Oxford: Basil Blackwell Ltd.

Frith, U. (ed.) (1991) *Autism and Asperger Syndrome.* Cambridge: Cambridge University Press. This book contains a full translation of Hans Asperger's original paper describing the patients he observed.

Gillberg, C. (2002) *A Guide to Asperger Syndrome.* Cambridge: Cambridge University Press.

Grandin, T. (1995) *Thinking in Pictures: And Other Reports from My Life with Autism.* New York: Doubleday.

Gutstein, S. (2000) *Autism/Asperger's: Solving the Relationship Puzzle.* Arlington, TX: Future Horizons.

Gutstein, S. and Sheely, R. (2002) *Relationship Development Intervention with Children, Adolescents and Adults: Social and Emotional Development Activities for Asperger Syndrome, Autism, PDD and NLD.* London: Jessica Kingsley Publishers.

Holliday Willey, L. (2001) *Asperger Syndrome in the Family: Redefining Normal.* London: Jessica Kingsley Publishers.

Holliday Willey, L. (2014) *Pretending to be Normal: Living with Asperger's Syndrome (Autism Spectrum Disorder).* London: Jessica Kingsley Publishers. First published 1999.

Klin, A., Volkmar, F., and Sparrow, S. (2000) *Asperger Syndrome.* New York: Guilford Press.

Ledgin, N. (2000) *Diagnosing Jefferson.* Arlington, TX: Future Horizons.

McKean, T. (1994) *Soon Will Come the Light: A View from Inside the Autism Puzzle.* Arlington, TX: Future Horizons.

Mesibov, G., Shea, V., and Adams, L. (2001) *Understanding Asperger Syndrome and High Functioning Autism.* New York: Kluwer Academic Publishers.

Newport, J. (2001) *Your Life Is Not a Label: A Guide to Living Fully with Autism and Asperger's Syndrome.* Arlington, TX: Future Horizons.

Shore, S. (2001) *Beyond the Wall: Personal Experiences with Autism and Asperger Syndrome.* Shawnee Mission: KS: Autism Asperger Publishing Co.

Slater-Walker, C. and Slater-Walker G. (2002) *An Asperger Marriage.* London: Jessica Kingsley Publishers.

ARTICLES

Articles such as Temple Grandin's "Choosing the right job for people with Autism or Asperger's Syndrome" (1999) provide immensely helpful advice for employment-related issues. Articles such as "The Geek Syndrome" (Silberman 2001), "Think different?" (Baron-Cohen 2001), and "Take the AQ test," (Baron-Cohen 2001a) all featured in *Wired* magazine (December 2001, 9.12, pp.174–187), provide excellent reading material that you can quickly and easily pass on to friends and family who need a brief, attention-grabbing synopsis of ASD. Browsing ASD-related websites will lead you to many informative articles.

COUNSELORS

Once you start looking for professional help, you may quickly discover that the general medical services population may not have deep enough awareness of ASD to give adequate help. Many may have a *Rain Man* image of a person with ASD, or perhaps see ASD as the diagnosis of a silent child locked in a prison of nonverbal seclusion, not recognizing even their own name. Although your partner may be high functioning, when the word Autism is mentioned, many negative traits may be inaccurately attributed to your partner.

While there are knowledgeable doctors, counselors, and therapists who can offer support, it may take some serious detective work to find them. It is extremely important to find a professional who has had experience with ASD in adults, since an uninformed professional could possibly do much more harm than good. For example, a general family psychologist may tell the partner with ASD to "Explore your feelings" and "Explain why you feel the way you do." Your partner with ASD may be perplexed, befuddled, and may respond with pure fiction, guessing at what the psychologist may want to hear. Or your partner could respond with confusion that appears as obstinacy. Or he could try to gracefully exit the situation, appearing evasive and dishonest. Or he could become defensive, realizing that, yet again, he is backed into a corner and does not know words good enough to convey his confusion. Without a solid understanding of ASD, incorrect assumptions may abound.

Keep in mind that traditional couples counseling is based on a verbal back and forth between patient and counselor. Reciprocity and social awareness are paramount in the mind of a couple's counselor. Since social communication is the number one defining difficulty for people with ASD, standard counseling can be extremely frustrating. You will need to find a counselor who is not only familiar with the ASD diagnostic criteria, but who is also experienced enough to find ways to reach your partner with ASD through logic, visual images, or whatever other areas happen to be strong for your partner. Merely talking about vague concepts of love and compassion will not be as effective as it would in a standard counseling session.

In "Meeting the challenge of Asperger's Syndrome," Maxine Aston, a counselor specializing in ASD marital relations, states:

> Due to the very nature of Asperger's Syndrome, it is quite likely that the couple relationship will soon become problematic and research has shown that the couple will often seek out couple counselling to try to sort out the problems they are facing. Unfortunately, in the past, this has not always been successful as the counsellor as well as the couple have often been unaware that Asperger's Syndrome is at the root of the problem.
>
> In the higher functioning adult with Asperger's Syndrome, recognition of this disorder can often go undetected and awareness of its existence can be clouded by the very capable, intelligent and hard working nature that adults with Asperger's Syndrome on the higher level can sometimes display.
>
> Counselling a couple when one of the partners has Asperger's Syndrome requires a very different type of counselling from that most usually practised by Relate counsellors. It also requires an understanding into which problems are a direct effect of one partner having Asperger's Syndrome and cannot be changed, and what is changeable and within the control of the couple.

Despite any difficulties you may encounter while searching for an ASD specialist, it may be well worth the effort. A therapist or counselor can reveal information that would otherwise be off-limits. A third party can get through to your partner when you cannot. For example:

> The therapist told him [ASD] the *exact same thing* that I have been telling him for years. Somehow, it got through to him!

A skilled psychologist will first assess each partner's level of basic interpersonal skills; second, teach the needed interpersonal skills, even if they are basic skills; and third, help both partners put these new skills to use in their everyday interactions.

ORGANIZATIONS

In your search for more information, you may need to rely on the services and information provided through the following organizations:

Autism Society
4340 East-West Hwy, Suite 350
Bethesda, MD 20814
USA
Tel: 301-657-0881
Tel: 800-3AUTISM (800-328-8476)
www.autism-society.org

National Autistic Society
393 City Road
London ECIV 1NG
UK
Tel: 44 (0)20 7833 2299
Fax: 44 (0)20 7833 9666
www.autism.org.uk

Autism Research Institute
4182 Adams Avenue
San Diego, CA 92116
Toll free hotline: 866-366-3361
www.autism.com

RDI Connect
4130 Bellaire Blvd. Suite 210
Houston, TX 77025
USA
Toll free: 866-378-6409
Phone: 713-838-1362
Fax: 713-838-1447
www.rdiconnect.com

Autism Speaks
1 East 33rd Street
4th floor
New York, NY 10016
Tel: 212-252-8584
Fax: 212-252-8676
www.autismspeaks.org

WEB

There are more ASD-related websites than can be listed in this book. The following sites are only a sampling of sites that have been active and informative for more than a decade and will probably continue to be informative long term.

OASIS (Online Asperger Syndrome Information and Support) @ MAAP
www.aspergersyndrome.org

Tony Attwood
www.tonyattwood.com

SUPPORT GROUPS

Some turn to online support groups for validation and information when in need. There are sites for people with ASD-only and their partners, professionals, non-professionals, people with ASD who have children, and others. Within these groups, you may find the solace and information you cannot find elsewhere, especially if you have not yet been able to locate an ASD professional in your part of the world.

As with all other forms of support, there is also a downside. You may wish to log on to a support group and share every intimate detail in order to receive help, but often this private information is recorded and cataloged in archives that can be referenced by the general public or by anyone who joins the group. If you do experience divorce or separation, these publicly recorded details could prove detrimental. As with all forms of support, be careful and be aware of the risks.

Support groups can come and go quickly. To find a list of all the ASD support groups currently available, do a quick search for "Autism" or "Asperger Syndrome" (also spelled "Asperger's Syndrome") on any search engine.

FRIENDS

A friend will be able to help you recognize when something is not quite right but may be unable to help you solve it unless the friend is well versed in the implications of the various criteria of the ASD diagnosis.

Although friends can help only minimally with the difficulties you face in an ASD-linked relationship, it is still strongly recommended that you make and keep solid friendships throughout your adult years. People with ASD typically have drastically lower needs for friendship—one or two friends may be plenty (Aston 2014, p.33). If you match your partner's level of friendships, you may find yourself feeling isolated, lonely, and seeking extra friendly affection from a partner with ASD who is already operating at a maximum level. Make and keep friends. Although the benefits are not immediately obvious, you will find more peace in your relationship if you are comfortable with the level of companionship you give and receive on a daily basis.

If you are fortunate enough to find close, personal friends who also understand the ASD diagnosis, consider yourself lucky. They will be able to offer you a genuine form of support that few can match.

Epilogue

I sit on my porch and feel the sun set at the end of each day, and I wonder if what I have said and done has been worthwhile. I wonder about the people who will read this book. I will never meet them. I will never meet you. I marvel at the level of intimate detail I have shared and in some way, you have shared back. You have read these words, then decided what to do with these concepts and beliefs. I hope that in some way the content of this book can help you and your partner build a stronger relationship. This book has helped me in many ways, both in writing it and in rereading it.

My husband with ASD has read and edited every word of this book. He is proud of my efforts and has supported me wholeheartedly. Every step of the way, I checked that he would not be embarrassed by the information contained in this book, pen name or not. He simply pointed me to the section of this book entitled "Mindblindness" and stated, "How could I be embarrassed?" He understands these concepts much better than I do and, if he were verbal, we could have co-authored this book, structuring it differently. As it is, this book is mainly for my benefit.

One unanticipated side effect of writing this is that now, when I slip up and forget that my marriage is different, my husband asks me, "Haven't you read your own book?" When I am angry with him for not understanding my NT-speak: "Haven't you read your own book?" And my favorite reaction: when I do something contrary to what I have stated in this book, he quotes passages verbatim. He may remind me, but I sometimes forget even my own best advice. I comfort myself with the realization that we all make mistakes and we all need gentle reminders.

In preparing to share my writing with others, I have tried to avoid sounding like an expert. I am not. I am an individual in an ASD-linked relationship, just as are the readers of this book. At times, I am just as unsure and just as shaky as anyone. I am also just as determined as others who are fighting for the survival and health of their relationships. I am among the crowd—the woman who blushes when her partner's ASD-ness shows, when his mask slips off momentarily.

There is something about a setting sun that helps us see our mistakes more clearly than at any other time. Some days I am too tired to look at the mistakes and I choose to look away or close my tired eyes. Other days I can stare down the mistakes until they wither into a little pile of solutions. Perhaps after my husband and I have been married 40 years or more, I will have boiled down the same nugget of wisdom that I have heard from countless other older couples: "Learn to live with it." When the sun sets on my life, I hope to look back, treasuring the moments when we turned a blind eye to each other's imperfections and held up a magnifying glass to each other's strengths.

Glossary

Adaptive behavior Behavior that enables a person to adapt to their environment, e.g. choosing to wear warm clothes on a cold day.

ADD Attention Deficit Disorder: neurobiological disorder characterized by short attention span and impulsivity.

ADHD Attention Deficit and Hyperactivity Disorder: similar to ADD but with hyperactivity.

AIT/AT Auditory Integration Training: a type of treatment that helps a person overcome sound sensitivities.

Apraxia Absence of speech, movement, or other functionality. Dyspraxia and apraxia are similar except "dys" means "some" and "a" means "none."

AS Asperger Syndrome, now classified as Autism Spectrum Disorder: neurobiological condition characterized by impaired social interaction and highly focused interests.

ASD Autism Spectrum Disorders: developmental disabilities characterized by difficulties with both verbal and nonverbal communication, social interaction, repetitive activities, stereotyped movements, resistance to change, and sensory issues.

Aspergated A term used to show that a person has developed ASD-like traits over time. It is a type of mock-ASD (not the real thing, but similar in appearance). A partner of someone with ASD may become "aspergated" over time.

Aspie Friendly term used to identify a person with Asperger Syndrome (Autism). Aspie identifies a personality type rather than a disorder, similar to "artist" or "intellectual."

BPD Bi-Polar Disorder (Manic Depression): mood disorder characterized by extreme high and low periods. The high periods can be identified by lack of sleep, hyperactivity, and highly creative ideas. The low periods often include suicidal thoughts and/or actions.

CAPD Central Auditory Processing Disorder: characterized by difficulty recognizing or understanding certain sounds, although hearing and intelligence are normal.

Differential diagnosis A diagnosis that is very similar to another, e.g. Social Communication Disorder is a differential diagnosis to Autism Spectrum Disorder.

DSM *Diagnostic and Statistical Manual*, produced by the American Psychiatric Association. Currently in its fifth edition (2013).

Dyslexia Difficulties decoding written information.

Dyspraxia Developmental disorder characterized by impaired motor function. Difficulty organizing and planning physical movement.

Echolalia Repeating or parroting of words or phrases (see also **Tics**).

Etiology The cause of a disorder.

Executive function The ability to plan, prepare, and execute tasks.

Experience sharing Engaging in interaction with another person for the sake of social contact with that person, e.g. chatting with a friend.

Extinction theory A behavioral theory which states that a certain behavior will cease if consistently ignored.

Faceblindness See **PPG**.

Fine motor skills The ability to manipulate small objects, e.g. handwriting or using utensils.

Fluid systems Social systems where the interaction is not predictable, e.g. a personal conversation with a group of people (see **Static systems**).

HFA High-Functioning Autism: indicates that the person with ASD has an IQ greater than 70. It is not a recognized diagnosis but is a commonly used term.

Hyperlexia An unusually precocious ability to decode written information. Hyperlexia is often associated with High-Functioning Autism.

Instrumental behaviors Things a person does to achieve a certain goal, e.g. talking with a person to gather specific information.

Large motor skills The ability to move larger muscle groups fluidly, e.g. running, jumping, dancing, or walking in sync with your partner.

LFA Low-Functioning Autism: Indicates that the person with ASD has an IQ less than 70. It is not a recognized diagnosis but is a commonly used term.

Mindblindness The inability to see others as having their own state of mind.

Modality Refers to the method through which a person perceives, e.g. sight is a modality.

NLD/NVLD Nonverbal Learning Disorder: there is often overlap between NLD and ASD. NLD teaching methods are often used for children with ASD.

NT Neurotypical: a term used in the ASD community to indicate a person who does not have ASD or other neurodevelopmental disorder, i.e. a person whose brain functions like the majority of people.

OCD Obsessive Compulsive Disorder: anxiety disorder characterized by persistent repetitive thoughts (obsessions) and/or the need to repeat certain actions over and over (compulsions).

ODD Oppositional Defiance Disorder: a psychiatric disorder characterized by excessive arguing and defiance.

OT Occupational Therapy: treatments that help a person improve their fine and large motor skills, sensory difficulties, and other related physical coordination issues.

PDD Pervasive Developmental Disorders: a term signifying that the disorder is evident during childhood, the developmental phase of life. Under the PDD umbrella are: Autism, Rett Syndrome,

Childhood Disintegrative Disorder and others, depending on the diagnostic tool used.

PDD-NOS Pervasive Developmental Disorder Not Otherwise Specified: a catchall category for a person who does not fit the Autism diagnosis but does fit under the PDD umbrella.

Perseveration Repetitive pattern of activity: i.e. focusing on a single object, thought, activity, or person (see also **Stim**).

PPG Prosopagnosia: also called faceblindness. A neurological condition that renders a person unable to recognize the faces of others.

Residual ASD Terminology used to identify a person who still has ASD, but who has managed to achieve a high level of functionality in everyday life, e.g. a person with residual ASD may be able to navigate a social situation, but may have disabling difficulties if not allowed to prepare for the event.

Schizophrenia A brain disease characterized by hallucinations and/or delusions. A person with ASD may be incorrectly diagnosed with Schizophrenia.

Scripting Using predetermined speech. The script can be predetermined by reading it, hearing it, learning it, or otherwise forming it mentally, e.g. if someone says, "How are you?" your script is, "Fine, and you?"

SID Sensory Integration Disorder: unusual perception of sensory input, e.g. tactile defensiveness, auditory processing abnormalities, taste aversions, etc.

SIT Sensory Integration Therapy: treatment administered by an occupational therapist to reduce tactile defensiveness, e.g. massage, deep pressure, rubbing.

Social referencing Looking to others for cues to help maintain fluid social interaction.

Spectrum Referring to a person as "on the spectrum" indicates they have ASD and are impacted on some level ranging from low functioning to high functioning.

Splinter skills Skills that are exceptional, e.g. being able to shoot baskets with high accuracy, being able to do complex calculations mentally, being able to absorb new content quickly.

Static systems Social systems where the interaction is predictable, e.g. going through the checkout line at a store (see also **Fluid systems**).

Stim The informal term for self-stimulatory behaviors, e.g. tapping your foot, rocking, pacing.

Tactile defensiveness An unusually heightened sensitivity to touch.

Theory of mind The inborn ability to realize that other people have unique thoughts and feelings. Theory of mind allows a person to infer mental states, have empathy, determine intention, etc.

Tics Repetitious, involuntary movements or sounds, e.g. blinking, rubbing, twitching.

TS Tourette's Syndrome: neurobiological condition characterized by involuntary verbal and nonverbal tics.

Unimodal Indicates that a person uses one modality at a time, e.g. a person can either take notes or listen to the speaker, but not both.

References

American Psychiatric Association (2013) *Diagnostic and Statistical Manual of Mental Disorders* (5th edition). Washington, DC: American Psychiatric Association.

Asperger, H. (1944) "Die 'Autistischen Psychopathen' im Kindesalter." *Archiv für Psychiatrie und Nervenkrankheiten 117*, 76–136.

Asperger, H. (1979) "Problems of infantile autism." *Communication, Journal of the National Autistic Society 13*, 45–52.

Aston, M. (2000) "Meeting the challenge of Asperger's Syndrome." *Relate News 66*.

Aston, M. (2014) *The Other Half of Asperger Syndrome (Autism Spectrum Disorder): A Guide to Living in an Intimate Relationship with a Partner who is on the Autism Spectrum.* London: Jessica Kingsley Publishers. First published 2001.

Attwood, T. (1998) *Asperger's Syndrome: A Guide for Parents and Professionals.* London: Jessica Kingsley Publishers.

Attwood, T. and Gray, C. (1999) "The Discovery of 'Aspie' Criteria." *The Morning News*, Fall.

Baron-Cohen, S. (1995) *Mindblindness: An Essay on Autism and Theory of Mind.* Cambridge, MA: The MIT Press.

Baron-Cohen, S. (2001a) "Take the AQ test." *Wired* 9.12, 180.

Baron-Cohen, S. (2001b) " 'Think different?' Interview by Oliver Morton." *Wired* 9.12, 184–187.

Bashe, P. and Kirby, B. (2001) *The OASIS Guide to Asperger Syndrome: Advice, Support, Insight, and Inspiration.* New York: Crown.

Bauer, S. (1996) "Asperger Syndrome." The Developmental Unit, The Genesee Hospital Rochester, New York. Available at www.aspennj.org/pdf/information/articles/aspergers-syndrome-through-the-lifespan.pdf, accessed on June 6, 2014.

CDC (2014) "CDC estimates 1 in 68 children has been identified with autism spectrum disorder." Available at www.cdc.gov/media/releases/2014/p0327-autism-spectrum-disorder.html, accessed on May 29, 2014.

Cline, F. and Fay, J. (1990) *Parenting with Love and Logic: Teaching Children Responsibility.* Colorado Springs, CO: Pinon Press.

Dimitrius, J. and Mazzarella, M. (1998) *Reading People: How to Understand People and Predict Their Behavior—Anytime, Anyplace.* New York: Ballantine.

Eyre, L. and Eyre, R. (1982) *Teaching Your Children Responsibility.* New York: Fireside.

Fling, E. (2000) *Eating an Artichoke: A Mother's Perspective on Asperger's Syndrome.* London: Jessica Kingsley Publishers.

Folstein, S. and Santangelo, S. (2000) "Does Asperger Syndrome Aggregate in Families?" In A. Klin, F. Volkmar, and S. Sparrow (eds) *Asperger Syndrome*. New York: Guilford Press.

Frith, U. (1991) *Autism and Asperger Syndrome*. Cambridge: Cambridge University Press.

Grandin, T. (1995) *Thinking in Pictures: And Other Reports from My Life with Autism*. New York: Doubleday.

Grandin, T. (1999) "'Choosing the right job for people with Autism or Asperger's Syndrome." Colorado State University, November. Available at www.iidc.indiana.edu/?pageld=596, accessed on June 6, 2014.

Gutstein, S. (2000) *Autism/Asperger's: Solving the Relationship Puzzle*. Arlington, TX: Future Horizons.

Holliday Willey, L. (2001) *Asperger Syndrome in the Family: Redefining Normal*. London: Jessica Kingsley Publishers.

Holliday Willey, L. (2014) *Pretending to be Normal: Living with Asperger's Syndrome (Autism Spectrum Disorder)*. London: Jessica Kingsley Publishers. First published 1999.

Klin, A. and Volkmar, F. "Asperger's Syndrome and pursuing eligibility for services: The case of the 'perfect misplacement.' " Available at www.aspennj.org/pdf/information/articles/the-case-of-the-perfect-misplacement.pdf, accessed on May 27, 2014.

Klin, A., Volkmar, F., and Sparrow, S. (2000) *Asperger Syndrome*. New York: Guilford Press.

Ledgin, N. (2000) *Diagnosing Jefferson*. Arlington, TX: Future Horizons.

Lerner, H. (1985) *The Dance of Anger*. New York: Harper Perennial.

Lynn, G. (1999) "Five survival strategies to help children with Asperger's Syndrome overcome inertia." Available at www.asperger.it/?q=node/122, accessed on June 6, 2014.

McKean, T. (1994) *Soon Will Come the Light: A View from Inside the Autism Puzzle*. Arlington, TX: Future Horizons.

Meyer, R. (2001) *Asperger Syndrome Employment Workbook: An Employment Workbook for Adults with Asperger Syndrome*. London: Jessica Kingsley Publishers.

Randell, P. (1997) *Adult Bullying: Perpetrators and Victims*. London: Routledge.

Ratey, J. and Johnson, C. (1997) *Shadow Syndromes: Recognizing and Coping with the Hidden Psychological Disorders That Can Influence Your Behavior and Silently Determine the Course of Your Life*. New York: Pantheon.

Silberman, S. (2002) "The Geek Syndrome." *Wired* 9.12, 174–183.

Slater-Walker, C. and Slater-Walker G. (2002) *An Asperger Marriage*. London: Jessica Kingsley Publishers.

Stanford, A. (2011) *Business for Aspies: 42 Best Practices for Using Asperger Syndrome Traits at Work Successfully*. London: Jessica Kingsley Publishers.

Stanford, A. (2013) *Troubleshooting Relationships on the Autism Spectrum*. London: Jessica Kingsley Publishers.

Tantam, D. (1991) "Asperger Syndrome in Adulthood." In U. Frith (ed.) *Autism and Asperger Syndrome*. Cambridge: Cambridge University Press.

Tantam, D. (2000) "Adolescence and Adulthood of Individuals with Asperger Syndrome." In A. Klin, F. Volkmar, and S. Sparrow (ed.) *Asperger Syndrome*. New York: Guilford Press.

Wing, L. (1981) "Asperger Syndrome: A clinical account." *Psychological Medicine 11*, 115–130.

Subject Index

abuse 155, 256
achievements, non-sharing of 96–7
"acquired ASD" 40, 252–3
adaptive behaviors *see* self-help skills
ADD (attention deficit disorder) 34, 40
"Adolescence and Adulthood of Individuals with Asperger Syndrome" (Tantam) 139
Adult Bullying: Perpetrators and Victims (Randell) 128
adult diagnosis 37–40
adultery 256
American Psychiatric Association 25, 29, 36
amygdala, role of 43
anger management (NT partners) 65, 83, 207, 208, 243–7
anxiety 34, 44, 52, 162–3
arguments 131, 212
  avoiding 60–1, 213
articles, on ASD 262
"aspergation" process 19
Asperger Marriage, An (Slater-Walkers) 235, 258
Asperger Syndrome (Autism Spectrum Disorder)
  acquired Asperger Syndrome 40, 252–3
  definition 25–8
  diagnostic criteria 28–45
  manifestations 26–7
  NT partner's view of marriage 45–6
  partner with ASD's view of marriage 46–7
  people's judgments of 57–60
  removal of term "Asperger Syndrome" 25
  viewed as a disability 56–7

Asperger Syndrome Employment Workbook (Meyer) 223
Asperger Syndrome in the Family (Holliday Willey) 51–2, 202
Aspie, use of term 18, 26, 36
"Aspie Wedding Vows" (Holliday Willey) 251
athletic ability 107, 108–9
attention deficit disorder (ADD) 34, 40
auditory sensory dysfunction 81
Autism/Asperger's: Solving the Relationship Puzzle (Gutstein) 88
Autism Research Institute 264
Autism Society (ASA) 51, 264
Autism Speaks 51, 265
autistic disorder 36
avoidant personality disorder 40

babies, as unwelcome additions 136–8
behavior
  decoding 118, 122, 216
  not learning from 84
  restricted, repetitive patterns of (diagnostic criteria B) 30, 143–82, 195–6, 200
  unimodal 229–30
"being there" 232–4
benefits, of ASD 50, 52, 55, 229
body language
  clumsiness 106–9
  complexity of 104, 119
  executive function and dyspraxia 109–12
  failure to read 84, 104, 105–6, 121, 135–6, 214
  inappropriate 104, 106

Author Index